*Mary Lyon and
the Mount Holyoke
Missionaries*

Recent titles in
RELIGION IN AMERICA SERIES
Harry S. Stout, General Editor

SUBMITTING TO FREEDOM
The Religious Vision of William James
  Bennett Ramsey

OLD SHIP OF ZION
*The Afro-Baptist Ritual in the African
Diaspora*
  Walter F. Pitts

AMERICAN TRANSCENDENTALISM
AND ASIAN RELIGIONS
  Arthur Versluis

CHURCH PEOPLE IN THE
STRUGGLE
*The National Council of Churches
and the Black Freedom Movement,
1950–1970*
  James F. Findlay, Jr.

EVANGELICALISM
*Comparative Studies of Popular Protes-
tantism in North America, the British
Isles, and Beyond, 1700–1990*
  Edited by Mark A. Noll, David W.
  Bebbington and George A. Rawlyk

RELIGIOUS MELANCHOLY AND
PROTESTANT EXPERIENCE
IN AMERICA
Julius H. Rubin

CONJURING CULTURE
Biblical Formations in Black America
  Theophus Smith

REIMAGINING DENOMINA-
TIONALISM
Interpretive Essays
  Edited by Robert Bruce Mullin and
  Russell E. Richey

STANDING AGAINST THE
WHIRLWIND
*Evangelical Episcopalians in Nineteenth-
Century America*
  Diana Hochstedt Butler

KEEPERS OF THE COVENANT
*Frontier Missions and the Decline of Con-
gregationalism, 1774–1818*
  James R. Rohrer

SAINTS IN EXILE
*The Holiness-Pentecostal Experience in Af-
rican American Religion and Culture*
  Cheryl J. Sanders

DEMOCRATIC RELIGION
*Freedom, Authority, and Church Disci-
pline in the Baptist South, 1785–1900*
  Gregory A. Wills

THE SOUL OF DEVELOPMENT
*Biblical Christianity and Economic
Transformation in Guatemala*
  Amy L. Sherman

THE VIPER ON THE HEARTH
*Mormons, Myths, and the Construction of
Heresy*
  Terryl L. Givens

SACRED COMPANIES
*Organizational Aspects of Religion and
Religious Aspects of Organizations*
  Edited by N. J. Demerath III,
  Peter Dobkin Hall, Terry Schmitt,
  and Rhys H. Williams

MARY LYON AND THE MOUNT
HOLYOKE MISSIONARIES
  Amanda Porterfield

BEING THERE
*Culture and Formation in Two Theologi-
cal Schools*
  Jackson W. Carrol, Barbara G.
  Wheeler, Daniel O. Aleshire, Penny
  Long Marler

THE CHARACTER OF GOD
*Recovering the Lost Literary Power of
American Protestantism*
  Thomas E. Jenkins

Mary Lyon
and the Mount Holyoke
Missionaries

AMANDA PORTERFIELD

New York   Oxford   •   Oxford University Press   1997

Oxford University Press

Oxford   New York

Athens   Auckland   Bangkok   Bogota   Bombay   Buenos Aires
Calcutta   Cape Town   Dar es Salaam   Delhi   Florence   Hong Kong
Istanbul   Karachi   Kuala Lumpur   Madras   Madrid   Melbourne
Mexico City   Nairobi   Paris   Singapore   Taipei   Tokyo   Toronto   Warsaw

and associated companies in
Berlin   Ibadan

Published by Oxford University Press, Inc.
198 Madison Avenue, New York, New York 10016

Oxford is a registered trademark of Oxford University Press

Library of Congress Cataloging-in-Publication Data
Porterfield, Amanda, 1947–
Mary Lyon and the Mount Holyoke Holyoke missionaries / Amanda Porterfield.
p.   cm. — (Religion in America series)
Includes bibliographical references and index.
ISBN 0-19-511301-2
1. Mount Holyoke College.   2. Lyon, Mary, 1797–1849—Influence.   3. Women missionaries—Education
(Higher)—Massachusetts—Holyoke—History—19th century.   4. Women missionaries—United States—
History—19th century   5. Missionaries—United States—History—19th century.   6. Women missionaries—
History—19th century.   I. Title.   II. Series: Religion in America series (Oxford University Press)
BV2416.M6P67   1997
266'.02373'0082—dc21   96-45425

1 3 5 7 9 8 6 4 2
Printed in the United States of America
on acid-free paper

For my mother
Emily W. Porterfield
And in memory of my father
John B. Porterfield
1916–1996

Acknowledgments

Many people helped in the writing of this book. I am especially grateful to Mount Holyoke College Archivist Patricia J. Albright for her help from the outset to the final stages of the project, and for her unflagging patience and good cheer. Special thanks to Robert F. Berkey and Rowland A. Sherrill, who read drafts of the entire manuscript and offered good encouragement and advice. Thanks, too, to Joseph A. Conforti and David Hackett for their fine comments on chapter 1, and to Jan Shipps for her help in conceptualizing the communitarian aspect of Mount Holyoke in chapter 2. Thanks to Yvonne Haddad and Edward L. Queen II for comments on Islam and Nestorian Christianity, and to Manorama Barnabas, Paul B. Courtright, Ann Grodzins Gold, William J. Jackson, Plamthodathil S. Jacob, and H. Daniel Smith for their efforts to help me understand nineteenth-century Maharashtra. William R. Hutchison, David Chidester, Dana Robert, Chris Lowe, and Gabriele B. Sperling contributed to the chapter on missionary influence in Natal, as did a number of fine colleagues at IUPUI—Thomas J. Davis, William J. Jackson, Jeffrey Kinney, Missy Dean Kubitschek, Miriam Z. Langsam, E. Theodore Mullen Jr., Jane E. Schultz, Susan Shepherd, James F. Smurl, and Marianne Wokeck. Kimberly Long provided helpful assistance in preparing the manuscript.

I am grateful to my parents for working hard to send me to Mount Holyoke as a college student, and wish my father had lived to see the publication of this book. Thanks to Mark and Nick Kline for their daily love and support.

Contents

Introduction 3

ONE The Place of Antebellum Missionary Women in American Religious
History 11

   The Puritan Roots of Republican Motherhood 15
   *The Role of New Divinity Thought in Motivating Enthusiasm for
      Foreign Missions* 16
   Distinctions between Religious and Political Imperialism 19
   *The Importance and Distinctiveness of Antebellum Missionary
      Women* 21
   The Myth of Puritanism's Morbidity 24
   The Feminist Distaste for Self-Denial 26

TWO Religious Community at Mount Holyoke 29

   *Education and Teaching as Means of Negotiating Social Stress
      and Change* 30
   *Mount Holyoke as an Instance of Antebellum
      Communitarianism* 32
   Mount Holyoke Compared to the Oneida Community 33
   *The Role of Community In Shaping Modern Society in
      the United States* 35

The Mechanics of Communal Life at Mount Holyoke   37
Anti-Catholic Sentiment at Mount Holyoke   39
Investment in the Scientific Validity of Protestant Orthodoxy   41
Building God's Work of Redemption at Mount Holyoke   44

THREE   The Conversion Process and the Self-Referential Character of
Missionary Zeal   48

Missionaries as Exemplars of an Advanced Stage of the Conversion
Process   49
Mary Lyon's Conversion   50
Precedents for Conversion at Mount Holyoke   54
Lyon's Strategies for Nurturing Conversion and Missionary
Zeal   62

FOUR   The Centrality of Women in the Revitalization of Nestorian
Christianity and Its Conflict with Islam   68

Fiske Seminary as an Outpost of Mount Holyoke   69
The New Culture Created at Fiske Seminary   72
The Place of American Intervention in the History of Nestorian
Culture   79
American Contributions to Changing Expectations of Gender
Differentiation   82
The Exclusivism of American Missionary Idealism   84

FIVE   The Presence and Impact of Mary Lyon's Students in
Maharashtra   87

Christianity in India   88
Abby Fairbank as a Cross-cultural Exemplar of Female Piety   90
Mary Lyon's Students as Religious Teachers and Pioneers in Female
Education   94
Conflict in the Maratha Mission and Its Implications for
Missionary Women   99
Coinciding Iconoclasms and Forces of Social Reform   103
The Syncretic Reach of Hindu Piety   107
The Role of Women and Women's Issues in Hindu Reform   109

SIX   Mount Holyoke Missionaries and Their Husbands in Zululand and
Natal   112

Charlotte Grout's Exhibition of Power   114
The African Context of American Involvement   115
The Nature of American Influence   120
Mount Holyoke Missionaries in Natal   124
The Centrality of Women's Issues in Cultural Change   128

Missionary Influence on Gender Role Differentiation and Sexual Behavior 131
The Entrenchment of Separate Communities and the Violation of Christian Fellowship 133

Conclusion 139

Notes 145

Index 173

*Mary Lyon and
the Mount Holyoke
Missionaries*

Daguerreotype of Mary Lyon,
from Mary Lyon Collection,
Mount Holyoke College.

Introduction

*A*s a student at Mount Holyoke in the late 1960s, I was aware that the college was America's first publicly endowed institution for women's advanced education, and also that it was founded as a religious institution. The exact nature of the original religious vision was vague, but I knew there had been such a vision and that it persisted, somehow, in the communal character of campus life and in the expectations of personal achievement my teachers transmitted. On my first day as a student at Mount Holyoke, President Richard G. Getell made an oblique reference to this original religious vision in a speech he delivered to new students that proclaimed us the new generation in a long line of "uncommon women." The exact meaning of the epithet *uncommon* was unclear to me, and I recall some jokes about it after the speech. The president had referred to our SAT scores, which he expected us to live up to, and to our virginity, which he expected us to keep, but he also meant something else by "uncommon," something spiritual and historic, although he was not very explicit. I had the sense of just having acquired a pressing but obscure responsibility, along with a peculiar female ancestry, whose spirits I imagined lurking in the rafters of the auditorium.

The feeling of belonging to something I did not well understand sometimes recurred when I passed the grave of Mary Lyon, the founder of Mount Holyoke Female Seminary in 1837, on my way to classes or the library. A monument marking her grave stood at the center of a rise at one end of the main quadrangle at the highest point on campus. To read the inscriptions on the

3

monument, one had to stop and peer across the low fence that put several yards of grass between the grave and passers-by. The words on one side of the monument read, "A teacher for 35 years; and of more than 3000 pupils." Another inscription from the last verse of Proverbs emphasized Lyon's ability to live through her students, and linked their achievements to her own: "Give her of the fruit of her hands and let her own works praise her in the gates." This connection between Lyon and her students was dramatized every year on Founder's Day, when the trustees and members of the campus community assembled to watch the senior class pass through the low gate of the little cemetery and gather around their class president, who respectfully laid a wreath on Lyon's grave.

Twenty years after graduating, when I was invited back to Mount Holyoke to give a lecture, I visited the grave again. I was struck by the simple beauty of the spot and by the authority it imputed to Lyon. During a visit to the college archives that day, I began the process of trying to better understand Lyon's religious vision and its place in the history of American culture. I wanted to explore the ways in which she and her students revitalized the New England tradition of female piety, which I had recently written about. I was also interested in cross-cultural transmissions of religious ideas in the nineteenth century, and therefore was particularly curious about those of Lyon's students who became missionaries, and about the impact they made on women in foreign lands. As a historian of American religions, I hoped that Mary Lyon and the early missionaries from Mount Holyoke would provide a manageable case study of a larger inquiry into New England women's piety in the antebellum era and the promulgation of their culture overseas.

American commitment to foreign missionary work escalated in the second and third decades of the nineteenth century as part of the religious enthusiasm of the second Great Awakening. While many young people from New England moved west in the early decades of the nineteenth century, contributing both to the proliferation of new religious groups and to the popularity of circuit-riders who made the Methodist Church the fastest-growing denomination in the United States, an idealistic and highly educated group of young New Englanders moved in the opposite direction as missionaries, often on merchant ships that were establishing Yankee trade networks abroad. While New Englanders who moved westward embraced a rich variety of religious faiths, the young people sent eastward as missionaries from New England churches strongly identified with the Puritan tradition and committed themselves to introducing that tradition in nonwestern cultures. Missionary enthusiasm became the defining characteristic of personal piety and a rallying point for inter-denominational organization in conservative New England churches during these years, and this enthusiasm coincided with renewed commitment to Puritanism. Thus the effort to carry American Protestantism overseas was "self-consciously a New England movement," as one historian concluded, "although it spread slowly westward with the movement of population and the growing momentum of the idea."[1]

Women were an important part of this early foreign missionary endeavor. Missionary work appealed especially to New England women because it enabled them to reaffirm the Puritan principles on which many New Englanders believed the best elements of the American republic were founded. At the same time, missionary work enabled women to break into public life, expand educational opportunities for themselves and other women, and acquire professional competence as teachers. Although the missionary movement was not the only context in which public life, education, and professional opportunities for women developed in antebellum New England, it attracted a much larger number of women than radical movements, like spiritualism, or secular ideologies, like natural rights philosophy.

Recognition of women's suitability for missionary work centered initially on the personage of Harriet Newell, who became America's first foreign missionary martyr when she died in 1812 at the age of nineteen on the Isle of France off the coast of southern India. In death, she became a major religious figure; no other woman in the second decade of the nineteenth century was so widely eulogized or emulated. Her piety was even more celebrated than that of her husband Samuel, whose prayer meetings while a student at Williams College and Andover Seminary led to the founding of the American Board of Commissioners for Foreign Missions, the largest and most influential American mission board in the early nineteenth century. As Leonard Woods, the Abbot Professor of Christian Theology at Andover Seminary, asserted in his memorial sermon for Harriet, "The *wife of a Missionary* when influenced by the Spirit of Christ, gives still more remarkable evidence of self-denial and devotion" than her husband, because "[t]he tie, which binds her to her relatives and her home, is stronger." The woman who "forsakes *all*, for the name of Christ . . . makes a higher effort," Woods wrote, "and thus furnishes a more conspicuous proof, that her love of Christ transcends all earthly affection."[2]

As Woods's sermon suggests, Christian self-sacrifice was one arena in which American women in the nineteenth century could compete with men and win. Self-sacrifice was an ideal deemed worthy of both sexes, but also one that women were more likely to attain because of their socialization as wives and mothers. The devotion to Christ exemplified by Harriet Newell dovetailed perfectly with the qualities of affection, submission, and self-sacrifice already ingrained in many New England women as part of their socialization as wives and mothers, and as part of their Puritan heritage. Missionary work celebrated these traditional Puritan virtues, offering women new opportunities for passionate self-expression and social activism, and enabling them to become virtuosos of Christian devotion with degrees of influence and public recognition to which they could not otherwise have pretended.

But while missionary work provided a doorway through which many New England women stepped out into new worlds of social activism, administrative responsibility, self-expression, and public renown, the requirements of female piety limited the extent to which they could succeed as public figures and still remain missionaries. Thus while women's proficiency in humility and self-sacrifice justified their place on a larger, more public stage, it also limited the degree to which they could enjoy and capitalize on their success. And while humility and self-sacrifice provided antebellum women an avenue to public life, once the presence of women in public life became more commonplace, public activism no longer demanded of women the extreme degrees of humility and self-sacrifice that missionary work required. But for a time, heroic self-denial was often a prerequisite for activism.

Although the number of its early missionary alumnae was not huge, no other institution was as closely associated with women missionaries as Mount Holyoke. When Lyon died in 1849, twenty-seven alumnae had become missionaries in foreign countries, and eight had become missionaries to American Indian communities. The next year, the total rose to forty. In 1859, the American Board of Commissioners for Foreign Missions listed sixty Mount Holyoke alumnae on its rolls, and Baptist and Presbyterian mission boards listed others. In 1887, fifty years after Mount Holyoke's founding, one-fifth of all women then serving as American Board missionaries were Holyoke alumnae.[3]

Men dominated the governance of all American mission boards before 1860, but women constituted approximately half of all missionaries commissioned by the American Board in the 1840s and 1850s, although before 1860 most were listed as missionary wives and not as missionaries in their own right. In the 1860s women founded their own mission societies independent of general mission boards, and concentrated on supporting single women missionaries. As a result of the increase in single women missionaries, the representation of women among American missionaries increased to sixty percent. But women's missionary influence functioned more conservatively than before the Civil War, when missionary idealism about world redemption was simpler and more radically egalitarian. Earlier women missionaries held less well-formed and more open-ended ideas about nonwestern women than their successors, and were more likely to be interpreted by nonwestern women in terms of indigenous traditions and patterns of female religious authority. As missionaries became more successful in controlling their image, and as the American culture out of which missionaries came grew less bold, less revolutionary, and less egalitarian, the presence and impact of American missionary women was increasingly inscribed within the confines of a "gospel of gentility."[4]

Focusing on the more plastic and egalitarian missionary movement of the antebellum era, this book examines Mary Lyon and missionary women trained directly by her. The book considers Lyon and her students as representatives of dominant trends in American missionary thought before the Civil War, and also as important actors in their own right. Lyon's missionary students clustered in a number of locales—Persia, India, Ceylon, Hawaii, and Africa being the most important—and this book focuses on three nonwestern sites where documentation about the activities of Lyon's students is especially rich, northwest Persia, Maharashtra in western India, and Natal in southeast Africa. All three sites figured importantly in antebellum missionary strategy; missionaries envisioned their converts launching the conquest of Islam from Persia, overturning

"Satan's seat" in India, and drawing the descendants of Ham in Africa into the fold of Christendom.

While the impact of their encounters with nonwestern women is not easy to determine, antebellum missionary women promoted female literacy everywhere they went, along with self-sacrificial devotion to Christ, belief in the superiority and scientific validity of Protestant orthodoxy, commitment to the necessity of monogamy and the importance of marital affection, and concern for the well-being of children and other women. Through their emphasis on these ideas, antebellum women missionaries contributed to cultural change in many parts of the world, and to the development of new cultures that combined missionary concepts with traditional ideals.

As this book attempts to demonstrate, American influence in the nonwestern world has been shaped more by women and women's issues than many historians have realized. R. Pierce Beaver, the missionary historian of thirty years ago, was one of the few to recognize the extent of American women's influence, although he overlooked the negative aspects of American missionary women's activities when he attributed a "colossal" global increase in women's "freedom and influence" to their work. If the diverse and often conflicting effects of their influence are acknowledged, it may be possible to agree with Beaver that "[n]o other form of American intervention overseas has made a more powerful cultural impact" than American women missionaries' "work for women and children."[5]

Of course, American missionary women were not alone in promulgating new ideas and triggering the development of new cultures; explorers, entrepreneurs, and missionaries from several western nations were also engaged in this process. In India especially, British missionary women led the way in inaugurating religious and cultural interactions that Americans built on. But efforts to trace the emergence of American influence in nonwestern cultures take on special interest in light of the global prominence that American culture attained after World War II. Early missionary activity gave initial shape to perceptions about America that persisted as its influence became increasingly ubiquitous and political, and interactions between American missionary women and nonwestern women played a significant role in determining these perceptions.

In the interest of better understanding their interactions, this book points to similar dynamics in the lives of both American missionaries and nonwestern women. Although the nonwestern women encountered by missionaries were more beleaguered by forces external to their own cultures that limited their opportunities to seize the momentum of social change, both Mary Lyon's students and the nonwestern women they tried to serve were caught up in dramatic forces of social change. Lyon's students were far less constrained by forces external to their culture, and unlike their nonwestern counterparts they were committed to aggressive programs of evangelization. But they shared with nonwestern women experiences of social transformation involving the breakdown of traditional patterns of community life and new controversies over gender role differentiation. Both Lyon's students and the nonwestern women they encountered were concerned to improve their own lives and the lives of other women, and they also shared an underlying conservatism and loyalty to traditional culture. All these women in transition between traditional and modern culture shared a similar allegiance to male authority and to ideal concepts of religious tradition and cultural stability through which male authority was defined.

❧

The first chapter of the book locates Mary Lyon and her students in the context of the American missionary movement. Focusing on the roots of this movement in both Puritan piety and the ideology of Republican Motherhood, the chapter shows how early-nineteenth-century American missionary women participated in the revival of Puritan piety during the second Great Awakening and also in the efforts to improve female education that were associated with the early-nineteenth-century ideal of Republican Motherhood. The chapter argues that several factors have obscured our understanding of the early stage of the women's missionary movement in America, including a tendency to discount the significance of religious arguments for women's education in the early nineteenth century, adherence to the myth of the Puritan tradition's decline in late-eighteenth- and early-nineteenth-century America, and the present-day culture of concern for women's self-esteem, against which missionary commitment to self-sacrifice seems perverse and irrelevant, even though it contributed indirectly to the emergence of the culture of self-esteem.

The second and third chapters of the book focus on Mount Holyoke and the commitment to missionary causes inculcated there. Chapter 2 examines the communal aspect of life at the seminary before Lyon's death in 1849 and describes her hope of participating in the creation of a global network of female societies that would help bring about a future age of harmony and justice. Locating the religious community Lyon established at Mount Holyoke in relation to other efforts to establish religious communities in antebellum America, this chapter argues that Lyon and her students participated in a widespread cultural attraction to communitarian ideals. These ideals were not just the property of religious radicals but also engaged nineteenth-century New Englanders representing a wide spectrum of religious positions. These ideals combined loyalty to the spirit of religious consensus characteristic of the Puritan ideal of family life with enthusiasm for modern industry and new forms of national and international culture.

Chapter 3 focuses on the psychology of commitment to missionary causes and lays the groundwork for understanding the need for mastery of other women that compromised the egalitarian aspect of missionary theology. Examining writings by and about Lyon and her students as well as some of the missionary autobiographies they drew inspiration from, this chapter describes the melancholy and self-doubt that beset missionary types as a result of their preoccupation with self-sacrifice and their attendant anxiety about putting themselves forward. This chapter argues that the missionary's hope of her own religious purification and desire for relief from melancholy and self-doubt were motivating factors in missionary commitment. While missionary commitment involved genuine concern for others, it was also a therapeutic process that required others to be objects of persuasion and malleable symbols of the missionary's own fears about herself.

Chapters 4, 5, and 6 follow Mary Lyon's students to Persia, India, and southern Africa, and consider the influence that they and other American missionary women exerted on women in these regions. Locating American influence in the context of social changes occurring in the three regions, these chapters trace the development of new cultures that emerged in response to American influence. The chapters show how elements of traditional cultures merged with Protestant ideas about social progress and Republican Motherhood, and how American and nonwestern women developed agendas that overlapped, intersected, and vied with one another to create arenas of mutual purpose and conflict.

The women of northwest Persia, Maharashtra, and Natal shared several traits with New England missionary women. Among the most important of these was allegiance to male authority. In its various forms, this allegiance offered women respectability, physical protection, and a means of expressing loyalty to the religious traditions and cultural stability of their historic communities. In addition, all the women considered in this book were forced to negotiate massive forces of social stress and change. Each group of women exerted a different degree of control over the direction of social change within their culture, and experienced a different degree of opportunity to benefit from new developments in education, communication, and industry. But all four groups of women developed cultures of service and social reform that were tied both to modern beliefs in education as the key to social progress and to traditional commitments to women's subordinate but nevertheless important roles in society.

Chapter 4 focuses on the role of Lyon's students in constructing an American alliance with Nestorian Christians in Persia that was defined by concern for women's welfare and hostility to Islam. The new culture that formed in northwest Persia as a result of missionary intervention involved both an emphasis on women's service to other women and a rejection of Middle Eastern attitudes toward women that came to be symbolized by claims about the superiority of American Protestantism over Islam. But the link that missionaries forged between women's elevation and hostility to Islam backfired as missionary triumphalism provoked considerable animosity among Muslims and contributed to the near elimination of the Nestorian community in Persia.

Chapter 5 examines the work of Lyon's students in Maharashtra in western India, where missionary intervention also produced a Protestant-inspired, reform-minded culture, but one with a very different historical outcome. Of all the missionary endeavors in which Lyon's students participated, their promotion of female education and other forms of social reform in Maharashtra had perhaps the greatest benefit for nonwestern women. In contrast to the Persian situation, where the weakness of Nestorian culture left the Nestorian people highly vulnerable to intellectual domination by missionaries, and to resulting Muslim hostility, the strength of Hindu culture in Maharashtra enabled Hindu reformers to exploit missionary influence and appropriate its culture of service in highly effective ways. Thus missionary efforts in Maharashtra functioned as a catalyst for Hindu reforms in female education and other forms of social welfare, but also coincided with a significant degree of failure to convert Hindus to Christianity.

Chapter 6 examines the influence of Lyon's students and the missionaries they worked with in Natal in southeast Africa. As in Maharashtra, the missionary emphasis on women's education, companionate marriage, and service to others held forth the possibility of freeing women from some of the difficulties under which they labored in traditional culture. But the instability of Zulu culture, along with destructive military, political, and economic forces external to it, hindered every effort the Zulu people made either to preserve their culture or to embrace Christianity and western forms of social progress. In this often desperate situation, Zulu women found themselves torn not only between loyalty to traditional culture and hope for social progress, but also between shoring up traditional culture against disintegration and fending off the grinding poverty, racial discrimination, and breakdown of family life that accompanied efforts to participate in westernization. A new culture did emerge to meet these challenges, and this culture drew on both on Protestant Christianity and western education. But its leaders often distanced themselves from American missionaries, who responded too little and too late to the problems that Africans faced.

As this last chapter makes especially clear, American missionaries failed to live up to the egalitarian aspect of their own religious message, and to the experience of Christian community that was so closely tied to their culture of service and to their own missionary vocations. This failure helped shape images of American culture abroad and contributed to the perception of Americans as not only culturally imperialistic but also hypocritical. At the same time, the failure of American missionaries to practice the egalitarianism and spirit of fellowship they preached set those conceptions free of missionary ownership. Thus in an ironic way, the failure of American missionaries to live up to the most progressive aspects of their message contributed to its universal development.

ONE

The Place of Antebellum Missionary Women in American Religious History

As an advocate of women's education, Mary Lyon expanded on two popular ideologies of her time, one centered on the theological concept of disinterested benevolence articulated by Samuel Hopkins in the eighteenth century and developed by other spokesmen for New Divinity theology, and the other centered on the patriotic notion of what historian Linda K. Kerber has termed Republican Motherhood. Lyon was not the first to link disinterested benevolence with Republican Motherhood, nor was she the first to justify women's education in terms of Republican Motherhood; disinterested benevolence was often presumed to characterize women's contributions to the public good, and advocates of Republican Motherhood argued that education would facilitate these contributions. Lyon's contribution was to build on these connections to establish a more reciprocal relationship between women and public life than had existed before. Thus she not only promoted women's education as the means by which women might best fulfill their maternal responsibilities to the nation, as other education reformers did, she also made women's education a matter of public concern. By soliciting small donations from a large number of New England women, with many of whom she was personally unacquainted, Lyon established Mount Holyoke as the first institution of women's advanced education whose endowment was "public," hence not dependent on a small base of wealthy donors.

Like other advocates of New Divinity theology, Lyon urged women to contribute to public welfare in a spirit of disinterested benevolence. But she went beyond others in conceptualizing undereducated and relatively impoverished New England women as appropriate objects of this benevolence. She appealed to married women in villages across New England to donate money to Mount Holyoke in order that younger women might have an education that the donors themselves never had. And once Mount Holyoke was established, she appealed to her students to extend themselves to women and children in the American West and overseas in the same spirit of disinterested benevolence in which donors to Mount Holyoke had extended themselves. Envisioning women as the cornerstones of a new world order grounded in benevolence, Lyon worked to establish religious ties among New England women, and between them and women abroad. Effort to establish these ties helped shape the development of women's education in the United States and in a number of communities overseas.

Like other proponents of New Divinity theology, Lyon understood disinterested benevolence as the defining characteristic of Christian life. Also like other New Divinityites, she hailed from a backwoods culture characterized by self-sufficient, family-based economies, arduous labor, and intense piety. Her commitment to disinterested benevolence involved an effort to apply the virtues of this culture to a new and expanding society. Thus she understood disinterested benevolence as a call to continuous personal sacrifice, and a righteous alternative to the "belle ideal" of womanhood and other notions associated with the emerging secularity, materialism, and consumerism of city life. Founding an academic community geared to women from backgrounds much like her own, she strove to replicate the virtues of backwoods culture while at the same time offering women firsthand exposure to theology, philosophy, history, and science. In Lyon's view, women would become the cornerstones of a new world order that combined the intense piety of the common folk of New England with the newest advances in historical knowledge and scientific investigation.

Like other New Divinityites, Lyon subcribed to the ideology of Republican Motherhood, which played an important role in shaping a nascent middle-class consensus about how women could best contribute to the virtue and vitality of the new nation. While the ideology of Republican Motherhood acknowledged women's patriotism and their importance in the life of the new nation, it also emphasized the circumscribed compass of their influence on public life. By insisting that women contributed best to the public good by rearing future citizens and statesmen, the ideology of Republican Motherhood emphasized the necessity and importance of women's maternal role.

This conceptual scheme emerged in the years following the American Revolution, and served to rechannel some of the political momentum that women had gained during and after the war when they had organized to raise money and provide supplies for the war effort and petitioned for various forms of government intervention and assistance. The ideology of Republican Motherhood worked against any further development of such explicitly political activity and defined women's contribution to the nation solely in religious, moral, and intellectual terms. In its refection of the full extension of natural rights philosophy to women, the ideology of Republican Motherhood made it clear that the public sphere of political life belonged primarily to men, along with all claims to political equality.[1]

As a result of this prohibition of women's public recognition, women shunned public speaking to mixed audiences, and only a few women dared step into arenas where power was publicly managed. On a remarkable speaking tour in 1837, Sarah and Angelina Grimké drew a few men as well as many women to their lectures on abolition, but it was not until the 1850s that a subculture of women consistently broke the taboo against public lecturing, and many of these pioneers justified their right to the podium by claiming to be controlled, or at least inspired, by spiritual forces.[2]

While it is crucial to recognize that the Republican notion of maternal influence contributed significantly to this limitation of women's direct participation in public life, it is equally important to see how amenable this notion was to progressive ideas about women's education. The ideology of Republican Motherhood proved conducive to belief in the compatibility of religious faith and higher learning, and could be invoked quite effectively to sanction the expansion of women's religious, moral, and intellectual influence on public life.

Advocates of women's education justified advances in female literacy and higher learning by invoking women's maternal responsibilties to the nation. If America was to retain its vitality and grow in strength through coming generations, so the argument ran, its women must be taught to read, write, and reason soundly. As Benjamin Rush put it early on, "The equal share that every citizen has in the liberty and the possible share he may have in the government of our country make it necessary that our ladies should be qualified to a certain degree, by a peculiar and suitable education, to concur in instructing their sons in the principles of liberty and government."[3]

Such concern for female education distinguished Republican thinking from the contemporaneous ideology of female delicacy and inadequacy. In fact, the argument for women's education developed in opposition to this "belle-ideal" of womanhood, and those who stressed the importance of education in enabling women's contributions to public good challenged the characterization of women as flirtatious, charming, dependent, and incapable of learning. As Kerber paraphrases this argument, "The Republic did not need fashion plates; it needed citizens—women as well as men—of self-discipline and of strong mind."[4]

Mary Lyon came up against the "belle-ideal" of female dependency in her efforts to enlist support for Mount Holyoke. Traveling through New England on fund-raising tours, she did not hesitate to try to enlist the support of fellow travelers on stage coaches and public cars. As one of her friends observed, "she could make herself heard easily." As far as women's education and her plans for a female seminary were concerned, she "would expatiate on the subject as freely as in her own parlor." In her defense, the friend continued, Lyon raised her voice no more "than many fashionably-dressed boarding-school girls do in public conveyances, the difference being that the latter inform the company of their own personal affairs, while she discussed principles as enduring as the human race." Lyon lashed out more angrily against complaints about her behavior. "My heart is sick," she complained, "my soul is pained with this empty gentility, this genteel nothingness." Invoking Nehemiah at Jericho, she asserted, "I am doing a great work. I cannot come down."[5]

Ready with biblical analogues to defend her efforts, Lyon exploited the well-established openness of Republican ideology to women's involvement in religiously motivated public activism. As early as 1787, Hannah Adams had insisted on the necessity of women's religious responsibilities to public welfare in a popular pamphlet, *Women Invited to War*, urging the women of the new American nation to unite in a spiritual war against Satan.[6] Such enthusiasm for the religious character of women's patriotism coexisted nicely with visions of American progress articulated by Whig ministers who painted a religious vision of America's role in world history that allowed for women's participation and influence. In conjunction with this tradition, Lyon called on women to take responsibility for the education of other women, emphasizing the compatibility between faith and knowledge and the importance of education in enabling women to exemplify faith.

In conceptualizing her educational efforts in religious terms, Lyon took the avenue to public life most clearly open to her. But religious belief was not simply a convenience for her. It was a passionate form of expression that shaped her understanding of the nature and purpose of knowledge and motivated her evangelicalism in promoting women's education. From Lyon's perspective, religion encompassed and underlay everything else—from emotional life to world history and scientific knowledge. In justifying advances in women's education on religious grounds, Lyon was not, in her own mind, marginalizing her efforts and those of her associates, but emphasizing their supreme relevance and centrality.

Justifying her outspokenness in behalf of women's education in terms of disinterested benevolence, Lyon attempted to forestall interpretations of her leadership in the cause of women's education as a bid for celebrity or even recognition for herself. Thus she wrote her colleague Zilpah Grant in 1833 about the importance of finding influential men to represent their plans for endowing a seminary. "I feel more and more that the whole business must, in name, devolve on benevolent gentlemen, and not on yourself or on myself. Fewer needless, unkind remarks will be thrown out, less jealousy will be excited, and our private influences will be more extensive and useful in directing matters for the good of the institution." She explained more specifically, "there is danger that many good men will fear the effect on society of so much female influence, and what they will call female greatness. They will think and say, 'Miss Grant and Miss Lyon want to do some great thing, to have a large sum of money raised, and a great institution established, and to see themselves at the head of the whole, and then they will be satisfied.' I imagine I have seen a little of this already, and if more interest were to be felt in the cause, more jealousy might be excited."[7]

Lyon's effort to allay concerns about any pretensions she might have to greatness fit within a longstanding New England tradition of self-sacrificial devotion to others. During the Revolution, women had endured considerable economic and physical sacrifice, often with patriotic pride, and the concept of Republican Motherhood memorialized these efforts in descriptions of American women as happy to give up pleasure and comfort for liberty's cause.[8] Even more fundamentally, submissiveness was an important aspect of Puritan piety in New England, and underlay the emphasis on disinterested benevolence that developed in the late eighteenth and early nineteenth centuries. A broken will was a basic constituent of Puritan piety, and Puritan writers celebrated self-sacrifice and suffering as characteristics of grace.

The Puritan Roots of Republican Motherhood

In seventeenth-century New England, women became exemplars of Puritan piety through their suffering and self-sacrifice and through their affection and submissiveness as wives. Their social roles as wives and mothers prepared them for careers of sainthood, which was often symbolized as espousal to Christ. Numerous Puritan ministers described Christ as a bridegroom, and Cotton Mather linked women's submissiveness and their suffering in childbirth to their special capacity for piety. As he put it in *Ornaments for the Daughters of Zion*, women's "[c]urse in the difficulties of *subjection & Childbirth* . . . has been turned into a Blessing." For Mather, there was no better expression of the relationship between suffering and redemption than the relationship between women's suffering and women's piety, which he represented theologically by the relationship between Eve, the mother of sin, and Mary, the mother of Christ.[9]

Women were attracted to Puritanism not only because they were practiced in the qualities revered in Puritan theology but also because of the egalitarian dimension of Puritan spirituality. In counterpoint to the feminized version of Puritan piety outlined by Mather, which presaged later ideas about the inherent spirituality of women's nature, many Puritan writers emphasized the sinfulness of all Christians, and the importance of suffering, piety, and charity for both men and women. As part of this line of thought, Puritan writers celebrated marriage as an affectionate union in which unequals might become equal. Moreover, they often rejected the assumption underlying religious celibacy that sexuality, and women's bodies, were inherently sinful. Certain aspects of the old equation between sin and female sexuality sometimes recurred, as in Governor John Winthrop's belief that Anne Hutchinson's religious deviancy caused her to give birth to a monster. But by making marriage and family life the core of society and the model for church and state, Puritan writers delivered female sexuality from some of the stigma associated with it in Christian tradition, and recognized the importance of women's participation in the construction of Christian society.

While both the egalitarian and feminized aspects of Puritan piety contributed to the high percentage of women in church pews in New England after 1660,[10] the imbalance between female and male church members was redressed to some degree during the Great Awakening of 1740–42, when George Whitefield's dramatic modeling of the conversion process brought a new influx of men into both new and established churches. Church membership declined in the decades following the Great Awakening,[11] but ministers concerned with revitalizing Puritan tradition gained new influence during the Revolutionary period by articulating a civil religion based on Puritan virtues of hard work and self-sacrifice. Forging a civil religion for the middle and southern colonies as well as New England, the "black regiment" of New England ministers cast the American struggle for independence in the framework of a (somewhat exaggerated) Puritan commitment to religious liberty. In the 1820s and 1830s, Whig politicians built further on this civil religion, invoking America's Puritan legacy by linking their own commitment to commerce to an (also exaggerated) Puritan enthusiasm for commercial venture.[12]

While Whig rhetoric encouraged men to identify with New England's Puritan heritage by defining it in terms of religious liberty and Christian commerce, the ideology of Republican Motherhood built on the tradition of Puritan piety and on the idea that women were important to the maintenance of Christian culture. Liberal interpreters of Republican Motherhood may have overlooked the Puritan roots of this ideology, but New Divinityites saw Republican Motherhood and the Puritan tradition as coextensive. Moreover, by interpreting the contrast between self-interest and true virtue more radically than ever before, New Divinity thought strengthened the egalitarian aspect of the Puritan tradition and made it part of an urgent mandate for social change. By rejecting the notion that true virtue was in any way natural, New Divinityites held both men and women to the same radical standard of selfless action on behalf of others. As relatively proficient exemplars of this standard as a result of their commitment to religion, women found an opening into public leadership.

The Role of New Divinity Thought in Motivating Enthusiasm for Foreign Missions

Mary Lyon stepped into this opening with the help of the New Divinity leader Joseph Emerson, who ran the Ladies Seminary in Byfield, Massachusetts, where she was enrolled for six months in 1821. Emerson had studied with the New Divinity teacher Nathaniel Emmons, whose commitment to disinterested benevolence led him to be an early supporter of women's advanced education and women's active participation in foreign missionary service.[13] Lyon embraced Emerson's ideas and joined the Congregational Church in 1822 as a result of his influence. The New Divinity concern for self-sacrificial benevolence as the quintessential element of Christian virtue became the guiding principle of her life, and Emerson's interest in education as a means of facilitating women's role in the process of global redemption became her cause. She transmitted these concerns in turn to her own students and, like other New Divinity teachers, she nurtured missionary vocations as dramatic examples of the spirit of disinterested benevolence that epitomized conversion.

Lyon, Emerson, and Emmons were all indebted to the theology of Jonathan Edwards, and to the theology of Edwards's most influential interpreter, Samuel Hopkins of Waterbury, Connecticut. Hopkins studied with Edwards in 1742, after being converted at Yale under David Brainerd's influence during the Great Awakening in 1741, and later collaborated in the editing of Edwards's work. From 1769, when he was called to a pulpit in Newport, Rhode Island, until a few years before his death during the second Great Awakening in 1803, Hopkins was the central figure in the New Divinity movement and the chief architect of the radical concept of disinterested benevolence characteristic of New Divinity thought. In making this concept the touchstone of Christian virtue, Hopkins emphasized the irreconcilable contrast between true virtue and the selfishness that permeated every natural affection. Disinterested benevolence involved nothing less than "willingness to be damned for the glory of God."[14]

Hopkins believed that the millennium would emerge from a Whig citizenry purified of self-interest, and he drew a line between Whigs whose political views were grounded in disinterested benevolence and those whose views were grounded in self-interest. In affluent Newport, where wealth was commonly tied to the slave trade, Hopkins argued that self-interest was epitomized by tolerance of slavery and belief in the inferiority of Africans. He attacked the complacency, racism, and classism of Congregationalists who believed themselves superior to Africans, and he made rejection of slavery an indicator of conversion. He also invoked the millenarian idea that slavery was an ingredient in the sixth vial described in the Book of Revelation, and that its overthrow would precede the opening of the seventh vial, the pouring out of which would bring God's kingdom to earth.[15]

In his efforts to cultivate a heroic selflessness in himself and others, Hopkins threw himself into missionary work, and he made commitment to it a prominent aspect of New Divinity thought. In his early life, Hopkins followed in the footsteps of Edwards and Brainerd and devoted several years to missionary work among the Housatanic and Mahican Indians. Later in Newport, he vigorously supported missionary efforts among Africans in both the United States and Africa.

Hopkins's most ardent supporters were women. During his trial period in the Newport church, Ezra Stiles and other liberal Congregational ministers in New England's coastal towns lobbied against his appointment, and a majority of the voting members of the church turned him down for ordination in 1770. But Sarah Osborne, Susanna Anthony, and other members of the women's prayer society continued to favor his candidacy. They prayed ardently for his ordination and sobbed openly during a surprisingly temperate sermon that he delivered after the negative vote on his ordination. These women succeeded in their appeals for a new vote overturning the first and secured the ordination.[16]

Hopkins's concept of disinterested benevolence celebrated a quality of self-sacrifice already familiar to his supporters from their social experience as women. His definition of Christian virtue as habitual selflessness and devotion to others made room for women to figure prominently in the spread of Christianity and the dawning of the millennium. Thus Hopkins's theology facilitated women's influence. If they could not compete with men in politics or law, they could work side by side with them in the arena of disinterested benevolence, which Hopkins claimed was the place where the victory of the American republic and the conversion of the world would be won or lost.

In their concern for global conversion, Hopkins and his followers revitalized an earlier missionary tradition within Puritanism that described Christians as ambassadors of Christ, responsible for helping to bring the rest of the world to a new level of faith, knowledge, and morality. In justifying their immigration to America, seventeenth-century Puritans had represented their missionary purpose on the seal of the Massachusetts Bay Colony with an image of an Indian wreathed by the words from Acts 16: "Come over and help us." Although missionary work in seventeenth-century New England was actually more limited than this advertisement might suggest, several New England men made heroic efforts to evangelize natives. John Eliot and Thomas and Matthew Mayhew converted Algonquian Indians in seventeenth-century New England and built towns of "praying Indians."

Mission societies based in England, Scotland, and Europe supported New England missionaries to the American Indians during the seventeenth and eighteenth centuries, and drew on American support for early missionary efforts to India and other foreign lands. Cotton Mather corresponded with Danish pietists engaged in missionary work in India, and he helped found a short-lived missionary society in Boston in 1721.[17] Jonathan Edwards was deeply interested in the spread of the Protestant gospel around the world and hoped, like Cotton Mather and other New Englanders, that the salvation of the world was commencing in America.[18] Although his own missionary service to the Housatanic Indians in Stockbridge, New York, was forced upon him by dismissal from his Northampton parish in 1750, the evangelical aspect of his theology helped establish the New Divinity idea that commitment to missionary causes was linked to conversion.

Commitment to missionary work flowered in the efforts of Samuel Hopkins and other New Divinity followers of Edwards, who recast Edwards's theology in social activist terms and pursued missionary work to strengthen the devotion to God he recommended. Four out of five of the mission societies established in Massachusetts, Connecticut, and New York before 1790 were founded by New Divinityites. In the 1790s, when the work of British mission societies drew considerable attention in New England and led to the establishment of spin-off societies in the United States, New Divinityites endorsed and supported these societies.[19]

While their descriptions of non-Protestant religions were wholly negative, New Divinity missionaries assumed that all peoples shared the same human nature, and that each individual was of equal importance in the eyes of God.[20]

This equality was one of shared sinfulness rather than innate goodness, but it undermined certain tendencies to racism, classism, and sexism, even as it established the religious grounds on which other people were to be treated as equal. The missionaries of the American Board offered equality to others, although only on strict Protestant terms. Believing in the truth of their theology, and in the inevitability of eternal damnation for those who did not embrace it, they did not see this offer as ironic, patronizing, or unjust. Any resistance they met was a sign of how much their work was needed, and an opportunity to prove their own willingness to be damned for the glory of God.

Distinctions between Religious and Political Imperialism

While complicated by Christocentrism, the egalitarian aspect of the gospel preached by these Americans distinguished them, at least subtly, from British missionaries, whose home country exercised a considerable political and military presence in many countries during the mid–nineteenth century. While antebellum American missionaries were religious imperialists who did not hesitate to impose their theological beliefs on others, their patriotic loyalty was antimilitaristic and independent of U.S. government support. Because their country's government was not a powerful force in foreign cultures, early American missionaries were further removed from political imperialism than many of their British counterparts. Thus in contrast to American missionaries, who despised the caste system in India, British missionaries often treated the Hindu castes as variants of British classes. Although individual British missionaries and government agents in India did strenuously object to the caste system, on the whole they were more deeply implicated in the British Raj and its hierarchical social structure than their American counterparts.

In addition to their independence from military and governmental support, American missionaries carried with them a powerful cultural tradition of resistance to social hierarchy and patriarchy, and specifically, a tradition of resistance to British imperialism. While Americans acknowledged the leadership of British missionaries in many places, and British-American cooperation established a transatlantic evangelical culture that counterbalanced political conflicts between the two countries, their anti-imperialistic political attitudes were rooted in the American struggle for independence from Britain.

Ironically, this lack of class pretense contributed to the Americans' sense of the superiority of their own life style and to their blindness to the richness of other cultures. New Divinity missionaries expressed ignorance and disdain of foreign cultures and reserved their egalitarianism for the people who inhabited them. As the earliest shapers of American foreign policy in Africa, Asia, and the Middle East, missionaries originated the continuing American tendency either to fail to understand or to make negative moral judgments about foreign cultures while sympathizing with the people of those cultures and working to free them for democratic, if not Protestant, life.

Long before the U.S. government had any influence in the Middle East, Africa, or Asia, or any ability to exert influence, New England missionaries systematically disseminated their beliefs about world history and individual salvation in numerous parts of the nonwestern world. By 1860, missionaries representing the theological lineage established by New Divinity writers had published hundreds of religious tracts in native languages and disseminated millions of copies, taught millenarian concepts of history to thousands of children in Persia, Turkey, Hawaii, Africa, India, and China, and preached thousands of sermons, in native languages, on personal responsibility for sin and the damnation in store for those who rejected the Christian gospel.[21] While the concerns of these writings, lessons, and sermons varied subtly according to the proclivities of individual authors, many of them preached that all people were sinful and damned to eternal life in hell unless they received Christ's grace, that God controlled the course of history, that opportunities for grace were often fleeting, and that those who received grace would transform the world as agents of God's redemptive benevolence.

The American Board had its most stunning success in the Hawaiian Islands, where thousands of natives converted to Protestant Christianity in the 1820s and early 1830s. Exploration and trade had precipitated a widespread loss of faith in the old deities and taboos, and this disenchantment made the New Divinity ideas of salvation and damnation more compelling to Pacific Islanders than they otherwise would have been. In the 1820s American missionaries convinced native leaders to condemn casual sexual relations between Island women and American and British sailors. When U.S. Navy lieutenant John Percival lobbied the Hawaiian king and his chiefs to reverse their ban in 1826, the American Board filed a formal complaint in Washington and broadcast their outrage in the American press. Responding to public sentiment, President John Quincy Adams sent a message to the young King Kamehamehan in 1829, urging him to support the Christian education of his people and to respect the missionaries, whose "motives are pure," Adams declared, "and their objects most friendly to the happiness of your people." In 1838 the king and his chiefs asked the missionaries to provide them with American political advisors to instruct them in "the science of Christian government." The missionaries declined this request because of their policy of noninterference in political matters, and they became increasingly concerned about the growing dependence of the Hawaiian leadership on U.S. government and business—even though the religious and educational systems they had instituted were deeply implicated in this dependence.[22]

The Hawaiian situation was unusual. Although the impact of American missionary activity was significant elsewhere as well, in no other country was the success of American missionaries in converting natives to American forms of Protestant Christianity as large or sudden, and in no other country before 1860 were American political, business, and missionary interests so quickly entangled. In other parts of the world where American missionaries were active before 1860, American economic involvement had less impact on social change, and American political power was virtually nonexistent. Far in advance of U.S. business and government, antebellum missionaries played the leading role in transmitting American culture and shaping perceptions of America in many parts of the world.

The number of missionaries in the antebellum era was small compared to the number during the peak era of American foreign missions, which began in the 1890s, when the missionary population swelled from 934 to nearly 5,000; it reached more than 9,000 in 1915.[23] But the relatively small group of antebellum missionaries were among the first Americans to reach foreign peoples, and their ideas had unpredictable and profound effects. Antebellum missionaries played a formative role in the establishment of concerns for democracy and progress that came to shape some areas of U.S. foreign policy; they also played a foundational role in establishing America's reputation for moral arrogance and hypocrisy.

The Importance and Distinctiveness of Antebellum Missionary Women

The entrance of women into missionary work contributed significantly both to enthusiasm for missionary work at home and to social change in many of the regions where American missionaries worked. In addition to being responsible for a considerable portion of the financial resources of missionary boards, antebellum women participated in missionary activity abroad at least as frequently as men. By 1860, the American Board had stationed 691 women and 567 men in various parts of the world.[24] As a result of women's enthusiastic participation and financial sponsorship, agents of the American Board were able to act more aggressively and systematically than American missionaries ever had before, producing a new level of support for missions and a network of missionary cultures around the world.

Through their roles as affectionate wives and hard-working teachers, missionary women modeled the piety that mission societies wanted to reproduce in foreign lands. As one missionary wrote, "The missionary's wife, as well as himself, should be a sort of moving commentary on the Bible; every thing she says or does should remind the hearer or beholder of something in the Bible; her whole life should be altogether a New Testament life."[25] Women missionaries strove to embody this idealism; it was not simply male rhetoric about how women should behave. Thus Mary Lyon's ailing niece Lucy reported from China that she felt it "a privilege to suffer anything, if by our sufferings, we could procure their [the heathen's] salvation."[26]

Women figured importantly in missionary work not only because they modeled Christian virtue and exerted strenuous efforts in behalf of the salvation of foreign peoples, but also because they had access to the women of other lands as missionary men did not. Men's approach to women was carefully restricted in all the cultures where American missionaries ventured, as well as in their own, and it was widely agreed that heathen and infidel women could only be taught by other women.

However naive and idealistic American missionaries were about the coming of the millennium and its reign of social harmony, they were realistic in their belief that the women and children of those cultures must be reached in order for religious and cultural transformations to occur. Because of their access to foreign women and children, American missionary women contributed significantly to changes in female education and gender role differentiation that underlay religious and cultural transformation, although the nature and direction of that transformation inevitably escaped missionary control.

Lyon helped facilitate both the mainstreaming of women into American missionary work and their impact on women and cultures outside the United States. When Mount Holyoke opened in 1837, the missionary martyrs Harriet Newell and Ann Judson were already legendary figures in American culture, and a few dozen other New England women had ventured into foreign mission fields. Lyon's efforts to nurture a missionary spirit in her students helped extend both the reach of the American Board and its emphasis on women's education. The success of her students in organizing and teaching in mission schools, and in garnering support from women at home, figured importantly in the explosion of American Protestant influence around the world.

Despite their importance in the establishment of American influence abroad, the records of antebellum women missionaries exist today in relative obscurity, overshadowed by accounts of the more populous cohort of American women missionaries in the late nineteenth and early twentieth centuries, who have been the subject of important and influential studies in recent years. Later missionaries were often less radical in their commitments to human equality, more professional in outlook and behavior, more committed to the comforts of middle-class domesticity, and further removed from the self-sufficient agrarian lifestyle from which many earlier missionaries came.[27]

Like other forms of women's benevolence, missionary activism also became increasingly rationalized in the course of the nineteenth century, and the old-fashioned willingness to be damned for the glory of God was slowly modified by concerns for professional objectivity and expertise, as missionary women came to identify themselves more completely as professional teachers, doctors, managers, and community organizers.[28] At the same time, missionary women identified themselves increasingly with middle-class American domesticity, partly in response to the growing popularity of Victorian concepts of Christian virtue, and partly as a way to distinguish themselves from what they perceived to be the degraded situation of nonwestern women. Even as the numbers of single women missionaries increased in the late nineteenth century, middle-class domesticity became an increasingly prominent goal of missionary evangelism.[29]

Lyon opposed the incipient forms of both professionalization and middle-class domesticity as they manifested themselves in her day. Against the protests of Catharine Beecher, she defended her plan to pay Mount Holyoke teachers a low salary with the argument that teaching required of women a kind of selflessness "which cannot be understood by the natural heart." Lyon's concern to insure women sufficient latitude for their public activism dovetailed quite explicitly with this commitment to religious humility. It also dovetailed with her endorsement of conventional assumptions about gender role differentiation. Thus she was happy to "make all due concessions, where god has designed a difference in the situation of the sexes, such as woman's retiring from public stations, being generally dependent on the other sex for pecuniary support, &c." in order that "we may plead constantly for her religious privileges, for equal facilities for the improvement of her talents, and for the privilege of using all her talents in doing good."[30]

Although Lyon agreed with Beecher that domestic skill and organization were essential aspects of women's work, she regarded disinterested benevolence rather than domesticity as the chief organizing principle of Christian culture. In contrast, Beecher sought to define both women and Christian culture in terms of domesticity, and developed a "science" of domestic economy. While Beecher's philosophy is consonant with the effort missionary women made in the late nineteenth and early twentieth centuries to replicate American middle-class domesticity as a marker of difference from heathen cultures, it sets her apart from Lyon and Lyon's commitment to the radical egalitarianism New Divinity thought.[31]

Beecher's enthusiasm for domestic culture and the professional development of women's work and morality does prefigure enthusiasm for those concerns in missionary work at the turn of the twentieth century, but does not represent the worldview of Mary Lyon or other antebellum supporters of missionary work, whose enthusiasm for foreign missions Beecher did not, in fact, share. Recent scholarship on nineteenth-century missionary women has overlooked this fundamental difference between Lyon and Beecher and its relevance for understanding the distinctive character of antebellum mission work. In *The World Their Household*, Patricia R. Hill quotes or refers to Beecher on numerous occasions, and Jane Hunter begins *The Gospel of Gentility* with a quotation from Beecher extolling women's "exalted privilege of extending over the world those blessed influences, which are to renovate degraded man, and 'to clothe all climes in beauty.' "[32] But Beecher resisted the process of conversion in her own life, and was never able to represent herself as inherently sinful.[33] She was certainly eloquent on the subject of sacrifice—she called it "the grand law"—but she did not recognize the sharp contrast between self-interest and self-sacrifice associated with New Divinity thought. Moreover, her discomfort with radical notions of original sin distanced her from the egalitarianism of New Divinity thought. Beecher believed that women were inherently superior as moral beings to men. In contrast, Lyon understood disinterested benevolence as something women could excel in because of their social experience, but not something that was more applicable or relevant to them than to men. For Lyon, disinterested benevolence was common ground between men and women as well as a legitimate field for women's activism.

The Myth of Puritanism's Morbidity

The failure to appreciate these points is not simply an accidental oversight, but an expression of the powerful myth of the decline of the Puritan tradition in New England that has persisted in the study of the Republican and antebellum eras for at least two generations, obscuring the activism of American missionary women and their role in disseminating American ideas abroad. More than sixty years ago, Joseph Haroutunian found the theology of the late-eighteenth- and early-nineteenth-century New Divinity leaders who revitalized the Puritan tradition to be inadequate in comparison with the magisterial intellectualism and existential authenticity of their seventeenth-century forbears. More specifically, Haroutunian argued that Jonathan Edwards's followers dissipated his lively defense of Calvinist piety and turned it into a dry and rigid moralism that attracted only the most unimaginative conservatives.[34]

Subsequent scholarship has embellished Haroutunian's interpretation of the intellectual rigidity and emotional insufficiency of the Puritan tradition after Edwards. Sidney Mead showed how Nathaniel William Taylor rescued New England theology from the fatalistic morass of consistent Calvinism by introducing more self-affirming conceptions of free will. More recently, Kathryn Kish Sklar linked Catharine Beecher's efforts to transcend her Calvinist background to her contribution to the advancement of women's education and to her own struggle for emancipation from her father's patriarchal Puritanism.[35]

In *The Feminization of American Culture*, Ann Douglas took a more positive view of Puritan culture, but she followed Haroutunian and her own mentor, Perry Miller, in portraying the theology of Jonathan Edwards as the high point of American religious thought, from which subsequent thought proceeded downhill. In contrast to Sklar, Douglas linked the decline of Calvinism not to the liberation of women but to women's overbearing influence. Contrasting the intellectual strength of Puritan theology with the intellectual weakness of sentimental novelists and preachers who seemed to her to dominate nineteenth-century American culture, Douglas explored the relationship between the ascendance of sentimentality in nineteenth-century American culture and the establishment of a materialistic culture of domestic consumption. In Douglas's scenario, the moribund giant of Calvinism was brought down not by the intellectual and emotional inadequacy of Edwards's successors, but by mobs of overwrought women and their allies, beneficiaries, and seducers in the pulpit.[36]

While Douglas overlooks the vitality of the Puritan tradition in the antebellum era, she is justified in pointing to the ascendance of a consumerist culture of domestic gentility and sentimentality. Social historians who understand the antebellum era in terms of the emergence of the middle-class family are not as acerbic about these values as Douglas, but Mary P. Ryan, Carol Smith-Rosenberg, and others rightly point to the institutionalization of "feminine" characteristics in the antebellum era and to the increasing importance of gender role differentiation in nineteenth-century America. In Ryan's analysis, images of Victorian womanhood played a crucial role in the American response to both urban industrialization and new patterns of immigration. "Women and gender symbolism propped up ethnic and religious differences" in antebellum America, Ryan argues, as "womanhood was subdivided along the axis of sexual propriety and social respectability into the dangerous and the endangered."[37]

In recent years, scholars have discovered challenges to inequality in nineteenth-century America in religious movements outside the mainstream. Studies of spiritualism and nature religion have pointed to the significance of these movements in nurturing strong traditions of gender and racial equality. But however welcome this attention to alternative religious movements, it has done nothing to challenge the idea that Puritan culture in antebellum America was moribund or to foster recognition of its egalitarian element. Indeed, scholars of spiritualism and nature religion have presented these religious movements as positive alternatives to all forms of mainstream Protestantism, and especially Calvinism, which is portrayed, in the words of one historian of spiritualism, in terms of its "repressive social [and] religious strictures."[38]

Working against this trend, a few scholars have begun to acknowledge the vitality of the Puritan tradition in Republican and antebellum America.[39] Most importantly, Joseph A. Conforti argues for the popularity of Edwardsean theology in the antebellum era, and for the importance of Edwards's disciple, Samuel Hopkins, whose reshaping of Edwardsean thought contributed significantly to the outpouring of benevolent activism in the second Great Awakening. Conforti points to the importance of Mary Lyon as a nineteenth-century representative of the Calvinist tradition, who framed her successful efforts to advance women's education in terms of Edwardsean theology. In his view, Lyon's success in establishing Mount Holyoke Female Seminary in 1837 as America's first publicly endowed institute of higher education for women is evidence not only of the vitality of Puritan thought in the nineteenth century but also of the effectiveness of that thought as "inspiration and legitimation for a new level of female self-assertion."[40]

As Conforti argues, Lyon's loyalty to Edwardsean theology has either been made to seem inconsequential or has functioned to obscure the importance of her contributions to women's history. Thus Kathryn Kish Sklar recognized the evangelical spirit in which Lyon founded Mount Holyoke, as well as Mount Holyoke's importance in the development of higher education for women, but failed to examine Lyon's theology or its role in shaping her ideas about women's education. Similarly, while providing meticulous detail about virtually all other aspects of Lyon's life, Elizabeth Alden Green's biography brushes Lyon's neo-Calvinism aside and fails to recognize its central role in shaping her educational philosophy. For example, in one of her few brief references to Lyon's religious views, Green notes simplistically, "Although she was an admirer of Jonathan Edwards and a believer in eternal damnation as well as eternal salvation, Miss Lyon talked to the students much less about the pains of hellfire than the sadness of being left out of heaven and the exhilaration of life animated by faith."[41]

Much as Lyon's biographer downplays the centrality of New Divinity thought in her worldview, other historians of women's education during the

Republican and antebellum eras tend to locate advances in women's education in the context of enlightenment rationalism. Ann Firor Scott's articles on Emma Willard show that Willard's plans for improving women's education were rooted in the Republican philosophy of the late eighteenth century. The Episcopalian mildness of Willard's religious temperament not only suited the liberal rationalism of her educational programs but also makes her a congenial protofeminist from Sklar's secular feminist perspective.[42] But while Willard and other religiously liberal advocates of women's education understood Republican Motherhood in relatively humanistic terms, Joseph Emerson, Zilpah Grant, Mary Lyon, and other neo-Puritans interpreted it in the context of the Edwardsean tradition and its antecedents in seventeenth-century Puritan theology.

Linda Kerber, the scholar who has done most to conceptualize the ideology of Republican Motherhood, has demonstrated its centrality in arguments supporting women's education. But she treats the religious aspect of Republican Motherhood as an indicator of women's marginalization rather than as the basis of their growing participation in public life.[43] Kerber and other historians have overemphasized the roots of Republican Motherhood in enlightenment rationalism, failed to explore the intersection between this ideology and New Divinity thought, and overlooked the roots of this connection in the religious tradition of New England Puritanism.[44]

The Feminist Distaste for Self-Denial

If Mary Lyon's loyalty to the Puritan tradition has obscured her importance as a spokesperson for Republican Motherhood, her intense interest in foreign mission work, and her success in making Mount Holyoke the foremost center for the training of American women missionaries in the nineteenth century, has not helped to elevate her reputation in late-twentieth-century historiography. Recent feminist studies emphasize the role that nineteenth-century missionary women played in carrying out the cultural imperialism of Anglo-Protestant culture, but overlook the egalitarian aspect of antebellum missionary theology and the intense concern missionaries had to conquer every impulse to self-aggrandizement. A balanced view of antebellum missionary women requires some understanding of this egalitarian impulse and its impact on other women. But it is precisely the missionary impulse to self-denial that distances antebellum missionaries both from feminist scholars today who are concerned about a usable past and from feminist theologians who call on women to be assertive, self-fulfilled, and conscious of personal worth. This ideological difference contributes significantly to the cloud of obscurity that envelopes antebellum missionary women and their place in American religious history.

In an essay published in 1960 that became the first landmark of feminist theology, Valerie Saiving challenged the long-standing identification of pride with sin in Christian thought, arguing that it is debilitating and inappropriate for women, who do not express lust for power and recognition, Saiving believed, as men do. The temptations to which women are most prone "can never be encompassed by such terms as 'pride' and 'will-to-power,' " because women's lives are filled with "moments, hours, and days of self-giving." If a woman is to experience a full religious life, Saiving argued, these moments of self-giving "must be balanced by moments, hours, and days of withdrawal into, and enrichment of, her individual selfhood." Without this requisite pride in herself, "a woman can give too much of herself, so that nothing remains of her own uniqueness; she can became merely an emptiness, almost a zero, without value to herself, to her fellow men, or perhaps, even to God."[45]

While subsequent writings in feminist theology have elaborated on this general argument,[46] some American Christian women writers have criticized the individualism of this approach. For example, Jacquelyn Grant has argued that feminist theology lacks sufficient appreciation of the strength that African-American women have derived from experiences of dependence on Christ. As Grant explains the nature and effect of this dependence, "In the experiences of Black people, Jesus was 'all things.' Chief among these however, was the belief in Jesus as the divine co-sufferer, who empowers them in situations of oppression." In the lives of African-American women, suffering and Christianity were entangled, but "the role of Jesus unraveled as they encountered him in their experience as one who empowers the weak."[47] On the other hand, pride also has a strongly positive value for African-American Christian women, as well as for other women in American churches today, and self-denigration is often viewed as inappropriate, especially in social and political relationships. Even among African-American Baptists today, whose concept of grace and sense of dependence on God brings them closer than many others to the sensibility of antebellum missionaries, the emphasis on taking pride in one's own identity and culture distances them from antebellum women missionaries.[48]

For these missionaries, the identification of pride with sin was unequivocal. The self-assurance so much encouraged in American culture today would seem to them antithetical to Christian virtue, which they understood as a radical rejection of self-interest, epitomized by the willingness to be damned for the glory of God. Like many Christians before them, these women believed that grace involved a willingness to sacrifice oneself for others and an evangelical faith that called others to the same self-denying love of Christ. In the tradition of Augustine, Calvin, and Jonathan Edwards, the women who are the subject of this book understood sin as the desire for self-gratification and empowerment, which, for them, constituted prideful rebellion against God. Their adamant rejection of pride distinguishes them from many women today, and especially from feminists who reject the traditional identification of sin with pride and perceive its function as a means of justifying women's oppression.

The selflessness embraced by antebellum missionary women locates them at a considerable distance from the commitments of present-day feminists, and this distance has contributed to their obscurity. It is important to recognize that they contributed to women's increasing prominence in American public life, and that this prominence contributed in turn to the development of a national culture in which feminist ideas of gender equity have come to command considerable, although certainly not universal, respect. It is equally important to note that the effectiveness of antebellum missionary women's efforts contributed to the erosion of that radical commitment to disinterested benevolence on which they had based their claim to public life. That is, as women succeeded in establishing their expertise as agents of public trust, the heroic selflessness that had once inspired and legitimated that trust ceased to be a requisite of public activism and employment. With their role in public life well-established, New England Protestant women continued to be religious, but they were not so preoccupied by the tension between their own self-interest and Christian virtue as were their predecessors. This shift in religious thinking made for a less punitive religious psychology but also undermined the egalitarianism implicit in the radical hostility to self-interest characteristic of New Divinity thought.

A similar set of observations can be made with regard to the ideology of Republican Motherhood that Lyon and other New Divinityites embraced. Women who benefited from the development of women's education and influence eventually broke free of conventional assumptions about the limits of women's public activism associated with the ideology of Republican Motherhood, but that ideology and its endorsement of limits on women's activism played a central role in the development of women's education and influence. It is equally important to note that the increasing freedom from deference to male authority that some educated American women enjoyed distanced them from women in other cultures who remained loyal to traditional customs. However problematic, the ideology of Republican Motherhood espoused by American missionary women resonated profoundly with the beliefs of many nonwestern women who were also endeavoring to improve their lives without relinquishing the deference to male authority that characterized their loyalty to traditional culture.

TWO

Religious Community
at Mount Holyoke

The intellectual worldview associated with Republican Motherhood and New Divinity theology offered Mary Lyon and other New England women a means of interpreting and negotiating social change. At a time when traditional communities based on economic self-sufficiency, ministerial authority, and interpersonal consensus were declining, and a national culture based on far-reaching and interlocking forms of industry, communication, and transportation was developing, Republican Motherhood and New Divinity theology enabled New England women to affirm their loyalty to traditional values while exploring new opportunities for work and influence. Through education and teaching these women both expanded the parameters of their lives and maintained significant experiences of community.

Female boarding schools were especially conducive to women's efforts to recreate the experience of community they associated with traditional New England culture. At the same time, boarding schools gave women a new degree of independence from male authority and enabled them both to define ideals of social progress in female terms and to pursue their own personal advancement more intensively than conventional family life allowed.

Education and Teaching as Means of Negotiating
Social Stress and Change

The women who galvanized the missionary movement in antebellum New England, and who were among the first to establish impressions of America overseas, came from backgrounds of both intense piety and considerable social and psychological stress. Mary Lyon became a passionate advocate for the education of these women; she had shared their experience of growing up in a sagging rural economy with a disproportionate number of women. Expressing her preoccupying concern for these women to her friend and assistant Hannah White in 1834, Lyon wrote, "During the past year, my heart has so yearned over the adult female youth in the common walks of life, that it has sometimes seemed as if there was a fire, shut up in my bones." [1]

Because they were more dependent on their fathers and more closely identified with domestic production, unmarried women could not move as freely as their brothers to the more abundant and less exhausted lands of western New York and Ohio. Moreover, as the economy of New England began to shift toward industrialization, the home began to decline in importance as an economic center. Women became increasingly less occupied in spinning cloth, making soap and candles, and taking part in other household industries, but without enjoying the degree of freedom men had to travel to cities for work or mechanical training. The emerging shift in economic production, coupled with the related phenomena of low male population and delayed marriage, created a new need among young women for meaningful employment. As David Allmendinger has shown, young women in antebellum New England often faced a period in their late teens and early twenties when they became economic burdens on their families. In this situation, they turned with increasing frequency to teaching. [2]

This increased interest in teaching among young women coincided with efforts across New England to implement laws passed at the end of the eighteenth century mandating public support for education. In many cases, girls' education improved dramatically when these laws were put into practice. Thus in 1812 the town of Northampton finally enacted a 1792 ruling by the attorney general of Massachusetts directed to the town's selectmen, which specified that "girls had rights and could not be excluded from school." [3] Such advances in public education stimulated an increased demand for teachers qualified to instruct girls. This new demand, together with an increasing supply of young women eager to be educated as teachers, led to what Mary Lyon identified as "an era in female education."

Kathryn Kish Sklar maintains that in 1770 only 45 percent of New England women were literate, compared with 90 percent of men, and that this gap was substantially diminished by 1850, when literacy in New England was almost universal for native-born Euro-American women. Because of the prevalence of home schooling, other scholars believe that female literacy in eighteenth-century New England was never as low as 45 percent, but they corroborate Sklar's finding that women were often excluded from public schools. As Sklar has shown, by 1810 many town and district schools had opened their doors to girls and begun to employ women as teachers. Even though some of the new classes for girls were only taught during special summer sessions, girls began to enjoy more academic equality with boys. And even though the pay that schoolmistresses received was often a fraction of what men received for similar work, the women who taught school enjoyed "a new kind of prestige" as publicly employed authorities.[4]

Mary Lyon understood the new opportunities for female teachers in early-nineteenth-century America as a highly significant example of God's work of redemption. "Without this wide and increasing field of usefulness," she wrote in 1837, the year Mount Holyoke opened, "that would be a dark providence, which, by manufacturing establishments, has taken from families so much domestic labor, which had its influence in forming the character of our maternal ancestors. But 'providence meets providence,' " she added confidently. Might not one see, she wondered appreciatively, "the hand of One, wiser than Solomon, in all the labor-saving machinery of the present day?"[5]

Lyon faced the first of her own dark providences in 1802, when she was five, and her father died on the family's relatively isolated farm in Buckland, Massachusetts. When her mother remarried eight years later, Mary took over the domestic work of the farm, which had been left to her older brother. Her domestic role became more tenuous when her brother married two years later in 1814. She began teaching summer sessions for girls in a district school; when her brother moved west with his family in 1817 and left her without a home, she entered the coeducational Sanderson Academy in Ashfield, five miles from Buckland, determined to prepare herself more systematically for teaching. She paid for her tuition at Sanderson with money she had earned by spinning, weaving, and teaching until these meager savings ran out, and then she received free tuition for one semester a year in exchange for supervising younger students.[6] In 1821, older at twenty-four than most female students, Lyon entered the Ladies Seminary at Byfield established by Joseph Emerson in 1818. As one who combined New Divinity thought with the promotion of female education, Emerson had a profound influence on Lyon. He renewed her positive sense of divine providence and inspired her with the idea that female teachers had an important role to play in God's plan.

Under Emerson's tutelage, the intense pressure Lyon felt to provide and account for herself began to be transformed into a sense of mission. The confidence in divine providence expressed by her mentors at Byfield rescued her from episodes of personal despair, prepared her for successful teaching, and inspired her eagerness to act on behalf of the young women of her society. As her concept of Mount Holyoke took shape, her mentors' millenarian view of history met her sense of perilousness and superfluity, and their vision of women's foundational role in the scheme of world redemption met her desire for education and meaningful work.

Joseph Emerson was committed to making women's education "more solid and much more extensive." The curriculum he instituted at Byfield included the study of Latin, which was widely recognized as the language of scholars and often considered inappropriate in women's education, as well as moral philosophy, history, geography, and some of the sciences. Drawing, dance, and French, taught in other female seminaries patronized by wealthy families with aristocratic tastes, were pointedly omitted. Concerned to teach young women to be agents of social and intellectual reform, not ornaments of polite society, Emerson viewed his seminary as a seedbed for a broader movement in women's education. "His object," wrote his brother and biographer, "was not merely to have a good seminary of his own, but also to benefit other teachers, and to raise up a multitude more, of the right stamp, and ultimately to fill the land with such seminaries and schools."[7]

Many elements of Lyon's conception of Mount Holyoke can be traced to Emerson's ideas. In her efforts to educate women teachers whose moral and intellectual influence would advance God's work of redemption, she followed Emerson in integrating Republican Motherhood with New Divinity theology. She also followed Emerson in establishing a boarding school that offered women new opportunities for advancement while at the same time reaffirming their connection to the cultural values of traditional New England society. But Lyon went beyond her mentor in creating a religious community that was deliberately and systematically modeled on the social order of the kingdom of God. In establishing an intentional religious community as well as an educational institution, Lyon encouraged unmarried rural women, who bore much of the stress of social change, to join their lives together to show the world how it could be redeemed.

Mount Holyoke as an Instance of Antebellum Communitarianism

In founding Mount Holyoke, Lyon not only promoted Christian benevolence among her students and faculty but also institutionalized it as a principle of social cohesion. As a religious institution that offered a model of Christian society for all to see, Mount Holyoke had much in common with the Oneida, Shaker, and Mormon communities of the same era. Like the leaders of these other religious communities, Lyon responded to the economic and social changes occurring in early-nineteenth-century America with an effort to manage those changes through a millenarian vision of social transformation and historical progress.

Mount Holyoke was unique among the other religious communities of the antebellum era in its intended appeal to young unmarried women, and in its responsiveness both to their desire for education and to the new demand for women teachers. Unlike other intentional religious communities of the antebellum era, Mount Holyoke offered a transition between life stages, and members arrived with the intention of completing some or all of the three-year course before becoming teachers, missionaries, wives, and mothers. But even though they entered with the expectation of leaving in a few years, the students at Mount Holyoke participated in a communal organization where the virtues of benevolence and mutuality were nurtured and expected of them at every turn. Moreover, a large number of alumnae retained ties to the seminary, and more than a few established satellite schools that replicated both the curriculum and the communal structure of their alma mater.

The communal organization of Mount Holyoke centered on Lyon's own authority and on the principle of self-sacrificial benevolence, which she expected her students and teachers to employ in their relationships with one another and to carry forth with them into the world. In teaching young women to embody this spirit of benevolence as well as to be knowledgeable about current advances in science and history, Lyon believed she was helping to create a middle-class culture that would inspire the world. "This middle class," she wrote in 1833, "contains the main springs, and main wheels, which are to move the world."[8]

Lyon's conception of the middle class was more of a vision of how the future would be organized than a description of social life in rural New England. The economically strapped farming families whose daughters made up the vast majority of Mount Holyoke students before the Civil War did indeed highly esteem thrift, industriousness, and personal conscience, which would come to characterize middle-class values, but they did not have the economic security, consumerist life style, or moral complacency commonly associated with those values.[9] Moreover, the antebellum families who sent daughters to Mount Holyoke had only begun to make the transition to an industrialized economy associated with middle-class society. The alterations in gender roles necessary to that transition were still very much in the process of being negotiated. Thus Lyon's concept of the middle class was a visionary and utopian one, which set thrift, industriousness, and individual conscience not in the context of a bourgeois lifestyle but within a traditional economy of reciprocity.

As a model of how society should be organized, Mount Holyoke combined innovative strategies with traditional ones. Women exerted new levels of influence as administrators and teachers, while respecting and cooperating with male authorities who praised and helped support the seminary. Thus Lyon capitalized on new economic trends that drew women out of the home and into schools by providing advanced education and teacher training at low cost to the daughters of poor farmers and artisans in New England who could not otherwise afford it, while at the same time reestablishing elements of the traditional New England family, such as shared and interchangeable labor, centralized authority, and consensual piety.

Mount Holyoke Compared to the Oneida Community

The social organization Lyon implemented might be compared to any one of a number of religious communities, but especially instructive comparisons can be drawn between Mount Holyoke and the Oneida Community established by John Humphrey Noyes in upstate New York in 1848, after the community's reputation for free love forced it to leave Putney, Vermont. Despite radical differences in their interpretation of Protestant doctrine, both Lyons and Noyes were steeped in the theology of Jonathan Edwards and his disciples, both attempted to institutionalize Christian principles in every facet of community life; and both were optimistic and millenarian about social change. Both fused the enthusiasm for invention and efficiency characteristic of the new industrial age with an ideal of psychological consensus and mutuality characteristic of earlier Puritan communities.

Like Lyon, Noyes invoked the concept of family life in establishing his community as a model of the world to come. As Lawrence Foster emphasizes, "life at Oneida" was based on "an enlarged family model," in which members woke together, ate together, did chores together, and "almost all necessary activities were carried out within the Community itself." Jobs rotated, not only for the purpose of discovering otherwise hidden talents in community members, but also, as Robert S. Fogarty pointed out, to "reaffirm the conviction of each individual that he was part of a larger scheme in which he had to fit." This larger scheme involved both the organic unity of the community itself, in which individuals were expected to fit, and a theological conception of world history in which the Oneida Community was a culminating event. Thus Noyes described his community as a "sortie or raid from the kingdom of God." As Fogarty put it, Noyes and his perfectionist followers were inspired by "the belief that by faith and example they might show a sinful world the road to regeneration." [10]

Noyes grew up under the tutelage of an intensely religious mother who instilled in him the ethos of the New England Puritan tradition. As a student at Andover Seminary in 1831–32, he underwent a conversion experience guided by his reading of Jonathan Edwards's theology, and joined The Brethren, a secret group of young men dedicated to missionary work who often found wives at Mount Holyoke before embarking for foreign mission fields. After he declared himself free of sin in 1834, Noyes resigned from The Brethren and distanced himself from Edwardsean restatements of the old Puritan belief that assurance of salvation was a sign of pride. But he retained the millenarianism characteristic of Edwardsean thought, along with Edwards's belief in grace as an indwelling, vital principle that irrevocably altered one's frame of reference. [11]

Both Lyon and Noyes adhered faithfully to Edwards's central idea that grace was an indwelling principle in the soul transforming every aspect of a person's behavior, thought, and feeling. For Edwards, Lyon, and Noyes, one of the most likely ways of receiving this grace was to see it in others in whom it worked. The true Christian embodied the beauty of God and represented it to others, these thinkers believed, and Christian society resulted from this principle of grace working in individuals. As a logical extension of this belief in the contagious and cumulative power of grace, Edwards, Lyon, and Noyes all understood that a golden age of Christian harmony and righteousness would occur within history, and that its construction had already begun. [12] But while Edwards had been able to encourage the contagious and cumulative power of grace in a society of eighteenth-century towns where individual identity was still largely shaped in face-to-face relationships with ministers and other community leaders, Lyon and Noyes found they had to establish independent communities of their own in order to facilitate the kind of personal transformations they desired.[13]

The enlarged family life at Mount Holyoke did not involve explicit sexual relations, as was the case with the system of Ascending Fellowship at the Oneida Community, where older members initiated younger ones into the spiritual and sexual practices of the community, nor did it, at the other extreme, equate Christian life with celibacy, as did the Shakers. But it did provide women with an alternative to marriage, for a few years or a lifetime, while at the same time offering them the experience and structure of a family. Lyon often referred to her students as daughters, encouraged them to regard each other as sisters, and identified these familial affections with Christian virtue. In her effort to "lay the whole foundation" of her seminary "on Christian principles," Lyon worked to "form a family, that from day to day might illustrate the precepts and spirit of the gospel." As at Oneida and in other religious families of the time, a tiered system of spiritual experience defined social structure at Mount Holyoke; at the top rank, Lyon encouraged students who best exemplified Christian life to be missionaries or to remain at Mount Holyoke as teachers, and from this latter cohort she chose special assistants with whom she was particularly intimate.[14]

Like Noyes, Lyon encouraged a "union of interests" in her community,[15] and urged community members to model their interactions with one another on the coherent and amiable social organization that characterized the kingdom of God. Avoidance of economic distinctions among students was essential to this union. "The principle of entire equality among the pupils is to be adopted," Lyon wrote eight months before Mount Holyoke opened. For this equality to be achieved, the spirit of mutual cooperation could not be violated by anyone's dependence on outsiders for basic needs and services. Equality among students required a system that would "reliev[e] them from the servile dependence on common domestics, to which young ladies, as mere boarders in a large establishment, are very much exposed."[16] In Lyon's view, the division of women in most boarding establishments into housekeepers, boarders, and hired domestics "endangers the simplicity, kindness & mutual confidence, which have been so tenderly fostered at home, & tends to cultivate artfulness, selfishness & distrust."[17] Lyon believed these flaws in female character were increasingly common, and linked them to the breakdown of the traditional family, where mutuality, consensus, and respect for authority had been part of daily routine.

The Role of Community In Shaping Modern Society in the United States

Lyon and Noyes were not alone in their millenarian views of history or in wanting to contain the ideas and behaviors associated with an emerging national economy within the context of family-style relationships organized around an authoritative leader. The Mormon leaders Joseph Smith and Brigham Young, the Shaker leaders at New Lebanon, the Methodist bishop Francis Asbury, the American Methodist Episcopal bishop Richard Allen, the founder of the Disciples of Christ Alexander Campbell, and even the Shawnee prophet Tenskwatawa represent this underlying dynamic. But historians often overlook this pervasive religious response to social change in antebellum America. A justifiable concern to understand the specific characteristics of particular groups and locales may be partly responsible for this oversight, but failure to appreciate the importance of religion in social and intellectual change is also at play. This failure has led, among other things, to the view that religion has been largely irrelevant to the emergence of modern society in America, and that traditional religious concerns for communal consensus have played a marginal or reactionary role in the development of American history.

Thus Bernard Bailyn and Gordon Wood, in writing about Revolutionary and early Republican periods, emphasized the movement away from consensual ideals and patriarchal religious authorities that dominated seventeenth- and early-eighteenth-century American culture. These historians leave little room to consider the emergence of new religious communities as anything more than reactionary opponents of the liberal forces of individualism and democracy that triumphed in the American Revolution and in the decades that followed. Even scholars of religious history concerned to document the vitality of religion in the antebellum era have been persuaded by this model to overlook the crucial role that religion played in generating enthusiasm for the new industrial era and shaping its contours. Thus Nathan O. Hatch emphasized the democratic egalitarianism of five religious movements of the Republican and antebellum eras—the Christian movement, the Methodists, the Baptists, African-American churches, and the Mormons—and stressed their hostility to Calvinist theology and its authoritarian ministry. But Hatch makes little mention of the hunger for community and communal consensus characteristic of these groups, and cannot explain why such democratic movements spawned authoritarian leaders.[18]

The antebellum belief in the possibility of wedding religious tradition to modern progress has often been obscured by a tendency among historians to perceive traditional community and modern society in mutually exclusive terms. The distinction between community and society was first articulated by Sir Henry Maines, who argued in the 1860s and 1870s that modernity entailed a shift from social organizations based on status and identification with authority to those based on contract and personal autonomy. Ferdinand Tonnies expanded the distinction in his book *Gemeinshaft and Gesellschaft*, published in 1877, which concluded that in the gemeinshaft of traditional community, people "remain essentially united in spite of all separating factors, whereas in *Gesellschaft* they are essentially separated in spite of all uniting factors." Emile Durkheim drew a similar distinction between simple societies characterized by interchangeable labor and more complex societies characterized by division of labor. In the twentieth century, Louis Wirth and Talcott Parsons interpreted these ideal types in the context of an evolutionary model that required gesellschaft to replace gemeinshaft in developing societies. Bailyn, Wood, and other historians of American culture change adhered to this evolutionary model in numerous accounts of the breakdown of traditional community in the face of the gathering power of modern society.[19]

In an important critique of such arguments, Thomas Bender argued that zero-sum interpretations of the relationship between gemeinshaft and gesellschaft cannot be justified on historical grounds, and that the relationship is actually a dynamic, interactive one. Thus in America after 1820, Bender writes, "The emerging national economic system, together with the increased mobility made possible in part by improvements in transportation, with national political parties, and with other regional and national voluntary associations, brought a new configuration to local life. Although the first impulse of the historian and social scientist is to describe this transformation as an eclipse of local life by larger and more important social aggregates, something different seems actually to have happened."[20]

Not only did local identity flourish after 1820, as Bender argues, so did intentional religious communities more or less separate from local towns. And the role of these religious communities with respect to the emerging national economy was not marginal or simply reactionary. At Mount Holyoke and elsewhere, the revitalization of an older style of social existence based on face-to-face consensus and authority made enthusiasm for industrial society possible.

The Mechanics of Communal Life at Mount Holyoke

Lyon's notion of the middle class as a kind of engine, whose mainsprings and wheels would move the world, reveals her enthusiasm for industrial modernization, as does her interest in "introducing system" into every aspect of life at Mount Holyoke.[21] This concern for system ranged from her careful compartmentalization of the day into a balanced sequence of activities, including calisthenics, long walks, and prayer meetings, to the layout of the domestic department, in which the ovens, sinks, crockery, cutlery, flour barrels, potatoes, ironing boards, tubs, doors, and post office were placed in the most efficient relation to each other possible.[22] Lyon took great pleasure in the way this department worked like a well-oiled machine. "Now I need not go into the kitchen once a month unless I prefer," she wrote the head of Monticello College, Theron Baldwin, in 1838, "though I do love daily to pass round from room to room in the basement story, & see how delightfully the wheels move forward."[23] A description of how she appeared to her students shows that they shared her penchant for industrial imagery. "She used to come sometimes driving into the Domestic Hall," one student wrote, "like a veritable steam engine."[24]

As in the Oneida Community, where the manufacture of steel traps, carpetbags, and other items involved both factorylike systems of production and modern systems of marketing and delivery, Lyon and other members of the Mount

Holyoke community were enthusiastic about labor-saving devices, advances in physical education, and new improvements in communication and transportation. Lyon swept up all these modern devices, advances, and improvements into her millenarian vision of a new world order ruled by Christian benevolence. As a model community designed to put the mechanics of benevolence to work, the Mount Holyoke Female Seminary would show how the millennium would be organized and thus help bring it about.

Crucial to Lyon's understanding of the mechanics of her seminary was attention to the proper relationship between the input and the output of benevolence. She wanted the subscriptions and donations flowing into the seminary to originate in the same spirit of benevolence that motivated the lives and labors of the students going out. This concern for a uniform quality of benevolence flowing through the seminary expressed itself in her argument that the "benefactors" of the institution should be of the same "class" as its "beneficiaries." Thus Lyon hoped that the example of benevolence provided by the donors would serve God's plan of promoting benevolence in her students who, in turn, would transmit it to others. Benevolence would be promoted in the people to whom she appealed for support, who would have to scrimp to contribute, and at the same time instill a special sense of gratitude and obligation in young women who knew their education was paid for by people who made personal sacrifices in order to be able to contribute. This concern for maintaining the flow of benevolence was theological as well as practical; in her effort to institutionalize and regulate its transmission, Lyon carried forward the Edwardsean idea that Christian virtue was not something that one could generate by herself; it had to come from a source outside the self, most commonly from meditation on the Bible or the inspiration of the example of a fellow Christian.

In her concern for the actual manifestation of theological ideas, Lyon orchestrated the mundane work of the seminary into a kind of symphony of benevolence. Students were grouped into "circles" devoted to particular tasks, such as washing, ironing, baking bread, making pies, setting tables, cleaning tumblers and dishes, washing floors, or sweeping hallways. This domestic program was the most controversial aspect of the seminary; Lyon answered numerous objections about the supposed drudgery of these assignments and repeatedly corrected the impression that Mount Holyoke was an institution of manual training. "It is no part of the design of this seminary to teach young ladies domestic work. This branch of education is exceedingly important," she wrote in 1837, "but a literary institution is not the place to gain it."[25] But if domestic work was not a topic of study, like astronomy, botany, or Latin, it was a necessary and eminently useful "appendage" of Mount Holyoke's system of benevolence.

Lyon regarded domestic work at Mount Holyoke "not as a matter of drudgery, but of elevated independence. . . . The thought of degradation or servility never seems to enter [the students'] minds, & why should it." Dependence on the labor of others for basic physical needs did not fit Lyon's notion of "An educated lady, who expects to be useful."[26] Such dependence also hindered happiness and sociability. Thus Lyon noted, "One young lady remarked last spring, that she had been rather homesick, but the first washing day, was an effectual remedy."[27] Most important, cooperative domestic work fostered that "obliging disposition" and "spirit of gratitude and . . . sense of obligation" so necessary, Lyon believed, to women's happiness and Christian virtue. Willing cooperation in the "continued scene of conferring and receiving favors" of domestic life overcame loneliness, produced happiness, and defined, in Lyon's view, "The excellence of the female character."[28]

Moreover, with students doing the domestic work, tuition could be kept as low as possible. "Could the expenses be reduced one third, or one half," Lyon wrote early on in the development of her plans for a seminary, "a great number, who now almost despair of ever being able to realize the object of their ardent desires," would be able to attend. In a circular addressed to the supporters of Ipswich Female Seminary, where she had taught for ten years with Zilpah Grant, Lyon argued that tuition might be sizably reduced by assigning the domestic work of the seminary to students, as well as by raising building funds by subscription, furnishing rooms with donations, providing tuition and board "at cost," and employing teachers with "so much of a missionary spirit" that they would gladly accept "only a moderate salary."[29] In response to Catharine Beecher's complaint that Mount Holyoke's low tuition put pressure on other seminaries to reduce their fees, she was impatient: "Shall we ask for higher tuition, at the same time that we are asking for benevolent aid?"[30]

As a strategy for attracting donors as well as an expression of her commitment to Edwardsean theology, Lyon located the founding of Mount Holyoke in the context of a great momentum of self-sacrificial benevolence that would "advanc[e] the Redeemer's kingdom." As she wrote in an 1835 circular advertising the seminary and seeking subscriptions for its endowment, "This institution is to be founded by the combined liberality of an enlarged benevolence, which seeks the greatest good on a large scale." Invoking "those great souls . . . whose plans and works of mercy are like a broad river . . . destined to give untold blessings to . . . the world," she described the contributors to the endowment of Mount Holyoke as Christians who were "advancing as fast as possible, the renovation of the whole human family."[31]

Anti-Catholic Sentiment at Mount Holyoke

Fear of Catholic competition contributed to the urgency of this argument and to its appeal to Lyon's many supporters. New England Protestants had long stigmatized the Roman Church for what they regarded as its inherent moral corruption and pompous, empty rituals, and made its defeat an essential step in progress toward the millennium. The Roman Church and her people were more legendary than real to New Englanders; they were largely removed from encounters with actual Catholics, whose residence during the colonial era was discouraged by various forms of anti-Catholic legislation. Longstanding Protestant beliefs about the Catholic Church sprang to new life in the early nineteenth century, with the establishment of religious freedom in the Constitution and the subsequent arrival of many Catholics fleeing war and poverty in Britain and Europe. Although the great influx of Catholics fleeing famine in Ireland did not reach its peak until the 1840s, Catholic immigration was significant enough in the early decades of the nineteenth century to prompt orthodox Protestants to suspect that final battles against the Roman Church had commenced in America. Especially alarming was the arrival of priests fleeing the French Revolution and the Napoleonic regimes who were viewed by many New Englanders as agents of political sabotage and purveyors of aristocratic decadence and immorality.

Although she exaggerated their influence and misunderstood their intentions, Lyon was aware of efforts made by Catholic women in Maryland, Louisiana, and Ohio to establish convents and open schools for Catholic immigrants to the United States. In 1837 she informed supporters of Mount Holyoke that the Catholic Church had already established "more than a hundred female schools" in the United States. Lyon believed that some Protestant mothers sought education for their children without being aware of the insidious moral effect of Catholic education, and "g[a]ve their children happily to Catholic schools."[32]

Lyon was clearly alarmed by the organizational scope of the Catholic Church, especially with regard to its interest in female education. In her circular of 1837, she described "the dangers to which our country is exposed" as an unchurched population was expanding westward, and thousands of Catholic dollars were being spent to educate female teachers "to lend their aid in converting this nation to the Church of Rome." Spurred on by the conviction that Protestant ministers could not sustain the work of redemption on their own, as well as by fear of organized competition from Rome, Lyon emphasized the urgency of establishing a Protestant female seminary. "This work of supplying teachers," she warned, "must be done or our country is lost, and the world will remain unconverted."[33]

Hostility to Catholicism was an important piece of the millenarian vision of history that Lyon shared with many of her Protestant contemporaries. Many New Englanders identified the Roman Church with the "man of sin" in the Book of Revelation, and linked Catholic opposition to Protestantism with the pouring out of the fifth vial of disasters during the final throes of Satan's struggles against Christ. Thus anti-Catholicism was a constitutive element in the Protestant conception of history that Lyon embraced, and was central to Lyon's vision of Mount Holyoke and its role in outstripping the efforts of Catholic sisters to educate American children.

Lyon's hostility to Catholicism was hardly an antidote to the assumptions about the inferiority of Catholic people expressed by at least one of her students. In a letter written soon after Mount Holyoke opened, Nancy Everett represented Lyon's emphasis on family life and mutuality in terms of its ethnic homogeneity, rather than in terms of the vision of a universal society that Lyon preached. "I believe if ever there was a happy family it is this!" wrote Everett in 1837. "We are so independent; that is if we wish *for* anything or to *do* anything we are at perfect liberty to get it, without a parcel of Irish girls scowling upon us, or wishing us out of the way."[34] While Everett referred to the domestic system at Mount Holyoke, and to the fact that students did not rely on a paid domestic staff as was commonly the case in boarding schools, she also alluded, without any discomfort, to social conventions in New England that presumed Irish Catholic girls would do the cleaning and waiting while Protestant girls did the learning.

Attitudes such as these existed in some tension with the New Divinity idea that a converted person never believed in her superiority or in another group's inferiority, as well as with the New Divinity belief that true benevolence led to a society of harmony and good will that incorporated all humankind. This kind of tension between ethnocentrism and benevolence characterized certain aspects of the foreign missionary movement as well as the attitudes of some students at Mount Holyoke, and lay at the root of the reputation for hypocrisy that missionaries later acquired. Lyon did not address these issues in her extant writings, and probably did not think much about how her intolerance for non-Protestant religions conflicted with her ability to help the women of other cultures. She had little firsthand experience of ethnic diversity herself, and she did not anticipate any of the ways in which the ethnocentrism of her religious vision would undermine its credibility. But this problem of credibility beset every foreign mission in which her students worked, and came to dominate the history of interactions between American missionaries and nonwestern peoples.

Investment in the Scientific Validity
of Protestant Orthodoxy

Whatever outsiders it excluded, the experience of mutuality within the Mount Holyoke community was so palpable that alumnae far away believed they were still tied to each other by invisible spiritual bonds. Missionary maps hung in all the common rooms of the seminary to encourage students and teachers to pray for their sisters abroad, and members of the faculty kept a journal recording seminary life to circulate among missionary alumnae and help structure their prayers. Lyon's colleague at Amherst, Edward Hitchcock, expressed the community's commitment to this journal in his description of it as "galvanic wires . . . through which the missionary spirit is transmitted back and forth." The Mount Holyoke community also joined with missionaries and missionary supporters around the world in concerts of prayer scheduled for specific times, in which women communed with one another and raised their prayers to God together. On her voyage to Persia to establish a girls' school in Urmiyah, Fidelia Fiske regretted that the time for group prayers on board her ship was "not in concert" with but two hours earlier than prayers in South Hadley.[35]

The realism that characterized Hitchcock's image of the journal as galvanic wires, and Fiske's notion of a concert of prayer, is indicative of the prevailing assumption at Mount Holyoke that spiritual experiences were as real and effective as any physical force. Such realism about the effects of spiritual effort reflected an underlying belief that religious experience and scientific fact were coextensive and mutually reinforcing. This belief was fundamental both to the millenarian outlook that characterized Mount Holyoke and other religious communities in the early nineteenth century and to the enthusiasm with which Lyon embraced the images, products, and processes of the industrial age.

Lyon went to great lengths herself to study geology, chemistry, and physics, arranging for special instruction in geology from Edward Hitchcock of Amherst and in chemistry from Amos Eaton of Rensselaer Polytechnic Institute in Troy.[36] The curriculum she developed at Mount Holyoke included physiology, algebra, chemistry, botany, astronomy, and geology as well as logic, geography, history, English grammar and literature, Latin, and theology. Some of these courses were not offered until 1846, nine years after the seminary opened, and even then students were enrolling who needed remedial coursework.[37] But from the beginning, Lyon aimed to offer coursework as advanced as that of any male institution, especially in the sciences. The courses in botany, geology, and chemistry at Mount Holyoke, taught by Lyon, Margaret Mann, Abigail Moore, and Edward Hitchcock, provided opportunities in science education at Mount Holyoke that were rarely offered to young women elsewhere. By the early twentieth century, when the conflict between religion and science was well established, and scientific enterprise had come to be dominated by an elite cadre of professional men, Mount Holyoke was one of the few colleges in the United States where women were still actively encouraged to pursue science. In establishing such a tradition of commitment to science education, Lyon anticipated neither the professionalization of science nor the conflicts that emerged between it and religion. She firmly believed that new discoveries in geology and biology would conform to the teachings of the Bible and the principles of Protestant theology, and she nurtured scientific curiosity in her students and faculty on the assumption that knowledge of the natural world served to glorify God and disclose his will.

No discussion of the appeal of the early Mount Holyoke to women should underestimate their hunger for knowledge, especially in the sciences. Lyon's own passion for knowledge was extreme. In 1817, at Sanderson Academy in Ashfield, it was remarked of her that "[s]he is all intellect; she does not know that she has a body to care for." In 1821 at Joseph Emerson's Ladies Seminary, she was too busy studying to write letters, and her roommate, Amanda White, sent messages for her. Under pressure from Emerson to frame her drive for intellectual mastery in religious terms, Lyon confessed to Amanda "that her unbounded thirst for knowledge had so absorbed every feeling, that there was no room left for a Savior's love."[38] But as she followed Emerson's lead and submitted herself to the systematic discipline of acknowledging God's power in everything she studied, the conflict between her piety and her thirst for knowledge disappeared. Lyon developed personal strength and self-confidence by defining her passion for knowledge as an expression of piety, and she found that other women were also energized by framing the knowledge they sought as a means of enabling their service to God.

Lyon found legitimation for her ambitious teaching program in Isaac Watts's *Improvement of the Mind*, which Joseph Emerson edited and published in 1832, and which she ordered for the first class of students at Mount Holyoke in 1837.[39] Utilizing the empiricism of John Locke and other Enlightenment philosophers, Watts recommended observation as the "first means of improvement." He also urged his readers to be aware of the "inestimable advantage of right reasoning," and to be diligent in discovering the underlying rational principles governing reality. "Let the hope of new discoveries, as well as the satisfaction and pleasure of known truths, animate your daily industry," Watts urged. There were many important discoveries yet to be made: "may there not be Sir Isaac Newtons in every science?" he asked.[40]

No less important in Lyon's worldview and in the curriculum she offered her students at Mount Holyoke was Joseph Butler's *Analogy of Religion*, which placed science and religion in analogical relationship to one another and served as a capstone reading in the senior course.[41] Butler's *Analogy* blended Protestant doctrine with a Lockean emphasis on empirical observation and a Newtonian view of the machinelike rationality of the natural world. But Butler went beyond both Locke and Newton in arguing that probable answers to questions about spiritual truth could be ascertained by identifying analogies to those truths in the natural world. Thus the certain evidence that life persisted through processes of transformation in the natural world could be taken as probable evidence of a future life after death. Given the certain evidence that worms change into flies and birds burst their shells to enter a new stage of life, and given the likeness, obvious to Butler, between the continuity of life in these transformations and the promise of personal immortality in Christian theology, he argued that the existence of a future life was rational and probable. No conclusive evidence of personal immortality existed, he admitted, but the evidences of nature, he argued, made disbelief irrational.[42]

As a central part of the early curriculum at Mount Holyoke, Butler's *Analogy* served its explicit purpose of providing argumentation for the probable truth of personal immortality, eternal punishment, and other aspects of Protestant orthodoxy, and also served the implicit purpose of legitimating scientific study as an important part of the education of well-trained female teachers. If nature provided probable evidence of religious belief, then its scientific study might be pursued as an extension of religious devotion, with which women were concerned as legitimately as men.

This religious approach to science was well exemplified in a prayer written by Margaret Mann, one of the early science teachers at Mount Holyoke: "May my Botany be the rose of Sharon, and the Lily of the Valley; my Geology the Rock of Ages in the Mount of the New Jerusalem; my Chemistry the invisible elements of the Mysterious Trinity."[43] These high-flown, mystical phrases elaborated on Butler's argument for an analogical relationship between science and religion, justified Mann's offering of science instruction for women, and showed how this instruction enhanced commitment to Protestant doctrine.

Belief in the existence of an analogical relationship between nature and religion also concretized the historical force of divine providence. As Butler suggested, the natural world was not simply an allegory for biblical revelation, but a material domain where the truths of revelation could be worked out and understood. Thus personal immortality seemed more palpably real when imagined as being like the fly transformed from a worm or the bird that had burst its shell. Similarly, the kingdom of God seemed more real when imagined as being like the benevolent community at Mount Holyoke, where each member cultivated mutuality in the most mundane as well as the most elevated activities and treated every other member as a mother, daughter, or sister.

Building God's Work of Redemption at Mount Holyoke

Central to Lyon's view of the building of Mount Holyoke was its analogical relationship to the work of redemption described by Jonathan Edwards. Lyon's enthusiasm for Edwards's *History of the Work of Redemption* was nurtured by Joseph Emerson, whose commitment to female education developed in the context of a worldview saturated with Edwardsean principles, and especially with Edwardsean ideas about the historical process of redemption. In 1806, in one of his earliest written expressions of interest in female education, Emerson encouraged his sister's desire for knowledge and identified Edwards's *History of the Work of Redemption* as her best guide. "Have you procured Edwards's History of Redemption? How much have you read in it? How much do you read in it every day?" he queried insistently. "Are you delighted with it and exceedingly edified? Press forward in your holy race," he urged. "Take fast hold of instruction. Cry after knowledge, and lift up your voice for understanding."[44]

Lyon's enthusiasm for Edwards's *History of the Work of Redemption* was no less than Emerson's. Fidelia Fiske, after fifteen years as a missionary in Persia, recalled how Lyon preached to the students at Mount Holyoke "with Edwards' History of Redemption in her hand."[45] The contents of this book were fundamental not only to the religious instructions Lyon imparted to her students but also to her conception of the nature and purpose of Mount Holyoke. Edwards's view of history provided the spiritual blueprint on which Lyon constructed her seminary. She envisioned the students, teachers, and buildings of that seminary as the living embodiment of the work of redemption that Edwards described. As a place that both emanated and represented benevolence, the Mount Holyoke community epitomized the work of redemption and hastened its progress.

In 1833–34, as her idea of founding the seminary took shape, Lyon was collecting subscriptions for a reprinting of Edwards's *History of the Work of Redemption*. Hoping to make the book available to persons of modest income, she found a publisher willing to reprint it for seventy-five cents a copy (sixty-two and a half cents a dozen), providing she secured a "definite number" of pledges. Her interest in disseminating the book was intense. "Perhaps you know that I have been exceedingly anxious that it should be published," she wrote her friend and former assistant, Hannah White, in February 1834. Six months later, Lyon had been successful in securing subscribers, but not in keeping her publisher. In August, she sent a letter of thanks to Sarah Brigham, who later became a student and then a teacher at Mount Holyoke, for her "great and good success in obtaining subscribers for History of Redemption." Lyon expressed her disappointment at losing the publisher she had informally contracted with and her difficulty in finding another who would agree to the seventy-five-cent price expected by her subscribers. But she was buoyed by a larger plan that incorporated her enthusiasm for Edwards's view of history even more completely. "The great object in which I am so much engaged, advances very slowly," she wrote Brigham. "To prepare the way for successful subscriptions in due time, we want an increase of interest an hundred fold."[46] Lyon did not need to name her great object. Brigham was obviously acquainted with Lyon's desire to found a female seminary, and could be counted on to subscribe to it, just as she had subscribed to the republication of Edwards's *History of the Work of Redemption*.

When construction of Mount Holyoke officially commenced on a Sunday in October 1836, Lyon reported to her close friend Zilpah "Polly" Grant, who had been Emerson's associate principal at Byfield, "We had a fine day for the laying of the corner stone." Lyon knew Grant would appreciate the relationship between that ceremonial event and Edwards's conception of redemption. "The stone and brick and mortar speak a language," she wrote, "which vibrates through my very soul." Lyon invoked this cornerstone analogy in other situations as well. She always referred to the first thousand dollars contributed to Mount Holyoke as the seminary's "cornerstone." And she used the same analogy to describe the community and people of Mount Holyoke. Thus in a promotional circular of 1836, in reference to the seminary's commitment to education of female teachers, she declared, "Another stone in the foundation of our great system of benevolent operations, which are destined, in the hand of God, to convert a world, will then be laid."[47] The first diplomas issued at Mount Holyoke pictured a palace with a quarry in front, with blocks of stone and a group of women standing beside them. Below this scene was printed the passage from Proverbs: "that our daughters may be as corner stones, polished after the similitude of a palace."[48]

Lyon's image of the graduates of Mount Holyoke as cornerstones of world redemption drew directly on Edwards's idea that the work of redemption was like a building. In *The History of the Work of Redemption*, Edwards wrote of God's plan for the world: "[F]irst the workmen are sent forth, then the materials are gathered, the ground is fitted, and the foundation laid; then the superstructure is erected, one part after another, till at length the top-stone is laid, and all is finished."[49] This plan of redemption had been in place since creation and was being systematically actualized in history, "from the fall of man," Edwards believed, "to the end of the world." The kings and prophets of the Old Testament were essential to this work, as was Jesus Christ. "We are told," wrote Edwards, citing Ephesians 2.20, that "the church of the Redeemer is built on the foundation of the prophets and apostles, the Redeemer himself being the chief cornerstone."[50] The superstructure of the work was the history of the Church to the present time, which Edwards believed was hastening on to "a time of great light and *knowledge*," when "all the world [will] be united in one amiable society."[51]

In appropriating Edwards's imagery, Lyon emphasized the foundational role of educated women in the work of redemption. While Edwards referred to Ephesians 2.20 in identifying Christ as the "chief cornerstone," Lyon made the alumnae of Mount Holyoke his principal representatives. Certainly she would not have disputed the centrality of Christ's role in the history of redemption, but in identifying her students so closely with his work, Lyon emphasized the importance of women's education and their role in building the future.

Lyon reached back to the tradition of the Puritan community to recapture the sense of authority, security, and belonging it had provided for colonial New Englanders. At the same time, she embraced the trends of her age in her systematic organization of individual development and in her enthusiasm for labor-saving devices and systems of domestic efficiency. She hoped that the union of interests facilitated at Mount Holyoke would manifest Jonathan Edwards's idea of redemption as "one amiable society." From her appropriation of Edwards's image of the work of redemption as a building to the practical system of domestic labor and happy spirit of cooperation carried on within it, Lyon worked to make her seminary a utopian representation of God's kingdom.

Like other leaders of religious communities in antebellum New England, Lyon felt enthusiastic about industrial ingenuity and improvement, especially with regard to the opportunity they provided to reconstruct expectations for women. If the Mount Holyoke family was less radical in its ideas about women's work and sexuality than the Oneida or Shaker families, its relationship to mainstream society was less marginal, and its influence was consequently more far-reaching. This influence on mainstream society was not accidental to Lyon's plans; it was central to her conception of the work of benevolence. She understood the work of redemption as a historical process in which society was gradually transformed by the benevolent actions of individuals. Consequently, her interest in the widespread acceptance of her ideas was inseparable from her utopian desire to make her community a living embodiment of Christian principles.

Lyon's efforts to disseminate her religious vision throughout mainstream society, and her pragmatic instinct for political process, distinguish her efforts from those of more radical spiritualists and utopian leaders. Although the spiritualists of her day were as graphic as she in their depictions of the spirit world, and no less convinced that spiritual and physical realms were coextensive, they called for complete equality between the sexes and sometimes compared marriage to slavery.[52] Lyon shared a tendency to spiritual materialism with spiritualists and with more radical communitarians in antebellum America, but not their enthusiasm for experiments in marriage and sexual practice. She never directly challenged the public or domestic authority of men, although she did establish a "family" over which she presided, and she exerted more influence on the public than most ministers of her day. She believed that the institution of marriage as it existed in New England was normative and that it honored women, even as she helped legitimate the lives and work of unmarried women like herself.

By linking women's education to the transformation of mainstream society, Lyon helped define a new role for American women, subordinate in certain respects to that of ministers, but perhaps more fundamental. Certainly ministers alone would never defeat ignorance and bring in the millennium. "Fill the country with ministers," she wrote in 1836, "and they could no more conquer the whole land and *secure* their victories, without the aid of many times their number of self-denying female teachers, than the latter could complete the work without the former." [53]

The combination of benevolence, learning, and millenarian enthusiasm nurtured at Mount Holyoke enabled its early alumnae to establish spin-offs of their alma mater in Ohio, Oklahoma, Persia, India, Africa, and elsewhere across the continent and around the world. In their efforts to reproduce religious communities that furthered, or even introduced, women's education in many locales, Mount Holyoke alumnae were among the vanguard in exporting American culture abroad. Along with other antebellum missionaries, these women spread the millenarian commitment to religious community that characterized the American transition to industrial society, and they helped shape that transition in other parts of the world.

THREE

The Conversion Process and
the Self-Referential Character
of Missionary Zeal

While antebellum missionary women contributed to women's negotiation of social change in other parts of the world, the self-referential character of their own religious experience worked against their ability to pursue sustained reflection about the similarities between their own social role and that of other women. Missionary women directed tremendous energy to improving the welfare of other women, but this outward extension of themselves functioned so importantly as means of testing their own state of grace that objective analysis of the effects of this extension was less developed than it otherwise might have been. Even though missionary women believed that benevolence toward others was a product of grace and not a means of building their own salvation, constant attention to their own motivations bound missionary self-criticism within a self-referential frame.

Missionary preoccupation with the attainment of a certain state of pure selflessness helps explain a spectrum of missionary shortcomings, including failure to establish communal bonds with people whose cultural orientations might have challenged their own. But the missionary's preoccupation with her own state of mind was not without its attractions and benefits. As the focus of the conversion process, the effort to analyze motivations objectively had an empowering and liberating effect for many New England women.

Missionaries as Exemplars of an Advanced Stage of the Conversion Process

By exercising their commitment to God in the most dramatic ways, giving their lives up completely to the spreading of God's word, and accepting whatever suffering came along as an opportunity to test and strengthen their faith, missionaries provided models for other Christians to emulate. Their religious zeal differed in degree, but not in kind, from the self-sacrifice and love of God believed to be characteristic of true christian life, wherever it was found. Indeed, orthodox Protestants like Mary Lyon understood every Christian to be at heart a missionary, even if she never left home. In this view, conversion was a never-ending effort for every Christian—to wean oneself from self-love and to exercise the benevolence toward others that characterized devotion to God.

In their exercise of benevolence, missionaries expressed the reciprocity universally characteristic of religion, in which believers feel obligated to give to others in response to gifts that they have received, as well as a typically Christian belief in the virtuousness of self-sacrifice.[1] In both its reciprocating and self-sacrificing aspects, conversion was not an event that isolated the individual from others but rather a process that involved others whom the convert aspired to emulate or elevate. Thus conversion entailed a network of people in which the missionary figured prominently, both stimulating other Christians' aspirations to self-sacrificing devotion to God and exercising herself in behalf of those who had not heard, or were still unable to fully respond to, the gospel call.

Conversion could lift a Christian beyond fears of death, and beyond some of the social constraints and emotional despair to which women especially were prey. In the conversion process, individuals drew strength from the millenarian view of history that orthodox Protestants espoused, which invited converts to identify their own lives with the progressive unfolding of a grand scheme of world redemption. Individuals engaged in the conversion process also acquired strength by locating themselves in relation to others who could either inspire and support them or serve as the objects of their benevolence. Orthodox Protestants in Lyon's day also derived energy from the relentless process of self-examination that organized each convert's emotional life and propelled her into active and intensely purposeful relationships with others.

For individuals prone to extremes of feeling, and especially to self-recrimination and melancholy, the process of self-examination could be salutary and transformative. By subjecting feelings to scrutiny as possible expressions of pride, the conversion process celebrated humility but held self-recrimination in check. Although exercises in discerning, analyzing, and seeking forgiveness for self-love played on tendencies to self-defeat to which women were especially vulnerable, the Protestant regimen of self-examination involved a longstanding distinction between humility and self-pity that challenged self-defeat and often yielded a self-understanding that was both rationally controlled and animated by eagerness to identify with the will of an all-powerful God.

Since Thomas Hooker in the seventeenth century, New England pastors had encouraged Christians preoccupied by feelings of unworthiness to recognize the element of self-pity in their claims and to relinquish it as an expression of pride and rebellion against God. In the case study of conversion that made him famous, Hooker focused on the self-pity in Joanna Drake's lamentations about her unworthiness for Christ, and identified her underlying anger about her lot in life as her real sin. Through these ministrations, Drake become more self-controlled and, by her own account, much happier.[2]

In its emphasis on self-discipline and responsiveness to the desire for personal achievement, the process of religious self-examination dovetailed with the desire for intellectual mastery that characterized the efforts of many New England women in the early nineteenth century to advance their education and become teachers. Indeed, the conversion process was partly a quest for intellectual mastery and thus quite similar to the other forms of intense and systematic study carried on at Mount Holyoke. In conversion, the self was the subject of study, and mastery of its desires was similar to mastery of knowledge about the stars, the properties of chemical agents, and the customs and histories of various peoples of the world.

At Mount Holyoke, this concern for intellectual mastery was supported by a communal structure that encouraged participation in the process of conversion, almost as a prerequisite of graduation. The pressure to convert was so intense at Mount Holyoke that only a relative few managed to resist some kind of engagement in the process. Emily Dickinson was the most famous of these, although even she was listed among those "hopeful" of conversion at one point during her stay. Having withdrawn from the seminary after one unhappy year in 1847–48, she called herself "one of the lingering *bad* ones," and closed one of her letters, "Your very sincere, and *wicked* friend, Emily E. Dickinson."[3] Most students had little interest in so distinguishing themselves.

Older students and faculty helped young women who entered the seminary identify and relinquish habits of jealousy, self-pity, and anger. Under Lyon's supervision, these older "sisters" encouraged self-examination and constant awareness of the need for God, as well as moments of interpersonal communion in which the boundaries between self and others dissolved, and individuals felt that they experienced God's power, beauty, and acceptance. Thus older women functioned as missionaries to newcomers, modeling the Christian personality and helping each initiate through the process of psychological transformation and strengthening that characterized a Mount Holyoke education.

Mary Lyon's Conversion

The relentless emphasis on conversion at Mount Holyoke was an extension of Lyon's commitment to her own conversion. The students, teachers, alumnae, and benefactors of Mount Holyoke provided a community of faith that served as the principal object of her religious devotion and mediated her experience of God. Lyon's concern for the conversion of her students expressed her desire to reciprocate gifts she had received and to sacrifice herself for the benefit of others. Like other missionary types, Lyon required objects of benevolence as means of furthering her own conversion.

Lyon's enthusiasm for the conversion process also involved longing for relief from depression. The strengthening agents of conversion helped save her, at several points in her life, from drowning in despair and led her to greater productivity and easier relationships with others. For Lyon and for some of the individuals who provided her primary models of missionary commitment, religious faith demanded a level of self-control and purposeful activity that relieved melancholy.

As a girl, Lyon was morbid, and spent time alone thinking about death in the Baptist graveyard in Ashfield. In more extroverted moods, she preached to other children while sitting on a branch of the beech tree behind her grammar school. Consumed by desire for intellectual mastery, when she was twenty in 1817, Lyon limited her sleep to four hours a night while a student at Sanderson Academy in Ashfield. Four years later she entered Joseph Emerson's seminary in Byfield with "many undesirable habits of person and manners." While her roommate, Amanda White, strove to improve Lyon's careless and uncouth appearance by inspecting her each time she left their room, Emerson and his assistant, Polly Grant, worked to bring her emotional volatility and intellectual drive under control.[4] They encouraged her to interpret her depressions and mood swings as self-indulgence, to define her passion for intellectual discovery as a means of glorifying the wisdom of God, and to develop her interpersonal skills.

The feelings of despair Lyon suffered were tied to constraints in opportunity that she lived with as a woman. The combination of economic stress prevalent in New England and the restrictions and dependencies associated with female gender made women especially sensitive to the gap between their own limited expectations and the expansiveness and millennial idealism of American culture. For Lyon and the missionaries she admired, the conversion process associated with the theology of Jonathan Edwards and his New Divinity followers provided a means of closing that gap.

In 1822, a year after the revival in Emerson's seminary made all forty students "solemn as eternity," Lyon joined the Congregational Church in Byfield with a strong hope of being able to give her self to God. Admonishing herself for being "easily discouraged," for not being able to "rise above disappointment," and for "yield[ing] to great depression, and . . . indulging in long seasons of weeping," she vowed to no longer "allow herself depression or tears," and carefully monitored her level of agitation. "I do not think it favorable to piety to have so much anxiety as I have had this winter," she wrote Eunice Caldwell in February 1825. The following September, she could give a better report: "My spirits have been unusually uniform for four weeks." As she told her mother, "I do not recollect an hour of depression," but she did feel "a kind of loneliness" lurking at the corners of her resolve, "which is ever ready to oppress my spirits." Eight months later, in May 1826, she had made the connection typical of missionary psychology between her own religious life and her promotion of religious life in others. Thus she linked the alleviation of her own spiritual darkness to her efforts to nurture the piety of her students: "The young ladies are so attentive to Bible lessons, that I sometimes hope there are good things in store for us; but my own heart is so cold I have reason to fear. . . . Do pray for us, and especially that I may have a heart."[5]

In the course of this process of self-reconstruction, Lyon developed an intense attachment to Polly Grant, who had been her religious guide at Byfield. In a letter to her sister Freelove in August 1827, Lyon described her love for Grant and hinted at sexual feelings she felt were wrong: "I love Miss Grant's society more than ever, and I believe we may love our friends very ardently, and love them according to the principles and spirit of the gospel. I also think we may love them in a manner displeasing in the sight of God." Four months later, in response to a rebuff from Grant, Lyon admitted that she had "been earthly and groveling in my desires." Entreating Grant to "supplicate the throne of mercy in my behalf," she expressed her desire to be "holy, harmless, and undefiled" like Jesus, and thus able to love her friends in a way that would prevent it from being "necessary to take them from me."[6]

This effort to restrain her feelings proved to be a valuable lesson in self-control. Her relationship with Grant remained one of the most important in her life, but it entered a new phase when she became Grant's assistant at Ipswich Female Seminary in 1828, and stood in as acting principal when Grant fell ill. As she wrote Grant in 1833, "Your society will always be to me a source of the *highest* earthly enjoyment, but I do not mean to make it 'my meat and drink.' "[7] While Lyon remained indebted to Grant for introducing her to supporters of Ipswich Seminary who would become donors to Mount Holyoke, as well as for a curriculum at Ipswich that would serve as an initial model for the curriculum at Mount Holyoke, her control over her feelings enabled her to extricate herself from Grant's authority. The autonomy Lyon gained by relegating her concern for Grant to a secondary position in relation to her concern for God enabled her to calculate other aspects of her life in similar terms. On the question of the religious dimension of female education, for example, Lyon went beyond both Grant and Emerson in her efforts to make the principle of benevolence permeate the life of her seminary, to facilitate religious professions and instill missionary interest among her students and teachers, and to raise an endowment from donors to missionary causes.[8] By dedicating herself and her seminary so completely to God, Lyon was able to go further than either of her mentors in making a place for her daughters in the Edwardsean scheme of redemption.

Another lesson in the importance of self-control occurred during the years Lyon taught on and off at Ipswich. In 1828 her sister Lovina Putnam entered the Insane Asylum in Hartford. Lyon helped to care for Lovina's five children, and for Lovina herself, when she returned home early the next year with her "mind still weak" but demonstrating "self-government" and expressing a "resolution to go forward in the path of duty." Lovina soon lost her resolve, and she was returned to Hartford, where she died in 1832, after seizures left her physically impaired. "My dear afflicted sister has finished her work and her sufferings," Lyon wrote in October 1832, and "now, I trust, she is sitting at the foot of Jesus, clothed and in her right mind."[9]

If Lyon inherited a tendency to mental illness, the example of her sister's dishevelment may have led her to ally herself even more completely with the emotional balance characteristic of Edwardsean theology. Its distinction between emotional excitement and the equanimity of benevolence supported her commitment to self-government and her own resolution to go steadily forward in the path of duty, without succumbing either to despair or wild exhilaration. Just a month after Lovina's death, she wrote, "There is an unusual evenness and uniformity in my feelings, freedom from excitement, or any rising above the common level."[10]

Later at Mount Holyoke, Lyon told her teachers that she had simply put to rest her tendency to depression. "At one period of her life," they recalled her saying, "she used to be dejected and unhappy; but she came to the conclusion that there was too much to be done for her to spend time in that manner. Since that, she had experienced but little unhappiness." Until the stress became too much for her in the late 1840s, Lyon was enormously productive as a fund-raiser and manager of every aspect of life at Mount Holyoke, from the sweeping of floors and baking of pies to the academic achievements and missionary interests of her students. If this all-consuming commitment to Mount Holyoke left no time for depression, it did have a compulsive aspect. As one of her students wrote, "I really do not know when she sleeps, for she is up the first in the house, sometimes before four, and once she rose at *one* thinking it was five! The bell rung—and we who heard it were in great consternation for a short time thinking the house was on fire."[11]

But even as the plans for Mount Holyoke were taking shape, Lyon succumbed temporarily to exhaustion. She fell into a "partial stupor" for several days in the winter of 1834–35, after reaching a state of mind "in which she seemed to lose the power of stopping the wheels of thought." She was relatively free of episodes like this over the next six years, as she presided over the endowment, curriculum, and domestic and religious life of the seminary, but in the late winter of 1841 she acknowledged a recurrence of her troubles: "I have tried to rest," she wrote Grant, "but all seemed only to reduce me more." In this state of "general prostration," she complained, "I could not read much, nor write, nor think, nor feel, nor talk." Episodes like this recurred, and six years later, on her fiftieth birthday in February 1847, after a long winter illness, she "took leave" of her "active life." But if Lyon was exhausted, her struggles to combat depression seemed as if they would finally end in victory. As she described her anticipation of the future "on this most solemn day of my life," she wrote: "There seemed to be no ladder between me and the world above. The gates were opened, and I seemed to stand on the threshold."[12]

Lyon's death two years later came after one of her students, Sarah Wingate, died suddenly of erysipelas, an acute streptococcal infection of the face and glands. The morning after Sarah's father left with the corpse, it became clear that Lyon "was suffering from severe headaches and intense mental excitement." The arrival, that evening, of the news that her nephew had committed suicide while deranged, without any sign of commitment to God, threw her into despair. He had lived with her in South Hadley a few years earlier; she had tried to help stabilize his behavior, and may have thought she had succeeded. After "a night of anguish," Lyon's "excitement increased until it became insanity; not the delirium frequently attendant upon fever," her biographer insisted, "but real mental derangement." For almost seventy-two hours "she talked day and night, without intermission, in a worried, excited manner," and often about the temptations of her soul. As one of her attendants wrote, Lyon would not take a drop of water, although she was desperately thirsty, because "she had all those days the strong impression that her Savior had *forbidden* her taking it—and all her friends were combined with Satan to tempt her to sin and destroy herself." Finally, she lapsed into exhaustion and semiconsciousness, and died.[13]

If the conversion process failed to bring Lyon any relief on her deathbed, it did contribute to the periods of equanimity she enjoyed before that, as well as to the sense of direction that enabled her productivity and her success in influencing others on the subjects of women's education, religious conversion, and foreign missions. These successes enabled her to identify further with Edwardsean models of effective, productive, and emotionally balanced Christianity. In both these successes and in her battles with despair, Lyon exemplified a life pattern similar to that of other missionary types. Her inner life was strikingly similar to that of one of her own models of Christian virtue, the intelligent and passionate Ann Hasseltine Judson, the schoolteacher from Bradford, Massachusetts, who, in 1812, became the first American woman missionary to teach in a foreign land.

Precedents for Conversion at Mount Holyoke

"Nancy" Hasseltine was a protégée of Lyon's mentor, Joseph Emerson, who was a longtime friend of the Hasseltine family. Emerson counseled her in 1810, when she was deciding whether or not to accept the hand of Adoniram Judson and sail with him as a missionary to Burma. Adoniram was one of the Andover men whose religious zeal led to the founding of the American Board of Commissioners for Foreign Missions. At the time of his proposal to Nancy, "[g]eneral opinion" was "decidedly opposed" to a woman engaging in such a bold venture: "It was deemed wild and romantic in the extreme, and altogether inconsistent with prudence and delicacy." But Emerson and one or two other "steady, affectionate advisers" urged her to go.[14]

Desirous of giving herself "entirely to God, to be disposed of according to his pleasure," Nancy wanted to be sure that, in accepting Adoniram's proposal, she would be responding to God's call for her as missionary and not to her attraction to Adoniram. Equally important in her decision was her desire to surmount her fears of loneliness and suffering. As she explained to herself, these fears were not a disqualification for missionary work, as she had thought at first, but a challenge from God "to gain an ascendancy over my selfish and rebellious spirit, and prefer the will of God to my own." The best way, it seemed, of submitting herself to God, was to become an emissary of the gospel in a situation where it seemed to be most absent and needed, and where the challenges to her own spirit were most extreme. Even if she converted only "a single soul" in that situation, the "danger and death" she would confront in heathen lands, and the "pain and suffering" she experienced, would test and purify her commitment to God. Like subsequent missionaries inspired by her life and writings, Judson invited persecution. And like other missionary types, she required unconverted souls and challenging terrain in order to work at her own salvation. Her investment in saving heathen souls was the means by which her own salvation might be achieved. As she wrote in her journal the summer she met Adoniram, "I am fully satisfied, that difficulties and trials are more conducive, than ease and prosperity, to promote my growth in grace, and cherish an habitual dependence on God."[15]

If neither her efforts to convert Burmese women nor her efforts to find assurance of her own salvation were as successful as she would have liked, Judson did make her mark as a talented educator and influential Christian. She became fluent in Burmese and Siamese, translated biblical stories into both languages, taught women to read, founded a women's religious society in Rangoon from which four women converted to Christianity, formed a friendship with the wife of a viceroy in Rangoon, established a school in Ava, became well-known to numerous political officials, and adopted two Burmese girls, whom she named Mary and Abby Hasseltine. Her concern for the souls of Burmese people was genuine, if not enlightened by any appreciation for their Theravada Buddhism or Burmese customs, or by any doubt that they would perish in hell if they failed to give themselves to Christ.

This concern for the souls of Burmese people did not diminish over time. "If we were convinced of the importance of missions, *before* we left our native country," she wrote to a friend in 1817, "we *now* also *see* and *feel* their practicability." Her "picture" of "the miserable situation of heathen nations" had been vivid from the outset, thanks to books like Claudius Buchanan's *Star of the East*, but firsthand experience showed her more clearly "a whole populous empire, rational and immortal like ourselves, sunk in the grossest idolatry; given up to follow the wicked inclinations of their depraved hearts; entirely destitute of any real principle, or the least spark of true benevolence." But for all her ignorant intolerance of Burmese religion and culture, she recognized the intelligence of Burmese women, even if she regretted their use of this asset to resist her religious entreaties. When one Buddhist woman responded that "she could not think of giving up a religion which her parents, grandparents, &c. &c had embraced," Judson asked her "if she wished to go to hell, because her progenitors had gone there." With greater politeness, the woman replied that "if with all her offerings and good works on her head . . . she must go to hell, then let her go." And "If I do, said she, I will then cry out to you to be my intercessor with your God, who will certainly not refuse you."[16]

Judson was more successful in constructing a persona of self-sacrificing commitment to Christ that Protestant women in America could identify with than in persuading Burmese women to give up their devotion to "Gaudama" and follow Christ. James D. Knowles's lively and well-paced memoir of Judson, first published in 1829 and reissued almost every year until 1856, included generous selections from the articulate and engaging writings of both Nancy and Adoniram, as well as details about Burmese life and history drawn from other sources. By 1833 the story of Nancy Judson's life was so constitutive of American Protestant culture that even the Unitarian Lydia Maria Child referred to Knowles's biography as "a book so universally known that it scarcely need be mentioned."[17]

Even before her death and the publication of this memoir, Judson was a celebrity in America, as well known and well respected as all but a few ministers and politicians. In an indirect and cautious way, she nurtured this celebrity, although her constant preoccupation with the inadequacy of her commitment to Christ and with her inability to relinquish her pride acted as a check on any desires for self-glorification she might have harbored and prevented her from deriving much satisfaction from her fame. When she returned to America for a visit in 1822, criticism of her boldness, along with poor health, kept her from making public appearances, but she made use of the press to publicize her life and work, and wrote up her "history" for publication before going back to Rangoon.

Excerpts from the Judsons' journals and letters were regularly featured in Baptist periodicals, such as the *Massachusetts Baptist Missionary Magazine*. Mary Lyon was undoubtedly familiar with these writings. Not only had she become a student of Nancy Judson's mentor in 1821, but Lyon herself was a Baptist until 1822, when she changed her denominational affiliation under Emerson's influence to Congregational. Lyon may have joined the Congregational Church because of its close association with the historical mainstream of Puritan tradition in America, which she envisioned herself helping to carry forward, but she remained a devoted daughter, sister, and aunt to numerous Baptist relatives, including her niece Lucy, who became a student and teacher at Mount Holyoke and later a Baptist missionary to China. Moreover, Lyon regarded the beliefs that Congregational and Baptist proponents of Edwardsean theology shared as far more significant than any points of doctrinal difference. She knew from accounts of Nancy Judson's life that Nancy identified with the writings of Samuel Hopkins and other New Divinity spokesmen and that she cherished a special fondness for Jonathan Edwards's *History of the Work of Redemption*.[18]

Nancy Judson's life was particularly relevant to intellectual and ambitious women, like Mary Lyon, who were seeking ways to expand their minds and activities without losing public approval. The moral sincerity and humility required by New Divinity Protestantism gave Judson and her emulators a broader scope of activity and leadership than American women were generally allowed. But however much her efforts to embody the New Divinity concept of sainthood legitimated her intellectual achievements and exciting life, the sufferings Judson underwent made it clear what price was required for such attainments and freedom. After her first year in Rangoon, she developed a liver complaint that eventually led to her death, but she left Burma only twice for her health, and she returned the first time as soon as the pain in her side subsided enough to walk. She also suffered as a result of being separated from her family and from the female companionship she had enjoyed in Bradford. After seven years in Rangoon, she wrote to her sister in 1819 that her memories of girlhood "are as fresh in my recollection as though it were but yesterday; and the wound then inflicted" by her decision to leave her loved ones "every now and then opens and bleeds afresh."[19]

Judson demonstrated her willingness to suffer for God even more fully after she and her husband moved up the Irrawaddy River to the city of Ava. Just before the Bengali invasion of Rangoon, which signaled the outbreak of the British-Burmese war in 1824 and eventually forced British occupation and British government on the Burmese, Adoniram was taken prisoner under suspicion of being a British agent, and held in prison long after the pregnant Nancy privately convinced the Burmese governor that her husband had no political association with the British. When their possessions were commandeered, she took pains to avoid telling a direct lie about the whereabouts of all her money and silver, and she hid enough to bribe officials, for visits with Adoniram with the governor's secret permission, and for provisions for him and some of his inmates. Soon after their daughter Maria's birth, Adoniram, feverish and bare-foot, was marched forty miles in the blazing sun to a more remote prison. After running through the streets of Ava searching for some sign of him or news of his destination, Nancy and her children and Bengali cook followed him to the prison, without furniture, food or water, and took up residence for six months in a room half-filled with grain. Nancy nursed her husband and Mary Hasseltine, who contracted smallpox, until she fell ill with the same disease. With her head shaved and blisters all over head and feet, she was taken for dead by her Burmese neighbors. Adoniram was released early in 1826, but Nancy never recovered. She rallied long enough to write a vivid narrative of her ordeal, and then died in a British garrison later that year.

There are important antecedents to Nancy Judson's suffering devotion to God in earlier Christian narratives; Christians have often have regarded Christ's death, and his willingness to suffer and die, as something to emulate as well as revere. Women and men throughout Christian history have embraced suffering and death as a means of attaining salvation and representing their love of Christ to others. Perpetua went willingly to the lions in Rome in 202 C.E., hoping that her martyrdom would not only bring others to Christ but also transform her soul and elevate it to manhood as well as salvation.[20] In subsequent centuries, the desert fathers and other male ascetics strove to mortify their bodies in the hope of purifying their souls. In Europe during the late middle ages, numerous women took up ascetic practices for the purpose of identifying themselves with Christ. For example, the thirteenth-century Flemish Beguine Hadewijch was so dedicated to the emulation of Christ's sacrifice that she gave herself over "[t]o founder unceasingly in heat and cold, In the deep insurmountable darkness of love [that] outdoes the torments of hell." Like Hadewijch, other female mystics from the thirteenth to sixteenth centuries deprived themselves of food and inflicted other forms of suffering on themselves as a means of identifying with Christ. As Caroline Walker Bynum argues, these mystics interpreted the physical sufferings of Christ as expressions of his humanity, and they demonstrated their own humanity as women by emulating his sufferings.[21]

If late-medieval female mystics made suffering a means of sacralizing humanity, thereby departing from earlier forms of asceticism designed to elevate the soul and leave the body in the dust, Protestant reformers and Puritans blended this sacrificial humanism with the more moderate and rational humanism represented by Erasmus and other Renaissance scholars. As a rational humanist before his conversion, John Calvin of Geneva joined classical concern for order in intellectual thought, and moderation in eating, drinking, and sex, with the Christian drama of sacrifice and redemption, in which faith entailed both belief in the efficacy of Christ's sacrifice and willingness to suffer and die in his name. Puritans embraced a similar blend of humanism and self-sacrifice, cast in terms of willing participation in the historical operations of divine providence.

Puritan suffering could not be deliberately constructed or self-inflicted, as it often was for medieval saints. Redemption was to be found in the ordinary sufferings of life, carefully interpreted as exercises of divine providence. In seventeenth-century New England, Anne Bradstreet represented this Puritan humanism in her blend of classical reasoning and personal identification with Christ. She interpreted sickness and grief as chastisements from God that prompted consciousness of sin, led to repentance, and represented God's government of all aspects of life. To express this Puritan sense of God's providential direction at work within her sickness and grief, she drew an analogy from her experience as a mother: Just as "[s]ome children are hardly weaned although the teat be rub'd with wormwood," she wrote, so "some Christians . . . are so childishly sottish that they are still huging and sucking" the sweet things of life, "that god is forced to hedg up their way with thornes."[22]

The life of Ann Judson derives from this tradition of welcoming suffering as a form of religious instruction, and bears important similarities both to Bradford's writings and to Mary Rowlandson's captivity narrative, one of the most popular texts of the Puritan era. Rowlandson's account of her captivity by Indians during the French and Indian War of 1675–76 exemplified the Puritan tendencies to interpret suffering and affliction as means of grace and to attribute providential significance to historical events. Thus Rowlandson consulted her Bible at various stages of her ordeal, and she interpreted her sufferings in the light of biblical episodes and teachings in which God tested Israel and led her toward a more righteous relationship with him. Judson's narrative is much like Rowlandson's in its attitude toward suffering and its respect for personal history as the arena of divine providence. But Judson's narrative also departs from Rowlandson's in ways that distinctly mark it as an early-nineteenth-century rendering of female suffering and conversion.

While Judson does her share of suffering, it is her husband, not she, who is actually taken captive by hostile forces. She negotiates with government officials for her husband's safety and for improvements in his treatment with a clearheaded and forceful self-confidence. Unlike both Mary Rowlandson and Adoniram Judson, who were completely at the mercy of their captors, Nancy Judson surmounted one obstacle after another in her efforts to protect her husband. The popularity of Judson's tale suggests that many admired this take-charge capacity in a woman, at least as long as it was accompanied by great suffering, and restricted to such emergencies and extreme situations as imprisonment in Burma.[23]

Judson's spectacle of self-reliance and organizational skill may represent a widespread, but cautiously promoted, eagerness for adventure, work, and self-mastery among antebellum Protestant women. While Rowlandson's narrative reveals that pious women were important in seventeenth-century New England and even were symbols of the righteousness of Puritan culture, the striking correspondence between Rowlandson's captivity and the political weakness of New England in the late seventeenth century also suggests the vulnerability of women in Puritan culture. Vulnerability was hardly unknown to antebellum women, but it was not Nancy Judson's most dominant trait. Although saturated with self-recrimination and heavy doses of suffering and self-sacrifice, Judson's life promoted a more aggressive and self-possessed image of female piety than Mary Rowlandson's. The stories of Judson's life also lacked the intellectual weakness associated with the helpless heroines in numerous sentimental novels of the time. For all its romantic aspects, Judson's life represents an attempt to break from sentimental expectations of female vulnerability and emotional debility.[24]

Judson's emotional strength was closely tied to the process of her conversion, which helped her to manage a prounounced tendency to depression. At sixteen, guilty about her enjoyment of dancing and pretty dresses, she sat in the corner of the meetinghouse where no one would see her and wept during religious meetings. Then she "lost all relish for amusements" and "felt melancholy and dejected." Distraught about her "deplorable state," she wrote, in her account of this crucial stage in her religious development, "I felt, that I was led captive by Satan at his will, and that he had entire control over me." When her earnest prayers of repentance failed to gain her any relief, she began to hate God. Fearing that she would be miserable if she had to live with God in heaven, she thought about ending her life. But with the help of readings in Edwardsean theology, she began to appreciate the coherence of God's plan of saving the world. Applying this plan to her own situation, she reasoned that, by sending his son as a model of self-sacrificial love for all to love and emulate, God had provided her a way out of despair. Reconceptualizing her self-loathing in constructive terms as the consciousness of sin requisite for grace, she became desirous of giving her life up to God to do with as he pleased. This attempt at self-transcendence was effective; it put her consciousness of sin in a larger, more positive perspective, and it relieved her from "that distressing weight which had borne . . . down" on her "for so long a time."

Judson's willingness to commit her life to the will of God helped turn her away from preoccupation with her insufficiencies and gave her a new sense of scope. Commitment to Christ removed some of her anxiety about putting herself forward in the world and legitimated her activism as a linguist, writer, teacher, and manager. Moreover, her activism as a missionary led her to become more interested in the lives of other people, and this social involvement contributed to the developing sense of worth that often kept her out of depression. But if she felt empowered by her religion, and if it saved her from falling into the kind of abject distress she had known in Bradford, she was never entirely free from the devil of melancholy. After seven years in Burma, she felt it a "privilege" to be doing Christ's work, but wished that she were more deserving. As she confessed to her sister in 1819, "I do at times feel almost ready to sink down in despair, when I realize the responsibility of my situation, and witness my short-comings in duty. If I have grown any in grace since I left America," she went on, "it has consisted entirely in an increasing knowledge of my unspeakably wicked heart." But when compared to the feelings of utter loss that tormented her before she consecrated herself to Christ, these self-reproaches seem more obligatory and ritualized, although not insincere. Judson's consciousness of her own sinfulness became balanced by a new sense of confidence. As she told her sister, "I do hope, however, vile as I am, to obtain an inheritance in that better world, where Jesus has prepared mansions for his followers, and will introduce them there himself, sprinkled with his blood, and clothed in his righteousness."[25]

One of Judson's own models was the well-known American missionary of the eighteenth century, David Brainerd. Like Judson, Brainerd turned to missionary work as a means of self-development and as a way to address his apprehensions about the adequacy of his devotion to God. He preached to several Native American communities in western Massachusetts, New Jersey, and Pennsylvania during the 1740s, and he died in Jonathan Edwards's home in 1747 at the age of twenty-nine, ending the long bout with tuberculosis that had made his missionary work a kind of martyrdom. Brainerd's diary, edited and published by Edwards, saw numerous printings and was revered by orthodox Protestants as a compelling account of Christian piety. When missionary vocations began to flourish in the early nineteenth century, it was often cited as inspiration. Nancy Judson read Brainerd's diary while depressed about her sinfulness and struggling to devote herself more completely to Christ. His piety inspired her, and gave her some relief from her preoccupation with her inadequacies: "Have had some enjoyment in reading the life of David Brainerd," she wrote in 1809. "It had a tendency to humble me, and excite desires to live as near to God as that holy man did." The idea of missionary work began to take shape in her mind as a way of increasing her devotion to Christ. "Felt my heart enlarged to pray for spiritual blessings for myself, my friends, the church at large, the heathen world, and the African slaves," she wrote. "Felt a willingness to give myself away to Christ, to be disposed of as he pleases. . . . O may I now begin to live to God."[26]

Like Judson's writings, Brainerd's diary is primarily concerned with the ebbs and flows of his own devotion. While he does describe the people he ministered to, these descriptions play only a secondary and supporting role. Similarly, Edwards's main purpose in editing the diary was to publicize Brainerd's piety, not the piety or plight of the Indians. Edwards found Brainerd's diary especially useful in demonstrating the point that longing after more grace was a distinguishing sign of conversion.[27]

Brainerd's attempt to devote himself to God sometimes exacerbated his sense of vileness and inadequacy, even though he did enjoy moments of rapture. His failure to achieve equanimity or any sustained transcendence of self-loathing was the one aspect of the diary that did not conform to Edwards's notion of Christian virtue. Thus Edwards warned his readers that Brainerd was "prone to *melancholy*, and dejection of spirit" and expressed concern about how skeptics might react to his tendency to depression: "There are some, who think that all religion is a melancholy thing; and that what is called Christian experience is little else besides *melancholy vapors*, disturbing the brain, and exciting enthusiastic imaginations." To counter this criticism, Edwards argued that melancholy and enthusiasm were opposing tendencies, and that Brainerd's tendency to melancholy worked against the tendency to unrealistic imaginings to which more excitable persons were prone. Moreover, Brainerd's imperviousness to excitement made him an excellent judge of the difference "between real, solid piety, and enthusiasm" in others. Thus Edwards saw in Brainerd "a talent for describing the various workings of this *imaginary enthusiastic* religion—evincing its falseness and vanity, and demonstrating the great difference between this, and true *spiritual* devotion—which I scarcely ever knew equaled in any person."[28]

Nancy Judson's editor expressed a similar concern about her tendency to melancholy. This tendency was so pronounced that Knowles thought it wise to exclude "a considerable portion" of Judson's account of her "conversion" from his compilation of her memoir. "The enemies of true religion," he feared, would interpret her expressions of despair "as inexplicable inconsistences, and as proofs that religion is the parent of melancholy, and is devoid of permanent and tranquil happiness."[29] In fact, orthodoxy may have done more to attract and help melancholiacs than, as some critics believed, to create them.

As the memoirs of Brainerd and Judson reveal, missionary life was a means of advancing the conversion of the missionary as much as of advancing the conversion of the people to whom the missionary preached. Thus both Brainerd and Judson felt they had begun to accomplish their religious work only when they felt God's beauty and his forgiveness of their sins. But while missionary work advanced the missionary's happiness in this way, it also elevated the site of grace, and the pressure to obtain it. The self-doubts of Brainerd and Judson persisted after they became missionaries, partly through a sense of failure in not being able to live up to the grace they had been given. With spiraling expectations and self-criticisms expected of Christian life, conversion was the work of a lifetime, in which moments of joy prompted ever greater effort to deserve them.

However torturous it was for the missionary, the unending nature of the missionary's own conversion added an element of equality to the process of converting others. The patience with which missionaries responded to the spiritual slowness of others was often much greater than their patience with themselves. While missionaries had little tolerance for the "Egyptian darkness" in which non-Christians lived, and while they condemned as false idols and heathen superstitions the devotions and beliefs of all who did not share their theology, they were no less sanguine about the darkness of their own souls, and they sometimes compared themselves to pagans.

Lyon's Strategies for Nurturing Conversion and Missionary Zeal

In encouraging the conversion of her students, Mary Lyon relied on this element of similarity between her students and heathen women, and she found that attention to the plight of heathen women facilitated her students' concerns for their own spiritual states. The high-intensity commitment of missionary life answered Lyon's own need for intense emotional focus, and the usefulness of missionary interest as a means of encouraging religious development in students became increasingly apparent to her. Although her initial plans for the alumnae of Mount Holyoke had focused on their prospects as teachers in the American West, when Fidelia Fiske, her protégée and one of the seminary's most popular teachers, answered a missionary call to Persia in the early winter of 1843, Lyon began to systematically utilize the lives of missionary women as means to her students' conversions. Foreign missionary work moved to the center of religious life at Mount Holyoke after Fiske's departure; according to Lyon's niece and philosophy teacher, Lucy Lyon, who started a journal for Fiske after her departure for Persia, "Miss Lyon's missionary interest seems (if possible) to have increased greatly since you left." [30]

As the niece of the famous Pliny Fisk, who died in Palestine in 1825 as one of the first American missionaries to the Middle East, Fidelia had special credentials for missionary work. When she offered herself as a missionary to Persia, she became a kind of celebrity at the seminary and the clearest embodiment, outside of Mary Lyon herself, of its ideals. Her willingness to leave family and friends, and perhaps die in a faraway land, prompted self-examinations in her students that led many of them to confess themselves not so willing to serve Christ as she, and much in need of grace. In various states of repentance, the students sewed as much as they could for Miss Fiske in the time remaining before her departure, then took their leave from her one by one. They expressed their hopes for themselves in a packet of letters intended for her to read as she crossed the Atlantic. As Fiske described those letters in a letter back to Abigail Moore, Lyon's niece and science teacher at Mount Holyoke, many of them expressed sorrow for not being sufficiently dedicated to Christ, and many entreated Fiske for her prayers. One student asked, "When your eye glances over these lines on the broad waters, will you not offer one petition for me, that I be not lost forever?" [31]

As she prepared for a trip to Boston to participate in Fiske's departure for Persia on March 1, 1843, Mary Lyon was concerned about the general progress of missionary benevolence in the country and about the religious state of her seminary. She worried that financial contributions to the American Board would fall short of what was needed to sustain the growth of foreign missions, and she was disappointed that Fiske's example of religious commitment had not yielded more firm commitments to Christ among the students at Mount Holyoke. "I made arrangements to be absent for a few days longer," she wrote Polly Grant, now Mrs. William B. Banister, "that I might have time to look over our sad, very sad state." [32]

The visibility of Fiske's piety may have raised Lyon's expectations for her students. While all her faculty and two-thirds of her students had professed their dedication to Christ, sixty others hesitated. There had been no new professions of faith in the weeks before Lyon and Fiske left for Boston, and the religious atmosphere at the seminary was strained. "I have thought that we seemed preparing for every thing else desirable," Lyon wrote Banister, "except for the reception of the special influences of the Holy Spirit. To this there seemed some great barrier." What her seminary needed, she continued, was more of "that living faith in the great atoning sacrifice without which it is impossible to please God." [33]

When Lyon returned to South Hadley on March 7, after seeing Fiske off, she convened her teachers to emphasize "the need of earnest and constant prayers" and "addressed the school in a similar manner for several days." Ready for a concerted movement of religious renewal, she offered a "vivid description" of Fiske's departure and conveyed her strong belief in "the necessity of an immediate work of grace among us." [34] While Fiske crossed the Atlantic, praying for her students' souls, they were finding their desires for stronger dedication to Christ realized in a collective surge of spiritual commitment in South Hadley. Lyon orchestrated this revival by carefully managing the spiritual crises and commitments that emerged among the members of her seminary. Her strategy of facilitating religious progress by grouping the women of the seminary according to the state of their souls seems to have taken shape during this time. In this arrangement, the professors of religion met separately to increase their commitment to Christ, as did those who had hope, and those who did not. [35]

"A spiritual change was passing over the face of things," Lyon wrote Banister two weeks after her return, "the Spirit of God was gently moving on the face of the waters." [36] This carefully managed change proceeded quietly but forcefully, affecting almost everyone in the seminary. "Out of sixty impenitent young ladies," wrote Lydia Pomeroy to her mother, "only five are left who do not express hope." Pomeroy was already a professing Christian familiar with religious experience when she entered Mount Holyoke, but she had never encountered such a work of grace before. Pupils known for being "wild . . . gay, and thoughtless" had become "so gentle and humble" that "it seems that their very natures are changed." And no wonder: "We have had prayer meetings every afternoon, and evening, and two or three days, were given up entirely to this object. Last Monday was appointed as a day of fasting, and prayer, and on that day five individuals found as we trust joy and peace in believing." And "of course" Miss Lyon, Lydia concluded, "has entered with her whole heart, and soul into the work." [37]

The first seeds of this revival had been planted in January, when the Rev. Justin Perkins visited Mount Holyoke seeking a teacher to accompany his family back to Persia to start a girls' school. Fiske was one of forty who responded within an hour of Perkins's appeal with a note of acceptance to Lyon. Lyon selected Fiske because of her success as a teacher at Mount Holyoke and because of the even-tempered humility evident in her note: "If counted worthy, I should be willing to go." In choosing Fiske, Lyon gave up one of the women on whom she most depended for personal as well as pedagogical support, but this sacrifice only confirmed Lyon's investment in Fiske's venture, and whetted her appetite for a deepening of religious commitment among the women around her. When Fiske's mother and minister in Shelburne objected to her going, Lyon traveled thirty miles in the snow to gain their consent. And when final decisions were being made to send Fiske, Lyon announced to her students, "This was the great object . . . for wh. the Institution was built—to prepare laborers for Christ's cause." [38]

Fiske's success in converting Nestorian girls in Persia became legendary and played an important role in altering conservative opinion about the propriety of unmarried women working as foreign missionaries. Missionary administrators were concerned that unmarried women would be left unprotected if they lived alone and that if they lived with a missionary couple, the arrangement might be misconstrued in polygamous societies. Most of all, missionary boards were concerned about the unseemliness of female authority. [39]

After celebrating Fiske's departure for Persia and orchestrating a revival around it, Lyon hung missionary maps in all the rooms of the seminary to encourage awareness of missionary ventures around the world. She had discussed the idea of purchasing maps for the seminary with Fiske just before her departure, and she probably ordered them while in Boston for Fiske's sailing. [40] Lyon also increased the number of copies of the *Missionary Herald* and the *Home Missionary* that the seminary received to seven each, and she devised a plan for integrating the contents of these periodicals in group discussions in which all students and faculty participated. [41] And she encouraged her students to write and speak about missions. Thus during the annual day of examination in August 1843, when students demonstrated their proficiency in geography, philosophy, chemistry, and other areas of study before an assembled audience of parents, ministers, donors, and other interested members of the public, Eliza Hubbell read an essay entitled "The Missionary's Farewell" written by Caroline Avery, the sister of one of Mount Holyoke's Cherokee missionaries, Mary Avery. The farewells celebrated in the essay were Pliny Fisk's death and Fidelia Fiske's departure for Persia, both of which exemplified the spirit of self-sacrifice and commitment to Christ encouraged at the seminary. [42]

Lyon further stimulated a sense of participation in missionary ventures by encouraging her teachers and students to make the largest contributions they possibly could to an annual gift to the American Board from the seminary, which the *Missionary Herald* recognized at least once in its pages. She wanted her students to feel obliged to give to others the kind of good-will offerings that had enabled them to attend Mount Holyoke, and she knew that the many contributors to the seminary's endowment had given their money in a spirit of missionary benevolence. "I sometimes feel," she told a group of alumnae at a meeting of the American Board, "that our walls were built from the funds of our missionary boards. Certainly much of the money expended upon them was given by those who hold every thing sacred to the Lord, and who, probably, would otherwise have devoted it to sending the gospel directly to the heathen."[43]

Lyon sought to establish a habit of sacrificial giving among the women of her seminary that would enable them to identify with the poverty of other women, and also to cultivate the denial of self-interest that she believed was central to Christian faith. She held up the "Bible standard of giving" to the members of her seminary, which she defined as giving to the point of pain and beyond "the point of poverty." She urged her teachers to contribute generously to the seminary's annual gift to the American Board, even though their salaries were already evidence of their willingness to live near the point of poverty for the sake of Christian work. Lyon led the way in this strenuous giving, with a salary of two hundred dollars a year, from which she contributed ninety to the annual mission fund. In the seminary's contribution for 1843–44, Lyon and her twelve teachers donated approximately four hundred and fifty dollars, which was 40 percent of the total donation. That year the teachers received, on average, a yearly salary of one hundred and fifty dollars, of which they donated, on average, almost thirty dollars, or 20 percent.[44]

In motivating her students and teachers to follow her own strenuous example in making contributions to the mission fund, Lyon sought to keep the spirit of reciprocating self-sacrificial benevolence constantly at work in her seminary and to attune each of its members to the sorrowful state of the world. According to Susan Tolman, who later became a missionary in Ceylon, Lyon urged this sort of strenuous giving because "she hoped we should all know what it is to suffer for Christ, to have the same feeling upon looking at a dying world as he had when upon the earth, so that . . . we could feel and weep."[45]

In this spirit, Lyon welcomed a series of visiting missionaries to South Hadley. Justin Perkins from the Nestorian mission visited the seminary on two occasions before Fiske left for Persia in the winter of 1843, and Ira Tracey preached twice during the following August in the Congregational Church in South Hadley about his mission to China. Rufus Anderson, the secretary of the American Board, discussed his recent trip to Armenia when he and his wife visited Mount Holyoke in July 1844, and the Baptist preacher William Dean, who had lost two wives and an infant daughter in China, spoke the following May. According to Lucy Lyon, who went to China herself two years later, Dean described his experiences so vividly that only "[v]ery reluctantly, did the people retire." The seminary's appetite for compelling scenes of heathen life was fed again in July 1845, when Mr. Sawtell spoke there about his years as a foreign missionary for the Evangelical Society in southern Europe.

He contrasted the "unimaginable splendor of the Vatican" with the "wretched, filthy, degraded" people held in its thrall. Lucy Lyon reported, "He says it is not strange for a Catholic mother to break the arms and legs of her infant, so as to make it a successful beggar."[46]

Such shocking portraits of life outside the Protestant world demonstrated the need for missionaries and their message of salvation and made foreign cultures seem to come alive for listeners. Vivid detail and horrible anecdote gave listeners a sense of immediacy and helped them imagine themselves as women in those cultures. Lyon fostered this sense of identification with hea-then women through the Missionary Society, which she established at the sem-inary for her most religious students and teachers. Members of this society read and discussed various published accounts of foreign cultures and missionary enterprises, and they followed closely the progress of Mount Holyoke mission-aries abroad.

The society also enjoyed spectacles of foreign life presented by members dressed in native clothes. Just three months after Fiske's departure, Tirzah M. Williams came in at the end of a Missionary Society meeting "dressed in Turkish costume, with her face veiled." With all eyes fixed on her, Williams "walked to the platform, laid off her veil and outer covering . . . and sat down in the Turkish manner on Miss Lyon's platform."[47] A second performance by Williams in the parlor at tea caused amusement, as did the appearance of Persis Thurston, the daughter of missionaries in Hawaii, at a meeting of the society several months later. Thurston "came in, in South Island attire" and, to the laughter of those assembled, "accosted Miss Whitney in the Hawaian tongue." Later, members of the society gathered around to watch her eat *poa*. Appreciation greeted Elizabeth Whaples during the second meeting of the society in the fall of 1846, when she entered "in the Nestorian costume. Her hair was braided in many braids, and hung down her back." According to Susan Tolman, "The ladies all seemed very much interested and thought the dress very becoming."[48]

These tableaux vivants dramatized the notions Mount Holyoke women held of foreign women converted to Christianity—exotically different on the out-side, but fundamentally like themselves on the inside. This perception of uni-versal sameness under external diversity involved elements of both democratic egalitarianism and psychological imperialism that, taken together, were para-digmatic of early-nineteenth-century missionary zeal. Much as the desire to help others was a necessary part of the missionary's own self-development, ide-alism about the potential equality of humanity was linked to faith in Protestant orthodoxy as the means of bringing that equality about.

Nancy Judson expressed both the egalitarian and imperialistic aspects of this paradigm when she took the Lord's Supper with a Baptist community soon after her baptism in Calcutta. The cultural diversity of this community was the most "striking display of the love of God" she had ever seen. Around the com-munion table "Hindoos and Portuguese, Armenians and Musselmans" gath-ered with "Europeans and Americans, in commemorating the dying love of Jesus." In Judson's mind, this community was a microcosm of that amiable, universal society that Jonathan Edwards had described in *The History of the Work of Redemption*. But admission to it required disavowal of any ideas that conflicted with Edwardsean Protestantism. "Surely nothing but divine grace," Judson concluded, with regard to religious difference, "could have removed prejudices, early and inveterate, from the minds of these different characters, and united them in the same sentiments and pursuits."[49]

The efforts Judson, Fiske, and other missionary women made to strengthen their own lives had an important referent in their preconceived images of women victimized by cruelty and superstition in foreign cultures.[50] The degraded heathen woman functioned as a kind of shadow image of the missionary—a symbol of her own fears about her vulnerability and just deserts. In helping to elevate the heathen woman, the missionary also experienced a simulated version of her own elevation. Ironically, investment in the elevation of heathen women, along with a narrowly Protestant definition of what constituted that elevation, often served to reinforce the self-preoccupation the missionary sought to escape. If the message of missionary Christianity carried elements of equality, community, and compassion that stirred hope for social justice in missionaries and in many of the people with whom they worked, the preoccupation with self-sacrifice within this message also subverted those elements, contributed to new forms of hierarchy, alienation, and cruelty, and frustrated the very hopes of social justice that the missionary message raised.

FOUR

~~~✦~~~

The Centrality of Women in the Revitalization of Nestorian Christianity and Its Conflict with Islam

Concern for self-sacrifice played a significant role in the new culture that emerged among Nestorians in northwest Persia as a result of American missionary intervention. As members of the Old Church of the East, the Nestorians were already familiar with the Christian concept of self-sacrifice, but missionaries encouraged a heroic interpretation that raised the profile of the Nestorian community and roused the animosity of the surrounding Muslim population. As missionaries encouraged their Nestorian students to conceptualize the repressions they endured from Muslims as means to salvation and participation in the Protestant ideal of global redemption, these ideas struck many Muslims as offensive and combative, and contributed to their persecution of the Nestorian community, and to its eventual decline.

The tensions that American missionaries exacerbated between the Nestorian community and the dominant Muslim population crystallized around attitudes toward women and gender differentiation that emanated principally from the Female Seminary established in the town of Urmiyah by Fidelia Fiske and her Mount Holyoke assistant, Mary Rice. In its replication of the educational system at Mount Holyoke, the Fiske seminary became an outpost of American Protestant orthodoxy and a staging ground for the implementation of ideas about the role of women in society that challenged traditional conventions of gender differentiation in Persia. At the "Holyoke of Oroomiah," as Fiske called her seminary, Nestorian women learned to read and write, and to expect companionship in marriage.[1] They also learned to identify with a form of Republican Motherhood that combined investment in self-sacrifice with new educational skills and leadership responsibilities for the transformation of their culture. As a consequence of a variety of reforms, many of which were associated with the concept of Republican Motherhood introduced by American missionaries, the Nestorian people became increasingly alienated from the dominant Muslim population with whom they shared a homeland. Because of their special relationship to America, and their corresponding relinquishment of certain Middle Eastern concepts of womanhood and customs of gender differentiation, the Nestorians became objects of envy and hatred. Many of them died violent deaths, while many others fled or emigrated to Europe and America.

Fiske Seminary as an Outpost of Mount Holyoke

In June 1850 the Female Seminary organized by Fidelia Fiske held its annual examination. A hundred and sixty Nestorian guests, including bishops, priests, and deacons of the Old Church of the East, squeezed into the seminary's recitation room, where the profusion of roses caused at least one of the guests to exclaim, "Paradise! Paradise!" The assembled visitors were impressed by the scholarly attainments exhibited by the seminary's thirty students, who answered questions about the Bible, usually without hesitation and often in minute detail. A few of the more advanced students read compositions demonstrating a solid grasp of Protestant doctrine.

These performances led a number of older women in the audience to inquire about learning to read. Sixty women asked for spelling books that day, and thirty of those, according to the missionaries, eventually learned to read the Bible in the vernacular Syriac edition distributed by the missionaries. This examination day also proved to be an important milestone in gaining the approval of influential men. According to the missionaries, some of the older men approached them after the recitations, saying, with tears in their eyes, "Will you forgive us that we have done no more for your school?" [2]

Fidelia Fiske had been recruited as a missionary to Persia by Justin Perkins, an enthusiastic advocate of the system of education that Mary Lyon had established at Mount Holyoke. Having visited Mount Holyoke twice, Perkins was drawn to the model of Christian society that Lyon had begun to establish in South Hadley, and to her idea of replicating this society in other parts of the world. In a letter written en route to Persia to one of the teachers at Mount Holyoke, Fiske reported, "Mr. Perkins takes an interest I should hardly have considered possible, in our Seminary." [3]

Perkins's interest in Mount Holyoke was shared by an influential bishop of the Nestorian Church, Mar Yohanan, who lived for a time with Perkins and his wife in Persia, taught them Syriac, and accompanied them on their second visit to the United States. Yohanan had learned English from Fiske's predecessor in Persia, Judith Grant, the wife of the missionary physician Asahel Grant. After her arrival in Urmiyah in 1835, Grant had acquired reading knowledge of ancient Syriac and fluency in vernacular Syriac and Turkish. She had also prepared several maps, one of which was reprinted in the *Missionary Herald*. A story persisted among missionaries that the bishops were amazed not only by Grant's erudition but also by her dispassionate concern for truth when "they saw her turn to her Greek Testament whenever the English differed from the Syriac." According to missionaries, it was this and other encounters with Grant that taught the Nestorian bishops to "honor womanhood."[4]

Mar Yohanan became convinced of the important role of female education in cultural advancement partly as a result of his study with Judith Grant and partly as a result of accompanying Perkins and his wife on their visit to Mount Holyoke in 1843. When queried by the Persian prince Malik Kassim Meerza, who spoke some English, about the marvels he had seen during his visit to America in 1843, Yohanan is said to have replied, "The blind they do see, the deaf they do hear, and the women they do read; they be not beasts." And he was remembered to have said, more than once, "Of all the colleges in America, Mount Holy Oke be the best; and when I see such a school here I die."[5]

The bishop's interest in the education of Nestorian women made the success of Fiske seminary possible. When Fiske arrived in the city, Yohanan promised to find students for the boarding school she hoped to establish. But he had difficulty locating parents who were willing to allow their daughters to abandon their agricultural work and extensive preparations for marriage and to give Fiske responsibility for their daughters' chastity. On the day the seminary was scheduled to open, Fiske had not a single student until Yohanan arrived with his seven-year-old niece Selby in one hand and ten-year-old Hanee in the other. "They be your daughters," the bishop told Fiske, and he admonished her to let "no man take them from your hand."[6]

The curriculum at Fiske Seminary, as it eventually came to called, was modeled after the curriculum at Mount Holyoke. The younger age of students in Urmiyah and the shortage of books in vernacular Syriac made it impossible to imitate the Mount Holyoke curriculum exactly, but Fiske did as much as she could through oral instruction to fill in the gaps caused by lack of books. The curriculum centered on Bible study, which included exercises in theology, history, geography, and singing, as well as reading, grammar, and writing. The curriculum also included arithmetic, physiology, chemistry, natural philosophy, and astronomy, although most of these subjects were taught without books. As a reward for good behavior at the end of the day, Fiske gave oral translations of her favorite religious stories and pieces of religious literature, and in some of these special sessions, her students heard excerpts from Jonathan Edwards's *History of the Work of Redemption*. They also imbibed Edwardsean theology more indirectly through other parts of the curriculum. In an account of her teaching methods and experience, Fiske described a lesson on "The Christ of the Old Testament" that she put together from her memories and notes of Lyon's lessons on Edwards's *History of the Work of Redemption*.[7]

Fiske taught her students to regard the women at Mount Holyoke as older sisters who encouraged their interest in learning, prayed for their spiritual growth, supported their efforts to teach others and reform Nestorian culture, and urged them on when rebuffed or persecuted. Fiske often reminded her students of the prayers offered in their behalf at Mount Holyoke, and she encouraged her students to remember their sisters in South Hadley during regular sessions of prayer for loved ones who were absent. Gifts from Mount Holyoke also fostered a sense of obligation in Fiske's students. Soon after her school opened, Fiske wrote to Abigail Moore, a science teacher at Mount Holyoke and one of Mary Lyon's nieces, requesting needles and material for book marks from Mount Holyoke students. Fiske hoped that those who sent donations would identify themselves, in order to "embalm their names in the memory of my little Syrian girls." As someone familiar with Mary Lyon's philosophy of the mechanics of benevolence, Moore would understand that "more gratitude is inspired when the name of the donor is known." Another source of gratitude was the melodeon donated by Mount Holyoke students, where the students at Urmiyah gathered to sing Protestant hymns translated into Syriac.[8]

Ties to South Hadley were further maintained by a flow of written correspondence. From the American side, the tone of these letters was often condescending. In August 1845 Lucy Lyon wrote to the students at Urmiyah, urging them to make the most of their religious opportunities. "God will be *very* angry with you," she warned, "if you do not love him now, when he is doing so much to make you happy. There are very many little girls in the world," she went on, "who never went to school, who cannot read, who know nothing of the great God their Creator, the blessed Savior who died on Calvary to save them, or what will become of them when they die."[9]

The Nestorian students entered enthusiastically into correspondence with their American sisters, and seemed eager to please and be accepted by them. "Many salutations and much love from the school of Miss Fiske to you, our dear sisters of the school at Mount Holyoke," wrote one group of students. Hoping the revivals that had occurred in South Hadley might be repeated in Urmiyah, the young women wrote, with characteristically vivid imagery, "[W]e beg you to pray that the Holy Spirit may visit us also, and our people, and strike sharp arrows into flinty hearts, that they may melt like wax before the fire." The young women expressed their gratitude to the students and teachers at Mount Holyoke, and to the people associated with them in America, "for so kindly sending us these missionaries. They have greatly multiplied our books and, as we trust, brought many souls to Christ." In closing, the students expressed their hope for the continued prayers of Mount Holyoke: "Please remember us in your closets and in your meetings, and ask your friends to pray for us and for our people. Farewell, beloved sisters."[10]

This correspondence reveals the emotional quality of Nestorian speech, which missionaries frequently commented on, as well as the hierarchical relationship established between the seminaries in South Hadley and Urmiyah. Fiske contributed significantly to the imbalanced nature of this relationship by treating her Nestorian students with condescension, and by presuming that they had to relinquish their own culture to participate in a relationship to which Mount Holyoke women brought everything of value. She conceptualized the relationship between Mount Holyoke women and her Nestorian students as a form of sisterhood, but the mutuality and reciprocity so important within the Mount Holyoke community never characterized the relationship between the two seminaries.

The New Culture Created at Fiske Seminary

Mount Holyoke women encouraged the students at Fiske Seminary to renounce numerous customs associated with their traditional culture and to pattern their lives on the New England Protestant model. In traditional Nestorian culture, girls began preparing for marriage as children and were often betrothed between ten and twelve and married a year or two later. Both betrothal and marriage were celebrated with food and wine, and whole villages or sections of towns participated in the festivities. A lengthy religious service as well as numerous folk rituals were performed at the time of marriage, with the bride swathed in white veils that signified her purity and the groom wearing red feathers in his cap that signified his fertility. The contrast between these ceremonies and the brevity and solemnity of orthodox Protestant marriages in America struck Mar Yohanan as quite remarkable when he visited the United States in 1842–43. After observing a wedding in the United States, the bishop jokingly asked Justin Perkins, "Do you *marry* people on *rail-roads* too?"[11]

Under missionary influence, Nestorian betrothal and marriage became more private, solemn, and brief. In 1849, when one of Fiske's older students became betrothed, and the ring of betrothal arrived at the seminary, the young woman disappeared during the excitement and could not be found for some time. Eventually she was discovered in a closet praying to God for his blessing on her new relationship. The missionaries were well pleased with this demonstration of serious piety at the prospect of marriage, and with their student's discreet but well-noticed avoidance of "the rioting and folly common on such occasions."[12]

The Americans also disapproved of traditional Nestorian attitudes toward death, especially the dramatic demonstrations of grief with which Nestorian women traditionally greeted it. Missionaries thought that death should be greeted with equanimity, and there was no mourning for the deceased at the funerals of reformed Nestorians; patterning themselves after their missionary instructors, reformed mourners took the occasion of death to share images of the happiness of their loved one in heaven, repent of their own sins, and draw closer to God. On one occasion, a group of Fiske's students declined to attend a funeral for fear that one of them would shame the others by not wailing or shedding tears. Missionaries were also troubled by the Nestorians' willingness to simulate emotion, which the missionaries thought dishonest. When asked how she could cry at funerals when she was not personally grieved, one young woman replied that she simply thought of other things that made her sad.

From the American perspective, this willingness to participate in mourning rituals without feeling personal grief seemed part of a general indifference to truth. Fiske and Rice were astonished by how easily and frequently their students lied to them. The missionaries seemed unaware that their students might be using falsehood as a way of maintaining their identity and some independence from their teachers. In her effort to promote truthfulness in her students and to encourage their submission to Protestant Christianity, Fiske followed a strategy Mary Lyon used to catch out offenders before they could lie or cover up lapses in the fulfillment of their duties. Rather than leading them "to temptation" by asking them to stand if they had failed to comb their hair, or arrive on time, Fiske caught miscreants off-guard and exposed their shame by asking everyone to stand and then asking those who had combed their hair, or arrived on time, to sit. "The faithful ones were delighted to comply. The others, mortified and ashamed, remained standing; but if one of them tried to sit down, a glance of the eye detected her." [13]

The missionaries complemented these painful exposures with encouragements to students to make use of the school's several closets for private prayer and introspection. Such a regimen of self-examination was new to girls little used to privacy and for whom religious experience was typically a communal phenomenon. While communal religious events also figured importantly in religious life at Mount Holyoke, they were more restrained, and emotional control was an essential part of the conversion process nurtured there. Fiske was profoundly disturbed by what she perceived as a lack of emotional restraint in her students, and she controlled their religious gatherings very carefully. She hoped that the intensity of these communal events would flow largely from the extended periods of private prayer and self-examination that preceded them and not from traditional Nestorian customs of raising feeling, which she thought insincere. After the first Nestorian revival of 1846, when fifteen or twenty students at the Boys' Seminary became so distressed with sin that they threw themselves on the floor and rolled around, "groaning and crying for mercy," missionaries carefully avoided language that might appeal to "the passions" of their students and were "fully aware of the danger of an unhealthy excitement, to which this people, from their ardent temperament, are peculiarly liable." [14]

Fiske and her missionary colleagues often remarked on the high-strung nature of the Nestorian people. The strictness with which missionaries monitored their students was partly a reaction to this perceived trait. Although the Americans tried to control the emotionalism of their students, they found themselves moved by the earnestness of their converts and by the lyricism of Nestorian piety. During a revival at the seminary in early 1850, the missionaries were charmed by the "wonderful transparency of feeling" that characterized the speech of their students, even though they were also alert to "a tendency to undue excitement that needed careful handling." [15] Missionaries were deeply impressed by their students' eagerness to please and to be good Christians, and by their affection. When the patriarch Mar Shimon became openly critical of the Americans in 1844 and threatened to tear off the fingernails of Fiske's students if they did not leave the seminary and return home, there was "a general burst of grief" at the seminary. The students "threw their arms around the neck of their teacher" as they left, "and there poured forth the deep sorrows of their hearts. . . . With affecting earnestness they said, again and again, 'We shall never hear the words of God more.' Weeping they left us," one missionary remembered, "and the breezes bore back their mournful sighs when they were out of our sight."[16]

Fiske was deeply gratified by the affection her students bestowed on her, and she became attached to them, often visiting and writing to them after they graduated. In a significant way, she found herself enlarged by the friendliness, emotional openness, and easy affection of Nestorian women. Thus one Sunday in the nearby village of Geog Tapa, during a long day of religious teaching and prayer, a Nestorian woman taught her a memorable lesson about the reciprocal nature of Christian love. When Fiske sat down on a mat on an earth floor, feeling too weary to think of deriving much benefit from the sermon that was about to begin, a woman seated herself directly behind Fiske and invited her to lean on her back for support. When Fiske declined, the woman pulled her back, saying, "If you love me, lean hard." The interchange was a sort of epiphany for Fiske; she identified the woman's words with the message of the gospel, and felt that through her insistent kindness, Christ "had preached me a better sermon than I could have heard at home."[17]

If missionaries were changed by their encounters with Nestorians, the Nestorians were changed even more. In addition to their demands for submission to missionary authority, private prayer, and the rejection of traditional rituals of celebration and mourning, missionaries also disrupted traditional habits of collective life by promoting new kinds of social interchange between men and women. Used to group activities where men and women were segregated, the Nestorians were initially uncomfortable when they followed the missionaries into situations where men and women were mixed together. For example, at a certain point during the day of examination at Fiske Seminary in 1850, the missionaries arranged for everyone present to sit down together for a meal of lamb roasted native-style, served with lettuce, cherries, and pilaf and followed by cakes baked by the seminary students that were "much discussed" during the meal. According to a missionary chronicler, "Many of the women had never before sat at the same table with men." While "their awkward embarrassment" was "amusing" to some of the Americans, for the Nestorians it was a significant moment of cultural experimentation and change. Willing to be present and join in the meal but unsure about how to proceed in mixed company, some of the women "snatched the food from the table by stealth, and ate it behind their large veils, as though it were a thing forbidden."[18]

Before the arrival of missionaries, only men preparing for ecclesiastical responsibility were literate, and the language they read was the form of Aramaic known as ancient Syriac, the language of the Nestorian liturgy and biblical texts. The missionaries promoted knowledge of this ancient language among both men and women, and also rendered into writing the dialect of vernacular

Syriac spoken by Nestorians in Urmiyah, which incorporated elements of Turkish and Farsi. Even the mountain Nestorians, who spoke a different dialect with many Kurdish elements, were taught to read the dialect spoken at Urmiyah. This dialect became the principle language of the mission, and hundreds of Bibles and other books and pamphlets printed in this language encouraged Nestorians to move away from their liturgical, highly formalized understanding of Christian scripture and to adopt a more individualistic and moralistic understanding consonant with Protestant theology.[19]

The missionary emphasis on religious literacy led both to the creation of a new generation of Nestorian women who participated in some of the same intellectual activities as men and to new literary ventures. Although for the first three years of her teaching in Persia Fiske was unsuccessful in teaching her students to do more than copy sentences, after the first revival in 1846 they began to express their thoughts in essays and letters and to take great pleasure in presenting their internalization of Protestant doctrine in artful and compelling ways.[20] The process of conversion led to a remarkable literary output among students at the Female Seminary, some of which the missionaries published in the United States. Mar Yohanan identified one of the students at the Female Seminary, Sarah from the mountain village of Chardewar in Gawar, who died before she could do much teaching, as one of the most gifted theologians of reformed Nestorian Christianity.

In their eagerness to foster a culture of missionary service among Nestorians, the Americans encouraged their students to identify with a vision of the future in which Christians who suffered persecution became leading agents in Christ's triumph of the world. This vision nurtured expectations of martyrdom and happened to coincide with the violence that Nestorians were actually suffering at the hands of Muslims, partly as a result of missionary involvement in Nestorian affairs. Missionaries took the massacre of mountain Nestorians by Kurds in 1843 as an opportunity to foster conversion experiences in the refugees who poured into Urmiyah, and Asahel Grant wrote positively about the effect of survivors' sufferings on their religious lives: "A new hope seemed to kindle in their bosoms," he wrote after the massacres; "they eagerly drank the encouragement I presented."[21]

Missionary hopes for the revitalization of Nestorian culture began to be realized in 1846, when revivals began almost simultaneously in both the Female and Boys' Seminaries and soon spread among other Nestorians in the town of Urmiyah and in the village of Geog Tapa, six miles to the southeast, where two Nestorian Church officials, Abraham, a priest, and Joseph, a deacon, had become affiliated with the Americans. The revival of 1846 occurred during an emotionally charged time of social stress and turbulence, and the missionaries' emphasis on suffering as an occasion for religious transformation encouraged Nestorians to interpret their fears, losses, and precarious economic and political situation as a needed correction from God for their sins and an opportunity for conversion and spiritual growth. Thus the Nestorians who participated in this revival used Christian concepts of sin and redemption, and Christian images of hell and heaven, to express their fears about the future, their preoccupation with death and grief, and their desires for escape, security, and happiness.

The revival was initiated by Sarah and another young woman from Gawar who were students in the Female Seminary. On the morning of the first Monday of the New Year, Fiske opened the school with the solemn announcement that prayers were being offered for the seminary that very day in America, and then she dismissed the students to their work. Sarah and Sanum approached her, weeping, and asked to spend the day in prayer. Hoping to nurture the religious concerns of the two girls and to facilitate their influence among other students, Fiske followed the strategy Mary Lyon used at Mount Holyoke of inviting students eager for salvation to a special session in her room. Other American missionaries encouraged similar concerns in the Boys' Seminary, and when the two schools met together for prayer a few days later, a revival caught fire. Experiences of heartfelt repentance and growth in grace continued for weeks among Fiske's students, and when news of this prolonged season of religious activity spread to the people of Urmiyah, many women flocked to the Female Seminary. Fiske turned the recitation room into a dormitory to accommodate the visitors, who received religious instruction from her during the evenings and often stayed through the night to pray.[22]

This involvement of older Nestorian women in the life of the Female Seminary marked an important moment in the creation of a Reformed Protestant culture in Persia. Nestorian women played an important role in cultivating interest in Protestant reform and in carrying forward American interest in female literacy and education. The involvement of dozens of women in the revival at the Female Seminary in 1846 prepared the way for the demonstration of support for women's education at the annual examination there in 1850.

The composition Sanum read at that examination illustrates how refugees influenced by missionaries interpreted their suffering as a providential means of their own conversion. In an essay entitled "The Lost Soul," Sanum described a dream of her own death that was so vivid and compelling that some of the women in her audience "beat on their breasts with half-suppressed cries for mercy." In the dream, Sanum resisted the efforts of her parents and teachers to make her repent of her careless pursuit of earthly pleasures until it was too late. "Then came a beautiful day in spring," when a voice broke through her complacence, announcing, " 'This night thy soul shall be required of thee.' " Stunned by this message, she collapsed and was carried home, where her parents wept over her, saying, " 'Sweet child, if you were only a Christian, gladly would we go with you to the gates of heaven, hoping soon to meet again.' " Fidelia Fiske and Asahel Grant were summoned to her side, and they joined her parents in weeping and praying for her soul. Fiske "pressed my hand; she could not speak. I said, 'You have ever shown great love; can you not help me now?' 'Dear Child,' " she responded, " 'have I not told you that though I love you, yet I have no power to help in this hour or hereafter.' "

As her teacher withdrew and the light dimmed, Sanum heard "a rushing, mighty wind" and began shaking with fear. "I discerned four fiends of darkness," she recalled. "I uttered a piercing shriek, and died. Then I found myself suspended between heaven and earth. Behind me, the world I loved so well had gone forever. Before me I saw the Ancient of Days seated on his throne, his raiment white as snow, his eyes as a flame of fire, his feet like brass glowing in the furnace, and a stream of fire issued from before him." This wrathful God "fixed his eyes on me glowing with holy indignation, while a two-edged sword proceeded out of his mouth." Bound and thrown into "outer darkness" until Judgment Day, she found herself with Cain, Judas, Jeroboam, and Jezebel and, like them, cursed and reviled. In reaction to this treatment, her "wicked feelings . . . kindled into a flame." These feelings set her tongue on fire, and she begged for water. "But instead of it came the word, 'Daughter, remember.' As I looked up, I got a glimpse of one of my companions in Abraham's bosom. Once we were together pointed to Jesus. Now the impassable gulf was between us." Sinking "down in unutterable agony," Sanum woke in a cold sweat.[23]

Sanum's description of being dead and looking behind herself to the world she had once loved corresponded to her social experience as a young woman whose mountain girlhood lay in the past. The happiness she knew there had been lost as a result of the violence that had destroyed the relatively peaceful existence of the mountain Nestorians. Moreover, the pleasant memories she had of this mountain life were tinged with guilt as a result of the alliance her family struck with American missionaries. Through this alliance, and through her education at the Female Seminary, Sanum came to embrace the orthodox Protestant concept of sin taught by the Americans and its damning interpretation of many aspects of traditional Nestorian life.

While missionaries praised the Nestorians for being "more simple and scriptural than . . . other oriental christians" and for holding "all image worship, auricular confession, the doctrine of purgatory, and many other corrupt dogmas and practices of the Papal, Greek, and Armenian churches" in the "deepest abhorrence," they also pointed to the Nestorians' belief in the spiritual efficacy of fasting, their frequent use of profanity, and willingness to lie as evidence that they lacked the proper concepts of sin and salvation.[24] As the Americans saw it, Nestorians understood forgiveness of sin as an external transaction rather than the deeply felt alteration in intentionality the missionaries presumed it to be. This impression was supported by the illiteracy of many Nestorians, the lack of Bible study, and the fact that most Nestorians could not understand the ancient Syriac in which the liturgies of the Nestorian Church proceeded.

The missionaries conveyed their disapproval of these aspects of Nestorian Christianity with the help of vivid descriptions of hell as a place of fire and brimstone where the absence of a genuinely existential commitment to Christ was eternally punished. These images of hell had a kind of immediacy as a result of the burning of villages and the physical sufferings, terror, and desperation experienced by mountain Nestorians. Sanum's image of staring at hell while her companions at the Female Seminary found safety in Abraham's embrace reflects the distance between the moments of chaos and horror in the mountains and the protection of the Female Seminary.

The conversion process that Sanum participated in at the seminary gave her a religious framework for interpreting the suffering of her people, as well as a commitment to missionary service. The hard times she later endured made her an exemplar of this culture of service. Thus in 1849, while home in Chadewar for a visit, Sanum wrote a correspondent in America, "I had bitter times this vacation, for our neighbors are all very hard-hearted, not listening at all to the words of God. When I opened my Testament to read to them, they would shut it, and begin to quarrel about the forms of religion. I entreat you to pray for my village," wrote this young missionary, "that I so unworthy, may see its salvation." Three years later, after she had graduated from the Female Seminary, Fiske and Rice visited Sanum in Chadewar and admired how she had formed a school of ten or twelve girls and captured the religious interest of almost the entire adult female population of the village. A brief account of Sanum's work was published in the *Missionary Herald*, which reported that "this young female, by her active and consistent piety, is exerting a happy influence in the village and the surrounding country." But only a few years later, after taking a family meal to a neighbor's oven to be heated, she and her family were poisoned with arsenic. Sanum and her husband survived, but her two children, Elisha and Jonathan, died. The letter Sanum wrote after Fiske visited her in 1859 illustrates the difficulty of her life. She recalled the sadness of their meeting, and how "the green grass was watered with our tears." Sanum claimed that she could not have born the separation from Fiske, who was returning to the United States, "but for the recollection of Him who prayed and wept in the garden of Gethsemane." [25]

By alienating Sanum and others from traditional Middle Eastern culture, the new culture that emerged as a result of missionary intervention prompted a backlash of resistance within the Nestorian Church, as well as an escalation of tension between Nestorians and Muslims. The Americans responded to this backlash by relinquishing their policy of working within the Nestorian Church. They established a separate communion ritual for Nestorian Protestants and, eventually, a separate church. The subsequent arrival of missionaries representing a variety of alternative Protestant denominations added to the fragmentation of Nestorian culture, as did the revival of Roman Catholic interest in the Nestorians, which occurred in response to the growing influence of Protestantism.

Throughout this process of cultural change and confusion, women's roles were crucial points of contestation. Missionaries promoting the American ideal of Republican Motherhood nurtured fundamental changes in Nestorian concepts of womanhood, and these changes figured centrally in the increasingly strained relationship between Nestorian and Muslim culture as well as in the polarization of Nestorian culture. The important role of American concepts of religious piety and Republican Motherhood in these changes can best be appreciated by locating the introduction of these concepts within the context of the history of the Nestorian people.

The Place of American Intervention in the History
of Nestorian Culture

According to popular legend, the Nestorians were converted to Christianity by the apostle Thomas when he stopped in Urmiyah on his way to India. The people named churches after Mar (Saint) Thomas in honor of his legendary visit and patronage. Whether or not this visit actually occurred, the origins of Nestorian Christianity can be traced to the earliest days of Christian evangelism. The Nestorian scholar John Joseph suggests that the spreading of Christianity to Persia and eastern Anatolia may have begun at the gathering of "Parthians and Medes, and Elamites, and inhabitants of Mesopotamia" in Jerusalem on the Day of Pentecost, mentioned in Acts 2.9.[26]

A distinct Nestorian Church was founded several centuries later by members of the Church of Antioch who continued to embrace the doctrines of Nestorius, bishop of Constantinople, after he was condemned as a heretic in the early fifth century by ecclesial authority in Rome. The western bishops rejected the arguments Nestorius made in behalf of the dual nature of Christ, and they opposed the theological and political reforms implicit in his emphasis on the humanity of Christ. The eastern church that become identified with the name of Nestorius established its patriarchal see in Seleucia-Ctesiphon on the Tigris, and then in Baghdad at the end of the eighth century. Missionaries of this church reached India in the sixth century and China in the seventh, and established several Christian communities in Arabia.[27]

Nestorian communities were greatly diminished by the persecutions of Tamurlane and other Mongol leaders who invaded the Near East and converted many of its inhabitants to Islam at the end of the thirteenth century. During the fourteenth century, Christian refugees from central Mesopotamia joined small settlements of Nestorians in Kurdistan that had probably existed there for centuries. Several pieces of evidence point to the longstanding existence of a Nestorian community in the area of Urmiyah—Azerbaijan was listed as a Nestorian diocese as early as the fifth century, Justin Perkins found an eleventh-century Christian manuscript in a mosque in Urmiyah that had once been a church, and Nestorian Church records note the residence of a bishop in Urmiyah in the early twelfth century. In 1840, two hundred and fifty thousand Nestorians lived on the plains of Urmiyah in Persian Azerbaijan, in scattered villages in the Hakkari Mountains on the border of Turkish and Persian Kurdistan, and in the area around Mosul in Turkish Kurdistan. Approximately six hundred Nestorians lived in the city of Urmiyah in 1840, along with two thousand Jews and several thousand Muslims. The Nestorians were recognized by Persian shahs, Kurdish amirs, and Turkish pashas as a religious minority, but they were subject to restrictions under Islamic law that prevented their political and economic advancement.[28]

Americans educated in church history at the turn of the nineteenth century were familiar with the name of Nestorius and with the reputation of his followers as early missionaries to India and China. But they were unaware of the continued existence of Nestorians until 1810, when Eli Smith and H. G. O. Dwight discovered them while touring Persia as scouting agents for the American Board of Commissioners for Foreign Missions. Despite the fact that the Nestorians were a small and poor population far removed from the centers of power, the Americans became excited about discovering people who were descended from early Christians. In the 1840s, when French and British archaeologists unearthed the palaces of ancient Assyrian kings and libraries of cuneiform tablets, the Americans pointed proudly to the Nestorians they were ministering to as "living Ninevehs."

The Americans linked their own religious history to that of the Nestorians, dubbing them the "Protestants of Asia," portraying Nestorius as a persecuted reformer, and saluting his emphasis on the humanity of Christ. As the Americans understood it, the Nestorians had possessed knowledge of the primitive truths of Christianity in ancient times, but they had subsequently lost some of that knowledge or allowed it to be corrupted. These primitive truths had been restored to western Christianity through the Protestant Reformation, carried forward through the Puritans, and passed on to the American missionaries, who, in turn, sought to restore Nestorian Christianity to its ancient integrity.

These American ideas were framed by the historical theology of Jonathan Edwards and his New Divinity successors, especially by their emphasis on the work of redemption as a historical process scripted since the beginning of time that was moving toward actualization through the efforts of orthodox Protestant missionaries. The Americans were also attracted by the pleasant climate and scenic beauty of northwest Persia. Except for the stagnant pools of water that bred disease, which the missionaries interpreted as a reflection of the stagnation of Nestorian religious life, the environs of Lake Urmiyah seemed like Paradise.

The Americans were enthused by the prospect of Nestorians recovering their ancient missionary heritage and assuming a leadership role in the conversion of the East. Situated in a geographical crux between the Sunni Kurds and Turks to the west and the Shi'a Persians to the south and southeast, the Nestorians seemed providentially positioned to conquer the Islamic world with Christian knowledge and benevolence. Thus Smith and Dwight described the Nestorians as the "prop, upon which to rest the lever that will overturn the whole system of Muhammadan delusion." Having "fixed himself" at the "centre" of this delusion, wrote Smith and Dwight, the American missionary would start "a fire which will shine out upon the corruptions of the Persian on the one side, and upon the barbarities of the Koord on the other, until all shall come to be enlightened by its brightness, and the triumph of faith will crown his labor of love."[29]

The destruction of Islam was to be complete, the Americans felt sure, and would be guided by the spirit of God, not by military, economic, and political forces, which the Americans felt their cause to be above. Guns and swords might be used if Muslims took them up, but Christians would wield them only in self-defense, if at all. Of course, American missionaries in the Middle East were incapable of mustering any military or political support from their government in the early and mid–nineteenth century. But they also believed that coercion was counterproductive and that conversion to Christianity would require heartfelt desire on the part of each individual to embrace Christ in the orthodox Protestant way.

As the result of this millenarian idealism about Christian history, the Americans rejected, or simply overlooked, the political interpretations that Muslims gave to missionary activity. Asahel Grant was oblivious to the political jeopardy in which his missionary work placed the mountain Nestorians, and he was apparently unconcerned about the role it played in fueling Muslim animosity. He angered Kurds and Turks by providing valuable educational services to the Nestorians that lifted them above their Muslim neighbors and by fostering a special relationship between the Nestorians and the West. In 1843 he stirred fears of immediate conflict by employing Nestorians in the construction of a school so large and well built that the Muslims suspected it was a military fortress. Tension escalated with the arrival of British missionaries, who gave promises of temporal as well as spiritual support to the patriarch of the Nestorian Church, Mar Shimon. Referring to Americans as "dissenters" from the Church of England, the British raised questions among Nestorian leaders about the religious legitimacy of American missionaries. Troubled by these allegations, and by the social unrest the Americans precipitated, Mar Shimon allied himself with the Turks and distanced himself from the Nestorians attached to the Americans. The Turks took the opportunity of this division among Nestorians to support Nurallah, the Kurdish amir of Hakkari, in his sacking of Nestorian mountain villages in 1843. After commandeering Grant's school as their own fortress, the Kurds killed fifty thousand Nestorians—one-fourth of the entire Nestorian population—and sent thousands more fleeing to Urmiyah.[30]

Not since the persecutions of Tamurlane in the fourteenth century had the Nestorians been so at odds with their Muslim neighbors. Before the Americans arrived the Nestorians had lived peaceably, for the most part, as a subjugated religious minority. They lived in separate sections of Urmiyah and of some villages or in villages of their own. Under Islamic law, their right to exist and enjoy limited forms of self-government were recognized, though they were discriminated against through special taxes, restrictions against selling wares and produce in the bazaars, and prohibitions against engaging any form of artistry other than carpentry or masonry. They were also subject to periodic attacks from the Kurds; in 1835, the year the first permanent American missionaries arrived, Kurds sacked villages in the district of Gawar. But their vulnerability increased dramatically as their self-perceptions changed under American influence and as Muslims became alarmed at the political and social implications of American favoritism. The relative security the Nestorians had enjoyed in the region disappeared. After the outbreak of violence against them in 1843, the Nestorians became more open to new religious attitudes from the West, and this angered Muslims further.[31]

American Contributions to Changing Expectations
of Gender Differentiation

The diminishment of gender segregation among the Nestorians that occurred as a result of missionary influence became a major point of difference between the Nestorians and their Muslim neighbors. As one scholar of Nestorian-Muslim relations recently argued, "The single greatest source of conflict . . . between the two groups involves the differential status and attitudes toward women. While neither Christian nor Muslim women play important political or economic roles, and are generally excluded from trade, commerce and positions of authority in the official hierarchy, the attitudes and values that each group attaches to their perceptions of women is an important line of cleavage separating the two religious groups."[32]

Some of this difference in attitudes toward women existed before the arrival of missionaries; the Nestorians' conception of marriage was strictly monogamous, but polygamy was protected under Islamic law. Whether or not women in polygamous marriages were always poorly valued, as missionaries believed, polygamy did foster gender segregation and restrict companionship between the sexes in ways that monogamy did not. American missionaries helped enlarge the existing differences between Nestorians and their neighbors by establishing schools for Nestorian girls and teaching their mothers to read, by encouraging companionship and mutuality in marriage, and by facilitating the breakdown of certain forms of gender segregation, such as separate eating.

Missionary women were shocked that Nestorian parents only celebrated the births of sons, and that when asked how many children they had, parents did not include daughters in their count.[33] This reticence about daughters was partly a matter of protecting them from exposure to men, especially Muslim men, who were not confined by religious faith to monogamy as Nestorians were, and who acquired rights to the wealth of a Christian family under Persian law if a member of the family converted to Islam.[34] But the absence of public enthusiasm at the birth of a daughter was also a public recognition of the idea of female inferiority. Missionaries may not have fully appreciated the ways in which women were respected in Nestorian culture, but they did understand that Nestorian men expected women to serve them and work for them — preparing food, but never eating until men were finished, and working in the fields all day, at what were often considered menial though necessary tasks, tending cotton, grapes, and other crops. When the first American missionaries to settle among the Nestorians arrived in Urmiyah in 1835, the only Nestorian woman known to be literate was Heleneh, the sister of the Nestorian Church patriarch Mar Shimon. The Nestorian women first approached by the missionaries had no interest in reading, which they considered outside the sphere of female activity; at least one woman turned down a missionary invitation to learn with the reply, "I am a woman."[35]

While American missionaries objected to the notions of female inferiority prevalent in Middle Eastern culture, they had no intention of freeing women from subjugation to male authority. Emphasizing the Christian virtue of humility as a model for women's behavior, Fiske argued that a wife's submission to her husband should be based in affection rather than coercion. To women who came reviling their husbands and complaining of being beaten, Fiske would say, "I did not come to deliver you from your husbands, but to show you how to be so good that you can be happy with them." She was appalled by the angry outbursts of Nestorian women. Although she acknowledged some of the injustices they railed at, Fiske regarded their displays of passion as sorry evidence of what women were like without the gospel. She recalled one "virago, who often, single-handed, faced down and drove off Moslem tax-gatherers when the men fled in terror." Recognizing in this woman's "stinging shrillness" and "frenzied gestures" the reason "why the ancients painted the Furies in the form of women," Fiske was amazed at the scene created by this woman. She was thankful for a gospel powerful enough to transform even a woman like that into a model of evangelical humility: "The hair of the frantic actors is streaming in the wind; stones and clods seem only embodiments of the unearthly yells and shrieks that fill the air; and yet it was such beings that grace made to be 'last at the cross and first at the sepulchre.' "[36]

Fiske was critical of what she perceived to be the desire for mastery of men expressed by Nestorian women, and she urged Nestorian women to be more, not less, submissive to their husbands. But the Americans also encouraged new kinds of interchange and mutuality between the sexes that undermined some of the assumptions about female inferiority on which Nestorian concepts of gender differentiation were based.

One of the signs of the growing difference between Nestorians and Muslims was the change in the use of the veil as a marker of group difference. The women who tilled the rich soil of northwest Persia did not wear veils when working in the fields; as Tajol-Saltaneh, the daughter of the Persian shah Nasser-e-Din, observed at the end of the nineteenth century. "In my journey through Azarbaydjan," she wrote, "I could see women working freely with men in the fields and without a veil. These peasants are the honorable and dignified people of this land. You could not find a single prostitute in all our villages."[37] Before American intervention, the veil was more a marker of class than religion. While Muslim peasant women worked bareheaded in the fields, some Nestorian women veiled their faces in mixed company. Thus some of the women who sat with men on day of the annual examination at the Female Seminary in 1850 ate their lamb and cake behind their veils. But this awkward moment marked a transition in Nestorian custom. Those who followed the Americans gave up the veil and became more used to participating with men in conversation and eating. Once a sign of protected womanhood shared by Muslims and Nestorians, the veil in Urmiyah came to be an exclusive mark of the religious identity of Muslim women.

Actual hostility between Christians and Muslims developed in the related phenomenon of female sequestering. When polite social interchange between Nestorian men and women became more common, this new sociability did not extend to Muslims. As a result of American influence, Christian girls were freer to socialize with Christian boys, but Christian parents were careful to restrict their daughters from contact with Muslim boys, warning them that any sign of friendliness might be interpreted as flirtation and frightening them with stories of Christian girls who were captured and forced to marry Muslims. While the Nestorian concern to protect daughters from Muslim men predated the arrival of missionaries, the missionaries exacerbated this tension by facilitating increased socialization between the sexes in Nestorian culture and by providing schools and events that catered primarily to Christians. Muslim children were welcome in missionary schools, and a few elite Muslim families chose Christian schools because of the literary and scientific education they offered, but the religious orientation of mission schools was unattractive to the vast majority of Muslims.[38]

If American missionaries to Persia helped shape a legacy of Muslim hostility to America, they also understood the crucial role that women, and women's issues, could play in the transformation of society. But while missionaries were deliberate and relatively shrewd in their facilitation of changes in the role of women and in their understanding of the central importance of women in cultural change, they were exceedingly obtuse and naive about the political implications of their religious idealism.

The Exclusivism of American Missionary Idealism

The importance of the difference between American and Muslim interpretations of the escalating tension between Nestorians and Muslims cannot be overemphasized. Because religion defined political identity in the Middle East, Muslims naturally interpreted the growing relationship between Americans and Nestorians in political terms. As a religious minority under Islamic law, the Nestorians lived within a system of limited self-government. Islamic law distinguished between "pagans," whom it did not tolerate, and Jews and Christians, or "people of the Book," who knew the one, true God, albeit misguidedly and incompletely. The millet system of Islamic law recognized the existence of Jewish and Christian sects and provided for members of these sects to be represented by their own leaders in Islamic courts.

For their part the Americans had little appreciation of Islam and little understanding of the role of Islamic law in Middle Eastern government. The Americans came from a system of government in which the state supported Protestant Christianity in a general and de facto way but remained independent of any particular religious body or set of religious doctrines. American missionaries also came from a religious system in which religious faith was primarily a matter of personal attitude, and in which ritualized forms of religious obedience were regarded as stupefying and wrong. Moreover, these missionaries were religious volunteers who acted independently of their own government. While elected representatives in the United States may have shared their values, the U.S. government had no Middle Eastern or Persian policy at mid-century. Compared with Britain's concern to establish influence in Persia and Turkey to protect its position in India, or with Russia's efforts after 1860 to woo Nestorians and Armenians into the Russian Orthodox Church as a step toward extending Russian command of Asia Minor, the U.S. government had no political, military, and economic interest in the Middle East before 1880 and little ability to pursue one.

Unlike the British and Russian missionaries, who followed government representatives of their countries into Persia, the American missionaries were far ahead of U.S. government policy. When the United States eventually did become engaged in Persian affairs, it was to secure the safety of American missionaries. In 1880, after an outbreak of Kurdish violence against Christians in the Urmiyah area, the Ohio congressman R. R. Dawes, whose sister and brother-in-law were missionaries in Urmiyah, appealed to the State Department to seek the aid of the Persian government in protecting them. With the encouragement of the shah, who did little to protect Christians in Urmiyah but was interested in American business investments, President Chester A. Arthur signed a bill in 1882 establishing a U.S. embassy in Tehran. The appointment of Samuel G. W. Benjamin, whose parents were missionaries in the Middle East, as the first American ambassador underscored the nature of the U.S. interest. Over the next forty years, while the shah's support of the British tobacco monopoly led to a revolution and to the establishment of the constitutional monarchy of Iran, U.S. policy in Persia continued to focus on the protection of missionaries and was often indifferent or hostile to American business investment.[39]

When other forms of government disappeared in Urmiyah during World War I, the American missionary William A. Shedd stepped in as temporary governor of the city of Urmiyah. He was unhappy about the conflict of interest he perceived to exist between this assignment and his missionary duties, which he considered not to be political, but he felt he had no alternative except to try to establish some government in Urmiyah that might save the Nestorians, and others, from destruction.[40]

This kind of protective action on behalf of Christian populations in the Middle East enabled the continuation of American missionary work to those populations, and came to shape U.S. policy in the Middle East. After World War I, the Americans' long history of missionary involvement with the Nestorians and Armenians became the driving force behind Woodrow Wilson's agenda in the Middle East. The secretary of the American Board of Commissioners for Foreign Missions, James L. Barton, successfully lobbied Wilson and members of congress in support of protection for the Christian minorities in Persia and Turkey that American missionaries had been cultivating for nearly a century.

While the Middle East was certainly not the only place were missionary influence played a role in transforming native cultures, the way in which that influence shaped U.S. policy was unusual. American missionaries contributed heavily to culture change in Korea and China, for example, but U.S. policy toward those countries was shaped more by economic and political interest than missionary concerns. In Liberia and Hawaii, American missionary influence played a larger overall role in reshaping the cultures of those countries than it did in the Middle East, where missionaries focused their efforts primarily on Christian minorities and had little success in communicating with surrounding peoples. It was precisely this narrowness, and the alienation of surrounding peoples, that distinguished the effect of American missionary influence on U.S. government policy in the Middle East from its effect in Liberia or Hawaii.[41]

When the United States developed its policy toward the Middle East after World War I, James L. Barton and Woodrow Wilson played decisive roles in defining that policy in terms of an underlying commitment to a Christian world. If Barton and Wilson were more accommodating in their attitudes toward Islam and its leaders than earlier American missionaries had been, they nevertheless persisted in singling out Christian minorities as special friends. The residual disdain for Islam inherent in this favoritism was expressed in explicit terms by Robert E. Speer, the secretary of the Board of Foreign Missions of the Presbyterian Church of the U.S.A., which had taken over the American Board's mission to the Nestorians in 1871. After a tour of Persia in 1922, Speer wrote, "Persia needs a greater friend than the Standard Oil Company or the United States of America and who can do more for her than build roads or develop oil or promote trade. She does need prosperity instead of poverty," Speer admitted, but what she needed most was "enlightenment." Persia "has had enough of Mohammed. She needs Christ whom Mohammedanism has praised, it is true, but has also effaced—long enough."[42]

The Christian internationalism that shaped U.S. Middle East policy in the twentieth century had roots in the conviction of Eli Smith, H. G. O. Dwight, and other early-nineteenth-century missionaries that Islam was a delusion to be toppled in the course of the historical progress of God's work of redemption. This attitude of Protestant superiority created resentment among Islamic peoples and contributed to the religious background out of which comes Islamic hostility to America in the Middle East today. It also confirmed the longstanding Muslim assumption that political and religious identity were one. Ironically, American involvement in the Middle East had originated in the religious idealism of missionaries who distanced themselves from politics. In their idealism about Christianity, American missionaries failed to see, or take seriously, the political implications of their influence.

But however naive and mistaken nineteenth-century missionaries in Persia were about the political implications of their influence, they were alert to the changes occurring in the personal lives of their followers, and they were adept at facilitating these changes. In their attentiveness to subjective and interpersonal life as the arena in which God's work occurred, missionaries recognized the importance, perhaps even the centrality, of women in the process of cultural change. The American missionary belief that interpersonal changes, in which women were centrally involved, would transform Nestorian culture from the inside, and that political change would follow as a matter of course, was not entirely off the mark.

~❧~

FIVE

The Presence and Impact of Mary Lyon's Students in Maharashtra

*A*merican missionaries also contributed to the creation of a Protestant-inspired, reform-minded culture in Maharashtra, the triangular region in western India known as the Bombay Presidency, which included the coastal region of the Konkan, the Sahyadri Mountains, and the arid plains of the Deccan. But this reform-minded culture had a very different shape and history than the new culture inspired by missionaries in Persia, where the weakness of Nestorian culture left the Nestorian people highly vulnerable to intellectual domination by missionaries. In contrast, the strength of Hindu culture in Maharashtra enabled Hindu reformers to exploit missionary influence to an extraordinary degree. Mary Lyon's students and their missionary associates exerted no less influence in this region than they did in northwest Persia, but in Maharashtra their influence was absorbed, to a considerable extent, within the context of the heterogeneous and powerfully syncretic tradition of Hinduism. Thus missionary efforts in Maharashtra functioned as a catalyst for Hindu reform, which coincided with a significant degree of missionary failure to convert Hindus to Christianity.

Missionary intervention in Maharashtra contributed to the revitalization of a longstanding Hindu tradition of iconoclastic piety that linked love of God with the attainment of experiential states of pure devotion and the repudiation of rituals designed to maintain caste. While missionary belief in the historical progress of God's work of redemption carried with it an unfamiliar and aggressive social agenda that called for new systems of social organization and welfare, the missionaries' emphasis on devotion to God was compatible with certain aspects of Hindu piety, and their habits of self-sacrifice were not entirely unlike Hindu ascetic practices designed to foster religious knowledge and experience. Given the variety of religious beliefs and practices within Hinduism, the respect that religious seekers commanded, and the important similarities between Hindu and missionary piety, Hindu leaders in Maharashtra were able to appropriate, more easily than might otherwise have been possible, some of the new concepts of social organization and welfare advanced by missionaries.

The concept of Republican Motherhood was an important extension of American missionary theology, and it resonated with certain aspects of Hindu female piety in Maharashtra. While the American emphasis on women's education was new, as was the notion of women's responsibility for nurturing an enlightened citizenry, the belief in the importance of women's devotion to patriarchal family structures was something that missionaries and Hindus held in common. This coinciding commitment to male authority provided the basis for translating various aspects of Republican Motherhood into Hindu terms. A shared belief in women's responsibility for maintaining the patriarchal structure of society established a framework within which Hindus drew on missionary concerns for social welfare and women's education.

Americans were not alone in promoting women's education or women's involvement in social reform. London missionaries in Calcutta established the first girls' school in India, and in Maharashtra they made significant contributions to female education both as donors and as teachers. But with the opening of a girl's school in Bombay in 1824, American missionaries became the first to introduce girls' education in Maharashtra. Ten years later they established an educational center in Ahmadnagar, a hundred and twenty miles east of Bombay, that drew many American missionaries as teachers, including six of Mary Lyon's students. While conceptions promulgated about women's role in society by British missionaries were often similar to American ones, the American commitment to Republican Motherhood had an anti-imperialistic element to it borne of the American struggle for independence from Britain. This anti-imperialism contributed to the national independence movement that developed in Maharashtra in the late nineteenth century, as did the Republican emphasis on women's education, and women's responsibility for helping to create a good society.

Christianity in India

In the 1840s women missionaries were a relatively new phenomenon in India, as were their concerns for female literacy and companionate marriage, but Christianity was not. As one authority claims, "Indian Christianity is almost as old as Jesus Christ himself and . . . as much a part of the Indian scene as the temples, tigers, bazaars and sacred animals." Some Christian communities in South India date back to the arrival of Syrian and Nestorian missionaries in the fourth and sixth centuries, and Christians in South India identify the beginning of Christianity in India with the arrival of St. Thomas in Malabar in 52 C.E. In the sixteenth century, Portuguese missionaries established a Christian presence in western India, especially among fishers in Goa. But the destruction of temples and confiscation of temple properties by these missionaries created much resentment, and high-caste Hindus were repulsed by the eating and drinking habits of the Portuguese, and by the infrequency of their bathing.[1]

In the early seventeenth century, the Jesuit missionary Roberto de Nobili made a systematic effort to integrate Christianity with Brahmanism in South India. In Madura he adopted Brahmanic dress, diet, and social customs, assumed the ascetic lifestyle of a native religious teacher, translated parts of the Bible into Sanskrit, and used the Upanishads as a basis for his lessons on Christianity. This accommodationist form of Christianity spread throughout southern India and into parts of Maharashtra as well, and helped prepare the way for accommodationist attitudes to American Protestantism among Hindus in the nineteenth century.

De Nobili's legacy dovetailed with the longstanding tradition of syncretism within Hinduism, but it was strongly criticized by other Christians both in his own day and afterward. As one historian summed up the objection, "[W]hile Roberto de Nobili was trying to convert Brahmans to Christianity he was in reality converting Christianity to Brahmanism." The Roman Church countered this pattern of accommodation with official intolerance of Hinduism in the eighteenth century, and in the nineteenth century Protestant missionaries made relinquishment of caste a requirement of conversion.[2]

After the East India Company established settlements in Calcutta, Madras, and Bombay, and Robert Clive established British military ascendancy at the Battle of Plassey in 1757, small numbers of British missionaries entered India to preach the gospel. But British officials opposed missionary work because of its offensiveness to Hindu elites and its potential to disrupt the social order upheld by religious adherence to the caste system. Agents of the East India Company and the British government banned missionaries from the cities over which they had control and prohibited English education until 1813, the year they allowed America's first missionaries to India to disembark in Bombay.

India had special appeal for orthodox American Protestants as "the place of Satan's seat," and the Bombay mission, as America's first foreign mission, occupied a special place in American mission history.[3] But not until 1830 was the first Hindu converted by Americans, Daji Nikant, baptized in Bombay. Despite meager success in securing conversions, the American Board expanded its Bombay mission into the Deccan in 1834 and established a mission in Ahmadnagar. By 1848 the American Board had sponsored fifty-nine missionaries in Maharashtra, producing an abundance of missionary leaders for a very small population of converts, and precipitating a crisis in missionary leadership that led to the dispersal of missionaries in Ahmadnagar to outlying stations in Bhingar, Satara, Kolhapur, and Wadaley. By 1854 the number of missionaries sponsored by the American Board had risen to seventy-one. These evangelists had disseminated millions of pieces of Christian literature, but out of a population of eight million Marathas, only "a few hundreds of men and women" had converted to Christianity.[4]

While they were relatively unsuccessful in making converts during this period, American missionaries in Maharashtra served as catalysts for important new developments in Hinduism. They established educational institutions and offered social services that became models for Hindu institutions and services. They also posed moral challenges to Hinduism—regarding the status of women, the morality of the caste system, and the abuses of priestly authority—that stimulated Hindu movements of religious and social reform. "The fear of the Christian missionary," remarked one editor of the *Indian Social Reformer*, "has been the beginning of much social wisdom among us."[5]

Some Hindu reform leaders were adamantly non-Christian, but others appreciated Christian missionaries for their role in revitalizing Hinduism. Referring to the reform movement in Maharashtra as a new "school of 'Hindu Protestantism' " in a speech delivered in the 1890s, N. G. Chandravarkar credited the missionaries with bringing the "light" that brought about the "awakening among us on the subject of religion and society." According to Chandravarkar, this awakening was a renewal rather than a repudiation of Hinduism. In its authentic spirit, Chandravarkar believed, Hinduism embraced the best aspects of Christianity. "Christ, too, was a Bhakta," he asserted, referring to the Hindu concept of the saint, "and the law of love which he preached has been the cardinal principle of the Bhakti School."[6]

The American bhaktas were often women. A significant line of American holy women in western India can by traced to America's first missionary martyr in a foreign land, Harriet Newell. Committed to "the great revolution about to be effected in this world of sin," Newell longed to tell "those dear benighted females" of India "what I have felt of a Savior's love and the worth of his blessed gospel." Vivid stories about Hindu widows being burned alive on the funeral pyres of their husbands contributed to her desire to rescue the souls of Hindu girls and women from the fires of damnation. Like many missionaries, she was preoccupied by her own unworthiness but also hoped to "meet a stingless death" in the service of Jesus.[7] She died in 1813 at the age of nineteen with her infant daughter on the Isle of France, just off the coast of India, after she and her husband Samuel, along with Nancy and Adoniram Judson, were denied admission to India in Calcutta. Although she never actually set foot on Indian soil, her religious writings, young life, and early death became a model for other women concerned about the plight of women in India and were part of the iconography that Hindu converts were expected to appreciate. The American missionary women who came after Newell not only followed in her footsteps as exemplars of Christian humanism and self-sacrifice, but also came to be appreciated by many unconverted Hindus as religious saints.

Abby Fairbank as a Cross-cultural Exemplar of Female Piety

Six women educated by Mary Lyon carried the tradition of female piety represented by Harriet Newell into Maharashtra. While these American women had only modest success in facilitating conversions, the similarities between their piety and that of many Hindus in Maharashtra made them effective catalysts of Hindu reform. As these women strove to convert and educate Hindu girls and women, and to promulgate an ideology of Republican Motherhood that made women responsible, through their maternal roles, for the common good, Hindus interpreted the activities of these God-saturated women in terms of their own traditions of piety and learning.

Thus in August 1852, when Mary Lyon's student Abby Allen Fairbank died in Bombay at the age of twenty-seven, news of her death spread rapidly among the natives in Bombay and in Ahmadnagar, where she and her husband Samuel had served from 1846 until they transferred to Bombay in 1851 in the hope that the coastal climate would improve her health.[8] In the week after her death, two hundred people came to the Fairbanks' house in Bombay to view the corpse. "Many were much impressed by the peaceful expression of the countenance," Samuel noted, and virtually "all went away in tears." Abby's language teacher, Hari Ramchandra Khiste, "was much affected" by the serene look on her face. "The religion that can impart such a look to the dead must be from God," he told Samuel. At the funeral a week after Abby's death, Samuel was "quite overpowered" by the "manifest sympathy of so many friends, and of strangers too, Christians, Parsis, Musselmans and Hindus, many affected to tears." Instead of riding in a carriage, as the English did on such occasions, he and his five-year-old daughter Emily followed the hearse on foot. Encouraged by this openness and lack of pretense, a long train of mourners followed them to the graveyard, "while the streets were filled with natives wondering at the unusual spectacle."[9]

In this region famous for its history of iconoclastic piety, Abby Fairbank had spoken and behaved in ways that Hindus as well as Christians could appreciate. She refused to leave India, against the recommendation of her doctors, in order to allow her husband to continue in his missionary work in India and to provide him with as much domestic happiness as she could, even though she was an invalid. Her blending of desire for her own salvation with devotion to her husband's happiness dovetailed with Hindu expectations of female piety as well as American ones. As it had in the United States, the respect that Mount Holyoke women received in Maharashtra hinged on their ability to demonstrate that female learning was not incompatible with male authority and happiness.[10]

At Mount Holyoke Abby Allen had been known as Miss Fiske's Abby, in reference to her special relationship to Fidelia Fiske and to distinguish her from Abby Moore, Mary Lyon's niece and assistant, who married Ebenezer Burgess in 1846 and became a missionary in Maharashtra in 1847. In a letter to Samuel Fairbank on the occasion of his wife's death, Abby Burgess recalled how "everyone loved" Abby Allen at Mount Holyoke, even the "wildest, gayest spirits." At Mount Holyoke eight years before her death, she ran up and down stairs "at least twenty times a day." But her energy declined sharply in India; even before the premature birth of her third child there and her final bout with dysentery, she had to stop for breath when she attempted a flight of stairs, and her husband often carried her. In her chronic illness, she became "prone to despond," fearful of death, and anxious about her unfitness for heaven. Like many missionaries she was preoccupied by a sense of unworthiness as well as by the intense desire to devote herself to God. In her last week she implored her husband, "Pray for me, Samuel, not for my body, but for my soul." When he broke down at the thought of being separated from her, she rallied to comfort him, assuring him, "We shall be there, together, and love each other forever." [11]

In her desire to overcome death and in her devotion to her husband, Abby Fairbank was like Savitri, the legendary wife of Satyavan whose faithfulness was celebrated by Hindus in Maharashtra each June. Charged by her father with choosing her own husband, Savitri set her heart on a blind prince who had lost his kingdom and was condemned to death. Through purity, strength of heart, and a certain ingenuity, Savitri succeeded in retrieving her husband's eyesight and kingdom from Yama, the god of death, along with Yama's promise to release Satyavan's soul. [12]

If Abby Fairbank's power was less than Savitri's, her desire for salvation was not. Her renunciation of worldly gain in order to find salvation for herself and others was consonant with the highly respected state of sannyasa, in which Hindus renounced their worldly responsibilities and privileges in order to devote themselves completely to religious life. While sannayis typically left home to make pilgrimages or wander the countryside teaching about religious life, either as students or, more often, as retirees whose children were grown, there were household sannayis in India who stayed married and owned property while fixing their minds on God and renouncing their spiritual attachment to household life. As pious women whose minds were fixed on God, who owned only a few personal possessions, and who renounced the comforts of worldly life to teach others and to purify themselves, Abby Fairbank and her missionary colleagues fit within the religious concept of sannyasa.

During her six years in India, Abby's exceptional ear for language had impressed a number of natives. She learned to speak Marathi with an accuracy and facility that delighted Hari Ramchandra Khiste, the first Brahman in Ahmadnagar to convert to Christianity, and her religious talk played a central role in his religious development. Although chronic illness kept her from the study she needed to acquire a large vocabulary, she communicated religious ideas clearly and forcefully to Haripunt, to the students in her schools, and to "the women she could bring under her influence." [13]

At her grave, surrounded by native auditors and fellow missionaries, Abby's mystically minded missionary colleague George Bowen spoke about her passage to heaven and the continuing influence of her soul. "This is victory indeed," he asserted; "Our sister bade farewell to death when she first found Christ; and made at that time a more wonderful transition than that over which she has this day made." Describing her suffering as a form of service to God, Bowen suggested that God may have made her "submission, resignation [and] patience" into a lesson in piety more useful in converting the people of Maharashtra than a lifetime of activism. He predicted, "The soul she hath scattered shall not be lost, but will in God's good time yield fruit—who can tell whether thirty fold, sixty fold, or a hundred fold." [14]

Bowen's concept of Abby Fairbank's saintly influence corresponds to Jonathan Edwards's belief that creation was an emanation of the "Being" of God, and that the saint represented God by turning toward God with complete devotion, reflecting God's beauty and power, and drawing others into consciousness of their place in God's Being. [15] Bowen also drew his image of influential soul from the writings of Goethe, Schiller, Carlyle, and the other romantic philosophers in which he steeped himself before his conversion to orthodox Protestantism in 1844. Belief in a cosmic soul underlying all reality and shining through the souls of gifted individuals was popular among romantic idealists in Germany and England in the early nineteenth century, as well as among Americans like Ralph Waldo Emerson, who studied Goethe and Carlyle. [16] Partly as a result of this romantic influence, Bowen understood pantheism to be an important aspect of Christianity, claiming in other writings that "[a]ll that is true in Pantheism is found in Christianity and there alone." [17].

Bowen's notion of Abby Fairbank's soul exerting a spiritual influence on the people of western India could also be interpreted in terms of the idealism of Hindu philosophy. The Upanishads identify *atman*, the essential human soul, with the divine and imperishable *Brahman*, out of which the world is created, and they recommend knowledge, discipline, and meditation as means of becoming aware of this *atman-Brahman* within the self. [18] Like Edwards's saint, the Hindu ascetic was able to live in the world conscious of being part of divine being and to reveal its ultimate reality to others. Many Hindu teachers venerated this divine being as a god or goddess, and the devotion they expressed marked a path to salvation that others could follow. As guides to salvation, they were vehicles of divine power, even incarnations of God. [19]

The similarities between the idealistic metaphysics of Hinduism and various streams of western thought may be more than coincidence. The transcendentalism of both Jonathan Edwards and the romantic philosophers familiar to George Bowen grew out of idealistic traditions in western philosophy that had roots in neoplatonism and classical Greek thought, on which Hindu metaphysics had exerted some influence in the ancient Mediterranean world. As one scholar remarks, "Indian thought was present in the fashionable intellectual circuit of ancient Athens, and there is every reason to suppose that Indian religious and philosophical ideas exercised some influence on early and classical Greek philosophy." [20] But however profound the underlying connections between the idealism of Bowen's Christianity and the idealism of Hindu philosophers and saints, his confidence in the final and exclusive truth of Christianity prevented him from considering the possibility that Christian theology was indebted in any way to Hindu metaphysics or finally compatible with it. His zealous evangelism also prevented him from imagining the degree to which Abby Fairbank's life and death could be assimilated within the context of Hindu thought.

The doctrinal narrowness that Bowen shared with other missionaries led not only to obnoxious behavior but also to obliviousness about the real contribution missionaries were making to Hindu reform. The missionary conviction that individual piety inevitably resulted in benevolent concern for others complemented Hindu ideas about love of God and helped galvanize Hindu efforts to link social reform with piety. But Bowen's denunciations of Hinduism hampered these connections and earned him the displeasure of conservative Brahmans who were angered by his attacks on Hindu belief and worship. A journal entry in 1849 describes the negative reaction that Bowen had grown used to: "As usual this morning, reviled, pushed, threatened, &c., and my books torn up." But in typical missionary fashion, Bowen took these vilifications as opportunities to identify himself further with Jesus, and consequently derived a certain religious pleasure from being the subject of priestly outrage: "In suffering these things, I do for Christ what He has done for me," Bowen wrote. "I stand in His place, and receive the reproaches meant for Him."[21]

Other missionary men were no less aggressive in their denunciations of Hinduism, and no less offensive to elite and conservatively minded Hindus. It is no surprise that missionary men often found it difficult to assemble large audiences of natives "after their first curiosity has been satisfied."[22] Missionary Robert Hume insisted that Hindus must "learn to reject" the Vedas and Puranas "with scorn and contempt." Henry Ballantine warned Hindus, "You may exhort your people as long as you please to reform," but "as long as the Hindu religion prevails, lust and avarice will increase, bribery will be practiced in courts of justice, and no one will be secure of obtaining his rights, until Christianity prevails there will be no change for the better." With reference to God's anger at Hindu idolatry, Ballantine also claimed that the outbreak of cholera in 1844 "can be traced almost universally to the pilgrimages made to Punderpoor." And Hume peppered his endorsement of female education with insult: "The general ignorance and degradation of females is one of the greatest evils of this land. What can a stupid, ignorant mother do for the moral and intellectual training of her children?"[23]

Mary Lyon's Students as Religious Teachers and Pioneers in Female Education

Abby Fairbank and the other women trained by Mary Lyon had no more knowledge or appreciation of the Hindu religion than their male counterparts, but they were less aggressive in reviling Hinduism. They were teachers rather than preachers, and their socialization led them to be more self-effacing and gentle than their husbands. Although missionary women were not much more successful in eliciting conversions than men, their demeanor conformed more closely to Hindu expectations of religious piety. Their demonstration that learning was compatible with piety and wifely devotion helped make female education acceptable, even though it challenged Hindu custom.

On a preaching tour in the Deccan in 1847, Royal Wilder brought his Mount Holyoke wife Jane along, with great effect. He reported that "Many females came out to Mrs. Wilder often uninvited, and the people generally listened to the truth with apparent interest." The following year, Royal noted that in a tour of fifty villages with his wife, natives received them, and especially his wife, with interest. "No female missionary had ever been among them," he wrote of village women. "They came to Mrs. Wilder in large numbers, even the wives of those who had been violent opposers." Similarly, in December 1846 and February 1847, Abby and Ebenezer Burgess made tours of outlying villages to the west, north, and northeast of Ahmadnagar, and "[m]any of the females came out to listen to Mrs. Burgess's instructions." In February and March 1847, the Ballantine family toured Cahnday, Niwasse, and Wadaley. According to her husband, "Mrs. Ballantine had frequent opportunities on this tour of meeting with companies of women and addressing them on the subject of religion."[24]

Similarly, in 1849 Martha Hazen accompanied her husband on a twelve-day preaching tour, during which she "had an opportunity of making known the truth to very many females, who are quite inaccessible to one of the other sex." During a visit in 1853 to an unnamed city north of Ahmadnagar, perhaps Aurungabad, the Hazens were impressed to find that "[m]any families here have given up idolatry." The relative absence of traditional Hindu means of worship in this city may have had more to do with the influence of Islam than with Christianity, and the Hazens made no mention of any potential conversions to Christianity, but the women of the city were especially attentive to Martha; she "had many opportunities for meeting with the women, and was much interested in the apparent advance which has been made in many places."[25]

While curiosity about exotic western women accounted for some of the attention that Hindu women bestowed on American missionary women, respect for religious piety and teaching was also a factor. On at least one occasion that the Americans were aware of, a missionary woman was approached by native women who wanted to make her their Hindu teacher. In 1849, when Elizabeth Ballantine and her husband Henry stopped to preach in a village on their way to Aurungabad, "the women came in such throngs to meet Mrs. Ballantine, and seemed so interested in what she had to tell them of the gospel of Jesus, that the brahmins were greatly enraged." Henry reported that "One came to me, and said that 100 women had collected around madam, and were about to make her their gooroo!" In a subsequent visit to the village of Wadaley, the Brahmans were friendlier and more accommodating. According to Henry, "the women of the higher classes received Mrs. Ballantine with great respect, and listened to her with great attention."[26]

There are no accounts of missionary women reviling Hinduism as their husbands did, and even in their tours of Maratha villages, they acted more as teachers than preachers, gathering women around them with short talks, prayer, and discussion. Except when they were interrupted by men, as in the incident in Aurungabad when Brahman men attempted to dispel the women gathered around Elizabeth Ballantine, the village sessions led by missionary women occurred apart from men. Moreover, there is no indication that missionary women ever spoke to mixed audiences, although there are numerous reports that village women "came out" to see and hear missionary women. The missionaries in Maharashtra did not force their way into *zenanas* (closed domestic spaces for women), as missionaries in Bengal did, but habits of gender segregation were sufficiently ingrained among both Marathas and Americans to make encounters between missionary and village women relatively quiet affairs.

If nineteenth-century American missionary women were less aggressive than their male colleagues, they were hardly tolerant. In the 1880s, Anandabai Joshee commented on the closed-mindedness and lack of compassion in missionary women: "I love these Mission ladies for their enthusiasm and energy," she remarked, "but I dislike their blindness to the feelings of others."[27] As this remark suggests, the piety that missionary women exhibited was often compromised by the rigidity of their theology.

Elizabeth Darling Ballantine was the first of Mary Lyon's six students to arrive in Maharashtra. She had been a student of Mary Lyon's at Ipswich, before Mount Holyoke was founded, and served as a missionary in Maharashtra between 1835 and 1870. In addition to supervising the girls' boarding school in Ahmadnagar, and raising six children, one of whom married Samuel Fairbank after Abby Fairbank's death, Ballantine carried forward Lyon's interest in maps, and published *A Small Geography* in Marathi in 1847. Along with other missionaries, she introduced significant innovations in the form and content of education in India, including regularly scheduled hours of instruction and new areas of study such as grammar, history, and geography.[28]

The second of Lyon's students to arrive in Maharashtra was Mary Grant Burgess, the niece of Lyon's senior partner at Ipswich Female Seminary, and Lyon's student in the Buckland county schools, and later at Ipswich. Mary Burgess died of cholera on June 24, 1842, three years after her arrival in Ahmadnagar, and only eight hours after being taken sick. In the wake of her death, feelings ran high among the girls and mothers who had attended her schools, and the missionaries were more encouraged than they had ever been about the possibility of gaining converts; the "great composure and joy" with which Mary Burgess met death "produced a deep impression" on many natives, according to the missionaries. When eleven-year-old Janya fell mortally ill, "she seemed to see Mrs. Burgess constantly before her," and the vision had a calming effect. Although her parents were unwilling for her to become a Christian and relinquish her caste, Janya met death with "peace and calmness of mind." According to Henry Ballantine, "the circumstances of her death" were "different from those of common Hindus" who typically greeted death with "alarm."[29]

The first alumnae of Mount Holyoke in Maharashtra were Abby Allen Fairbank and Eliza Jane Smith Wilder, who landed together in Bombay, along with their husbands, in September 1846. Jane Wilder organized schools in Ahmadnagar and Kolhapur, published in the American missionary periodical *Dayspring*, and established a friendship with the sister of the king of Kolhapur, whose wife was a descendant of the military hero Shivaji, founder of the Marathi empire.[30] A third Mount Holyoke alumnae, Martha R. Chapin Hazen, arrived in February 1847, five months after the Fairbanks and Wilders. The

Hazens worked in Maharashtra from 1847 until 1872, sent both their daughters to Mount Holyoke, and saw them return to Maharashtra as missionaries. Martha's sister Mary became principal of Mount Holyoke after Mary Lyon's death.[31]

Accompanying the Hazens to India was Mary Lyon's niece, Abigail Moore Burgess, and her husband Ebenezer, whom Abby married in 1846 after he visited Mount Holyoke on a furlough from India after the death of his first wife, Mary Grant.[32] The second Mrs. Burgess followed much the same path as the first, dying in 1853 from a breast abscess after a brief but influential career as a teacher of Hindu women and children. According to Henry Ballantine, Abby Moore Burgess was "peculiarly fitted for the training of children." When she became interim principal of the girls' boarding school in Ahmadnagar during Elizabeth Ballantine's absence, she was "encouraged by the aspect of the institution," and it was on her watch that the missionaries reported, "Female education is becoming more and more popular." When the Burgesses were relocated to a remote site in Satara at the end of 1849, Abby took the transition in stride, commenting that "she has as interesting a field as she had at Ahmednuggur." According to William Wood, who had preceded the Burgesses to Satara, "her labors in her schools, with the native women, and with the church members, were unceasing."[33]

The work of these six women complemented that of Cynthia Farrar, a friend of Lyon's beloved Polly Grant Banister, and the first single woman sent anywhere by the American Board. During a thirty-five-year career in Maharashtra from 1827 to 1862, the "indomitable and illusive" Miss Farrar did not write many letters that survived, and her educational work was not reported as extensively as that of her male colleagues. But she organized and taught in dozens of schools for Hindu girls. She and Elizabeth Ballantine took charge of the education of girls in Ahmadnagar, with Farrar's schools serving as feeders for the boarding school run by Ballantine.[34]

Farrar was often disappointed in her inability to facilitate conversion; in fact, in a revealing disclosure of just how disappointed she could get, Sarah Hume recalled Farrar "rolling on the ground in discouragement and agony of spirit." But her teaching efforts did have results; in 1853, in response to the challenge of the Farrar schools, and in keeping with developments among reform-minded Hindus of the time, two Hindu schools were established in Ahmadnagar for high-caste girls. In their report that year to the American Board in Boston, Henry Ballantine and Allen Hazen noted that the establishment of the new Hindu schools "has been rather injurious to Miss Farrar's schools." But they were pleased that Marathas had begun to appreciate the importance of female education, and no doubt hoped that this interest would lead Marathas to reject Hinduism and embrace Christianity. "We cannot view with regret the efforts made by the natives to promote female education," wrote the missionaries, "we only wish that these efforts may be very much increased."[35]

The contributions of Mount Holyoke alumnae to female education in Maratha continued into the twentieth century, although after 1854 they were more narrowly focused on Christian converts. The boarding school in Ahmadnagar stayed in the hands of women educated by Mary Lyon until 1867, and the Hume, Bissell, Ballantine, and Fairbank families were interlinked for decades in Maharashtra through intermarriage and through ties to Mount Holyoke and Wellesley. By 1881, when the number of Christians in Maharashtra had become more respectable to American Board administrators, the Young Ladies Boarding School in Ahmadnagar was enrolling one hundred fifty students annually and was housed in a large, well-equipped building. When a separate building to house single women missionaries was added at the end of the nineteenth century, missionaries called it the Holyoke Bungalow.[36]

But the earliest American efforts to teach Hindu girls had been greeted with incredulity. In Bombay in the early 1830s, Caroline Read's "efforts to get up a girls' school, were treated by the natives as a perfect absurdity, and by some scoffed at." According to her husband Hollis, "She was asked if she supposed a *donkey* could be taught to read!" As a last resort, Hollis admitted, his wife had paid her students ten *pice* a week to attend school. The activities in the schools Caroline supervised "were narrowly watched" by Brahmans, who almost succeeded in destroying the schools by circulating the story that Caroline planned to sell some of the girls as slaves. In 1839 the idea of female education still had not made much headway. Sendol Munger expressed little optimism with regard to his wife Maria's efforts to introduce reading among the women of Jalna: "The subject of female education is so novel a thing in this place, that she cannot expect to proceed very rapidly."[37]

During the 1840s and early 1850s a sea change in native opinion occurred. In 1850 Robert Hume reported from Bombay, "One of the most encouraging signs of the times in India, is the change which is gradually taking place, in the feelings of the people, in regard to female education." The following year missionaries in Ahmadnagar reported that "Female education is becoming more and more popular." By 1854 the journal of the American Board could report that in Maharashtra "a great change has taken place in the sentiments of the people regarding female education. When the missionaries began this work, they encountered great and general opposition. But now the most influential natives subscribe for the support of female schools, attend the examinations, and even send their own daughters to receive instruction."[38]

As reform-minded Hindus in Maharashtra began to think positively about female education, the vulnerability of girls to Christian conversion generated great concern among high-caste Hindus of both reformist and conservative bent. The few Brahmans who converted to Christianity were often regarded by other Brahmans as subversives and traitors because of their deliberate involvement in caste pollution. In 1831 the first Brahman to be baptized as a Protestant, Babaji Raghonata, publicly marked himself as a Christian by following missionary instructions to take the Lord's Supper with the Mahar woman Gopabai, an outcaste who had been baptized at the same time. According to the missionaries, representatives of the two castes had never before "come to the table of the Lord" together "acknowledging themselves a brother and sister."[39]

Some Brahmans were quick to retaliate against any of their number who converted. Between 1831, when the first Brahman was converted by Americans, and 1850, when the British government in India passed an "Act for the Preservation of the Civil and Natural Rights of Any British Subject Who May Change His Religion," Brahman converts were disinherited, treated as outcastes, and denied any contact with their families. The missionaries behind these conversions opposed such treatment but also celebrated the heroism and sacrifice they prompted. Thus the Americans broadcast news of the ordeals endured and obstacles surmounted by the Ramchandra Khiste brothers, Hari and Narayan, the first Brahmans in Ahmadnagar to convert to Christianity, as evidence of their Christian character.[40] In 1850 the missionaries reported the existence of a "brahmin plot" to discourage any further converts. Angry crowds gathered around Brahmans hired to teach in mission schools and around their students, especially female students perceived to be vulnerable to conversion.[41]

In 1842, when three girls who attended Elizabeth Ballantine's boarding school were baptized, the school suffered a temporary but drastic decline in enrollment. The expectations of missionaries, who viewed education as laying the groundwork for conversion, differed considerably from the expectations of Hindu students and their families involved in mission schools. These Hindus prized the knowledge and skills imparted in those schools and were open to reforms within Hindu practice, but were firmly resistant to conversion. In a few cases, missionaries succeeded in helping their students defy the wishes of their parents; with Elizabeth Ballantine's encouragement, eleven-year-old Janya "replied to her mother in very strong language for a girl of her age, and showed remarkable decision on the subject of religion, and a willingness to encounter disgrace rather than give up." But in most instances the girls in mission schools were not interested in defying their families, and their parents encouraged them to learn from the missionaries without relinquishing loyalty to Hinduism. As one historian of this process noted, Marathas who were interested in social change and mobility "quietly exploited" the skills of missionary women.[42]

Conflict in the Maratha Mission and Its Implications for Missionary Women

Because of their vocation as teachers, missionary women suffered most from the decision made by the men of the American Marathi Mission in 1854 to restructure the mission around preaching and away from teaching. The American Board sent a special deputation to India in 1854 to confront the missionaries in Maharashtra with their lack of success in converting Hindus and to demonstrate that their failure was the result of the excessive attention they had lavished on education. Before 1854, the missionaries had justified their efforts to establish schools as appropriate means of preparation for conversion; indeed, the American mission in Ahmadnagar was founded as an educational center for Hindus as well as Christian converts. As Henry Ballantine wrote, in reply to a letter from the secretary of the American Board, Rufus Anderson, questioning the mission's emphasis on education, the "object of our schools and seminaries [is] the extension of the knowledge of the truth." Focusing on the mission's efforts to foster female education, Ballantine argued that "considerable labor and expense" was justified "[t]o remove the prejudices· against female education, to raise the character of females, to bring this part of the community to a participation in the blessings of education and Christianity, and thus to prepare the way for a more rapid spread of the gospel."[43]

In December 1854, when Anderson arrived in Ahmadnagar to press his concerns, the men and women of the mission gathered for meetings with him for nineteen straight days. The men were the only ones to speak formally or vote, and all of them came around to Anderson's position, except Royal Wilder, who was bitterly opposed to Anderson, and George Bowen, who resigned from the American Board when the meetings were finished and stayed in Bombay as a missionary free agent until he joined the Methodist Church.[44] Anderson asserted that the policies of the American Board prevented him from allowing its limited resources to become entangled in educational programs, except as these programs served converts who needed the education to become pastors and pastor's wives. While Anderson was progressive in recognizing that Christianity should be indigenized within each local culture, and that religious leadership should be in the hands of native pastors as soon as possible,[45] his concern to separate conversion from education involved an all-or-nothing notion of conversion that was very different from Mary Lyon's notion that conversion was an ongoing process of self-criticism, pursuit of truth, and interaction and outreach toward others.

Anderson's simplistic attitude toward conversion was reinforced by his imperious and condescending attitude toward women and women's education. Lyon cultivated a respectful relationship with Anderson, and she knew that, as the single most powerful figure in American missions during his day, his approval of Mount Holyoke was essential to its success. She did not disagree that there were certain spheres of activity that were appropriate for women and others that were not, but Anderson's emphasis on the limitations of women's activity and status struck a very different chord from her emphasis on women as the cornerstones of world redemption. As he stated rather emphatically in his commencement address at Mount Holyoke in 1839, "All has not been yielded, on the score of *education,* that is due to the [female] sex; though I know of nothing due on any other score."[46]

But if Anderson was more emphatic in insisting on male dominance than others in the missionary movement, women were rather successful in making emotional appeals to his authority. During his visit to Maharashtra in 1854, he exempted some of the girls' schools run by missionary women from closure without granting similar exemptions for men. Hannah Hume was allowed to keep her boarding school in Bombay going because a number of her students had converted.[47] Cynthia Farrar's schools stayed open because they were financially supported by Englishwomen, and because she was so successful in appealing to Anderson's ego. She wrote Anderson's wife shortly after his departure, "The pleasures I felt on seeing Dr. Anderson in India . . . were to me greater than anything of a social or religious nature I have ever before enjoyed on earth." With obsequious gratitude and admiration, she referred to his visit as a "sweet foretaste" of our "Father's house above," likening his presence to the Holy Spirit that "seemed to pervade our little community."[48] And Jane Wilder took Anderson on daily drives during his stay in Ahmadnagar, which led to his provision for the continuation of her schools in Kolhapur, and to some easing of the extreme tension between Anderson and her husband.[49]

The competing egos and leadership ambitions among missionary men, coupled with a dearth of native followers to absorb these ambitions, created a set of internal problems in the Maratha mission that surfaced most visibly around Royal Wilder and led to Anderson's intervention. In 1850 and 1851, the Prudential Committee of the American Board became aware that there were too many missionaries in Ahmadnagar and that the business meetings of the mission "were divided, controversial, and painful." Wilder found himself in "frequent collisions" with Ebenezer Burgess, Allen Hazen, and Sendol Munger, and this unhappiness resulted in the relocation of the Mungers to Bhingar, the Burgesses to Satara, and the Wilders to Kolhapur. Further controversy developed over Wilder's translation of a theology textbook, which he was accused of plagiarizing from Ramakrishnapunt, a convert employed as a teacher in mission schools. After Anderson's visit, Wilder accused Henry Ballantine of manipulating Allen Hazen's vote on Anderson's program to scale back educational effort, and he caused further animosity by building a house in Kolhapur that was larger, more comfortable, and better roofed than other missionaries thought seemly.[50]

In 1860, a subcommittee of the American Board, charged with investigating Royal's charge that Anderson had forced the missionaries in Maharashtra to scale down their educational work against their wills, described Royal as "a sharp and willing controversialist" who was "self-reliant, inflexible in purpose, and of marvelous industry in carrying out his purposes." In this missionary "[a] conscience, energetic and comprehensive in its action, rendered an impracticable man still more impracticable. And honesty, coupled with boldness and plainness of speech, augments his power to annoy others. Harmonious cooperation with such a mind," the subcommittee continued, "would seem to be possible only on the condition of quietly following."[51]

In 1883, as editor of the *Missionary Review*, Royal criticized the American Board as having a mechanistic, penny-pinching obsession with the number of conversions. Instead of "enlisting and developing self-sacrificing, self-controlling, soul-loving missionaries," Wilder believed the Board was cultivating "clerks and money agents to do the bidding of the officers in Boston." In this situation "like begets like," and missionaries in the field behaved toward their native converts as the officers in Boston behaved toward them. These "missionary clerks and money agents organize what they call native churches and unions, but make them inferior and subordinate, and control them as masters too often control their servants, with sheer authority and secular motives."[52]

While Wilder's criticism exposed the calculating, narrow-minded tendencies of mission policies instituted by Anderson and carried forward by other officers of the American Board, and pointed to their aggressiveness, offensiveness, and empire-building mentality, he was obviously prey to an overreaching self-importance of his own. Allen Hazen recalled Wilder's own account of preaching tours in which "he would go up to a village gate in his bullack cart, send the *mhar* for the *Patil* (the headman)—and when he came he would preach to him and others as they gathered around, *sitting in his cart*."[53] Even Samuel Fairbank, whose wife's close friendship with Jane Wilder facilitated a better relationship with Royal than other missionaries enjoyed, was repelled by the book Wilder wrote in 1857 about mission schools in India, attacking Anderson's misguided policies in India and authoritarian rule. "I do not wish to soil my fingers by touching Mr. Wilder's Book," Fairbank wrote. It is "full of gross misstatements and what I believe to be malicious falsehoods."[54]

In the battle of wills among the missionary men in Maharashtra, and between these men and the commanding Dr. Anderson, missionary women played a subservient but important role in nurturing the elements of communal good will that did exist. It may be more than coincidence that the 1854 crisis in the Maratha mission came in the wake of the 1852 death of Abby Fairbank, whose friendship with Jane Wilder made Royal more acceptable, and the death in 1853 of Abby Burgess, whose "uniform cheerfulness and happy countenance" was an important resource for the missionary community.

While Abby Fairbank's death was not unanticipated, the death of Abby Burgess was a shock. From the perspective of Henry Ballantine, the oldest missionary and official spokesman in Ahmadnagar, she had played a crucial role in the missionary community. "I shall never forget the cheerfulness of her manner," wrote Ballantine. "She was the life of our mission circle" during her years in Ahmadnagar, and she "carried joy with her, wherever she went." Her cheerful manner was legendary, and no less intense than her husband's tendency to melancholy, which was significant. Mary Lyon had known Ebenezer Burgess at Amherst in the 1820s, when they had both studied geology with Edward Hutchinson. As fellow boarders in the Hutchinson home, they were fellow sufferers from the melancholy so common in missionary types. Although she seems to have welcomed Abby's marriage to him in 1846, Lyon had had doubts about his stability and suitability as a husband ten years earlier when he had proposed to Mary Grant, and she had discouraged Mary from accepting. Ebenezer's tendency to melancholy seems never to have entirely disappeared. When Abby died in 1853, he succumbed to a depression that kept him from working, and his colleague William Wood reported that "her loss to her afflicted, weeping broken-hearted husband is great beyond expression." But Wood was also distraught by Abby's death; she had taken him and his children into her domestic circle when Lucy Wood died. "Next to the death of my own dear wife," wrote William, "never have I felt so sorely bereaved as now."[55]

William recalled that Abby Burgess had spoken "most eloquently of the joy she felt in looking up to God as her Father, and in being enabled to trust in him with all the confidence of a child."[56] If this piety was disarming, it was also an effective interpersonal skill that gave her a certain authority among

Hindus as well as among her fellow missionaries. As a God-lover, teacher, and community organizer, her influence extended beyond her own circle.

After the departure of the special deputation in January 1855, missionary women continued to operate in a teaching mode when they accompanied their husbands on village tours, but except for the schools that Anderson exempted from his censure, missionary involvement with Hindu women and girls for the purpose of fostering education was discontinued. When the majority of the voting brethren in Maharashtra agreed with Anderson and decided to close mission schools that drew unconverted students and employed unconverted teachers who were supervised by missionary men and women, the American women in Maharashtra lost the primary context of their teaching and administrative work.

From the Maratha perspective, and from the perspective of the subsequent history of United States-India relations, this missionary withdrawal from education was a positive turn of events. In providing a catalyst for women's education and then relinquishing the field, the negative interference of Americans in the development of Hindu education was minimized.[57] But if the withdrawal was positive in its most important effects, it decreased the status and effectiveness of missionary women in relation to missionary men. Later in the century, this erosion was partly compensated for by the involvement of missionary women in Christian schools with increased enrollments and by the arrival of missionary women doctors, whose medical skills were highly prized. But the immediate effect of American withdrawal from education was to force missionary women away from their vocational identity and to define them more in terms of their domestic roles. When missionaries later recovered the momentum of their educational work, Hindu schools for girls were well established in Maharashtra, especially among the upper castes, and missionaries directed their education efforts to Christian converts.

The hope cherished by Lyon's students that education would enable Maratha women to play a foundational role in the Christianization of India never materialized. But the impact of American missionaries on women's education in Maharashtra and elsewhere was significant. As one Indian scholar claimed, "The credit for pioneering the cause of female education in the early nineteenth century goes to Christian missionaries."[58]

Coinciding Iconoclasms and Forces of Social Reform

Deistic and utilitarian philosophies current in Bombay in the nineteenth century also contributed to more liberal attitudes about female literacy and education, and competed with the more conservative missionary commitment to Republican Motherhood, which emphasized women's self-sacrifice and contributions to the maintenance of male authority. John Stuart Mill's *The Subjection of Women* (1869) played a role in generating momentum for women's reforms at Elphinstone Institute, named after Monstuart Elphinstone upon his retirement from the governorship of Bombay in 1827. Elphinstone believed that a utilitarian western education would destroy Hinduism and eventually lead to political independence, and his philosophy helped establish a secular movement of reform. At Elphinstone Institute, liberal young Brahmans learned to celebrate science and rationality over against faith and superstition by reading Voltaire and Thomas Paine.[59]

While they welcomed the challenges to the caste system and the veneration of religious statues that British and Hindu rationalists provided, American missionaries were distressed by the antireligious attitudes of these freethinkers, their indifference to orthodox Protestant notions notions of female piety, and their eagerness to subject Christian beliefs to the same kind of rationalist analysis as Hindu beliefs. In the 1840s, at least one Elphinstone scholar proclaimed the belief that "the Jesus of the English and the Krishna of the Hindus" were both "impostors." Another Hindu rationalist quoted by missionaries argued that Noah's ark could not really have held representatives of all the animal species of the world, and that the star of Bethlehem had to be a fabrication because its presence would have thrown the solar system into chaos. The scientific fallacies contained in the Bible were compounded by ethical ones; we "ought not to hope for salvation through the sufferings of another," the same author asserted, "without any efforts or sufferings on our part." A Parsee theologian took an even more adamant stance in his treatise on the Bible: "Christianity and Christian ministers as a body," he wrote in 1845, ought to be "charged with immorality."[60]

To aid teachers in mission schools in combating this antireligious rationalism, the Americans published numerous articles in their Marathi-English paper, *Dynanodya* (Rise of knowledge), which was printed monthly from 1842 through 1844 and semimonthly from 1845 to 1873, when it became a weekly. The *Dynanodya* responded to "the scurrilous attacks on Christianity" published in the Gujarati and Marathi periodicals that had sprung up in Bombay since the missionaries' arrival, while at the same time endorsing the criticisms of Hindu caste and idolatry emanating from this liberal Brahman press.[61] In 1844 the *Dynanodya* quoted an editorial from the liberal *Oopadesh Chundrika*, in which a Brahman author criticized his fellow Hindus for maintaining the existence of many gods. The following year the *Dynanodya* quoted a letter from the *Prubhakur*, another liberal paper, lamenting the "present degraded and depressed state" of the Hindu religion, and citing, as the cause of this unfortunate situation, the "oppression from caste and countless restrictions" forced on the people of western India by Brahmans whose invidious actions and corrupt characters were comparable to those of Roman Catholic priests.[62]

The Americans hoped such criticism of Brahmanic authority would eventually lead Hindus to Protestant conversion, but Protestant orthodoxy was often unappealing to liberal Brahmans. Even more important, the Americans' antagonism to caste went beyond what most liberal Brahmans endorsed and made conversion unacceptable to the vast majority of the Hindu elite. Concern for caste purity prevented Brahmans from engaging in Christian rituals, even if they liked Christian ideas. "Hundreds of my acquaintances among the higher castes have told me that they would be baptized to-day, and unite with the Christian church," wrote R. V. Modak in his history of native churches in Ahmadnagar, "if there were no Mahars or Mangs in it."[63]

As the ordained pastor of the Second Church in Ahmadnagar and one of the few Brahmans who did convert, Modak claimed that there were "thousands of educated Hindus, graduates of the government schools, having become Deists, openly denying many things of the Hindu religion." These enlightenment iconoclasts "are simply regarded as followers of a new sect of Hinduism," reported Modak in 1854, "and are honoured among the people." But while their rejection of image worship and miracles was widely known and often praised, these iconoclasts kept the appearance, at least, of maintaining the dietary rules and other restrictions of their caste. If they ignored these rules and restrictions in private, Modak observed, they would not admit it for fear of persecution.[64]

Fear of ritual defilement was widespread but not universal among Maratha Brahmans. In one radical Brahman sect, men and women met together to worship Shakti, the Great Mother, believed by her devotees to have authority over Vishnu, Siva, and other deities. The sect required men to violate orthodox concepts of ritual purity by eating meat and drinking liquor, and on special days the men met for ritual drinking with men of lower caste.[65] These Shakta practices were not means of denying the validity of caste rituals, as was the Christian practice of taking the Lord's Supper with converts from other castes, but were rather efforts to "storm" the divine by outrageous but only temporary breaking of caste rules. Shakta rituals also involved explicitly sexual elements that were hardly compatible with orthodox Protestantism.[66] Nevertheless, the coexistence of Shakta practices with the caste-breaking ritual of communion practiced by Christians living in Maharashtra encouraged the notion that Christianity could be interpreted in the context of Hinduism.

Even more significant similarities existed between Protestant piety and the bhakti movement in Hinduism, which emphasized the sufficiency of devotion to God. Far more widespread in Maharashtra than the deliberately outrageous practices of Shaktas, bhakti devotionalism, was the principal context out of which Hindus in Maharashtra interpreted and appreciated elements of the Christian gospel preached by Protestant missionaries. Many outcastes and members of the lower castes oppressed by the caste strictures of orthoprax Hinduism already believed in the sufficiency of devotion to God, and they were responsive to criticisms of formalistic rituals long before their acquaintance with Protestant preaching.

Religious teachers emerged out of the ranks of the Mahars with an abundance that rivaled that of the Brahmans, who regarded teaching as their own birthright and often believed that others were unfit to read the *shastras* (Hindu scriptures). Mahar gurus reacted to this Brahmanic arrogation of religious privilege by maintaining that love of God was all that was required for salvation. Among the Mahars were many religious teachers who were, even the missionaries realized, "opposers of idolatry." According to the missionaries, these gurus had "discard[ed] the Hindu system of incarnations and the belief in the efficacy of pilgrimages and other Hindu rites to secure salvation," and they preached "the doctrine of one God."[67]

Americans had their greatest success with the Mahars. An outcast group within the context of orthoprax Hinduism but also part of the "official corps" of every village, the Mahars were responsible for dealing with visitors, arranging transportation, and providing police service. They had "more intercourse with the outside world than any other class," and the missionaries regarded them as an "enterprising" people who were "much in advance of the Korrabees, or cultivators, in respect to general intelligence" and second only to the highly literate and philosophically sophisticated Brahmans.[68]

The greater receptivity to Christianity among the Mahars, and their "willingness to acknowledge" what the missionaries regarded as "reasonable and true," was as much the result of similarities between their gurus and Protestant teachers as of the transformative power of missionary preaching. One missionary reported that "[m]any Mahars, on hearing us preach, have explained that this was just the doctrine taught them by their own religious leaders, and it is only when we tell them of the Savior of the world, that they perceive the discrepancy of their system and ours." When a Mahar guru converted to Christianity, his devotees still followed him. Thus the guru Bhagoba Powar continued to draw "crowds of Mahars" after he converted to Christianity. "As soon . . . as his conversion was known among the people," wrote Henry Ballantine in 1844, "crowds of that caste came to see us and wherever we went accompanied by him we had great numbers of Mahars in our audiences."[69]

Religious iconoclasm was not only the province of the Mahars, but extended to many Marathas of elite background as well. Since the thirteenth century, Maharashtra had been a center of the bhakti movement, which emphasized the sufficiency of love to God, and home to many saints who criticized caste and preached the sufficiency of devotion to God. The poet, saint, and founder of devotional Hinduism, Jnaneshwar, wrote a vernacular commentary on the Bhagavad Gita that made the teachings of Krishna available to the humblest Maratha, and he was cast out of Brahmanism for his belief that all people (and animals) were essentially the same. Through the centuries, Maratha gurus and saints followed Jnaneshwar in defining piety as an alternative to the correct performance of ritual in the quest for salvation.[70]

Since the thirteenth century, pilgrims from all castes in western India had traveled to Pandharpur, the home of Jnaneshwar and of other Maratha poets and saints who followed him in believing that all earthly disabilities could be overcome by love of God, and that caste was nothing in God's eyes. In one important festival held in Pandharpur, pilgrims honored the thirteenth-century meeting of the Maratha saint Pundalik with Krishna, who appeared after Pundalik joined his parents on their pilgrimage. Pundalik had made his parents walk while he and his wife rode in the parents' cart, and abused them in other ways as well, until he discovered that nothing was as important for salvation as serving his parents with affection and humility. After this realization, Krishna appeared to Pundalik, who greeted him by throwing out a brick for him to stand on as he waited for Pundalik to finish attending to his parents. Krishna demonstrated his approval of Pundalik's sense of priorities by asking to be worshiped as Vithoba (he who stands upon a brick). In commemoration of this iconoclastic event, Pandharpur became a center of devotional Hinduism and home to many saints.[71]

The Syncretic Reach of Hindu Piety

Pandharpur was a focus of American interest in 1847, when Sendol Munger and Royal Wilder timed their preaching tour through the town to coincide with the "time when pilgrims had assembled from all parts of the Deccan to worship the god Vithoba." Without suspecting that the pilgrims who gathered around them might view Jesus as another incarnation of Krishna and see the resemblance between the human qualities Jesus prized and those praised by Vithoba, Munger and Wilder handed out three thousand tracts and booklets containing portions of the Bible. The Hindu pilgrims listened respectfully as the Americans preached about the iconoclastic nature of religious virtue and the importance of a pure heart in gaining salvation, messages similar to those they had traveled to Pandharpur to celebrate.[72]

The bhakti movement played a central role in creating the cultural milieu in which religious reformers in Maharashtra assimilated certain Christian ideas, while resisting conversion. The respect for individual freedom implicit in the bhakti tradition had kept certain aspects of Muslim domination at bay, including the seclusion of women, a custom rare in Maharashtra but typical elsewhere in India. Moreover, the bhakti tradition nurtured the seventeenth-century warrior and national hero, Shivaji, who freed Maharashtra from Muslim rule and devised a plan to unite India. The memory of Shivaji's liberation of Maharashtra, his aspiration to unite all of India against foreign domination, and his iconoclastic piety helped inspire the movement for national independence that began in Maharashtra in the late nineteenth century.[73]

While the bhakti tradition in Maharashtra was associated with political resistance to Muslim domination, Mahrathas responded to the religious piety of their Muslim compatriots with much the same tendency to syncretic appreciation with which they later responded to the piety of Protestant missionaries. Islamic devotionalism flourished under bhakti influence. And Maratha Hindus often celebrated Islamic holy days and venerated Muslim pirs, incorporating them into the Hindu calendar and belief system.[74] Any resemblance between Islam and Christianity perceived by Hindus of Maharashtra was reinforced by the fact that the first missionaries to take up residence in Ahmadnagar were installed in "an ancient Mahomedan Palace, called the Ferrie Bagh, about a mile from the city."[75]

Conversion to Christianity was never as prevalent in Maharashtra as conversion to Islam, but the reasons for it were similar. The Muslim and Christian emphases on salvation and life after death were intriguing to Hindus, who were also concerned about these issues. If the assurance with which both Muslims and Christians denied multiple paths to salvation, and multiple cycles of rebirth, seemed fanatical, the idea that piety was sufficient for salvation resonated with the ancient teachings of Krishna in the Bhagavad Gita, predating the development of bhakti, as well as the emphases on total submission to God in the Qur'an and on the supreme importance of loving God in the Bible.

When Muslims dominated the government in Maharashtra between the thirteenth and seventeenth centuries, conversion to Islam permitted new opportunities for civil service, and Hindus were attracted to Islam at least partly because of these. As one Brahman who converted to Christianity remarked, "[M]any Hindus became Mussulmans for the sake of gaining favor with those in authority."[76] In contrast, neither conversion to Christianity nor British education led many natives to civil service opportunities under the British raj, and the exclusion of all but a token group of natives from the government created a widespread unrest among educated people that was instrumental in the emergence of the Indian freedom movement.[77] But if conversion to Christianity was of little help in obtaining positions in civil service, it brought opportunities for employment in mission compounds. Indeed, conversion to Christianity often entailed economic dependence on missionaries. Despite sermons on the need for a self-reliant and evangelical lay ministry that accepted hardship and persecution as part of the price of salvation, the problem of dependence on missionary welfare persisted, and the early-nineteenth-century millennial vision of India filled with middle-class Christians faded.[78]

American missionaries had a more dynamic impact on the revitalization of Hinduism. During the 1860s, Hindus' respect for Jesus and the enjoyment of biblical stories and Protestant hymns was relatively widespread in Maharashtra, and did not necessarily entail conversion. When one of the converts in Ahmadnagar, Krishnaraw Ratnaji Sangale, began to revise Protestant hymns according to Marathi rules of poetry and set them to native tunes, many Hindus were delighted. Initially, the missionaries resisted these innovations because of their "vile associations" with idolatry, but, as the Americans warmed to them, these *kirtans* (songs) played an important role in breaking through missionary hostility to Hindu culture. Eventually the missionaries joined in singing kirtans with native Christians, discovering "that many of their earnest words of praise, set to native airs, are full of sweetness, and promotive of devotion." At the annual meeting of the American Marathi Mission in 1862, Krishnaraw "gave his first Kirttan . . . on the subject of 'Christ the excellent Teacher,'" accompanied by drum, cymbals, guitar, and native violin.

Kirtans based on Christian stories were a means of gaining some much-desired converts to Christianity, but they were far more successful as new additions to the Hindu repertoire of songs about the feats of gods and goddesses. Christian kirtans were especially popular among Hindu women; according to the missionaries, women "who otherwise would not sit in the company of men, would come and listen with delight." Christian kirtans became so popular among Hindus that the "heathen crowded out Christians" during performances, and the doors and windows were "so filled up by listeners" that the air became "stifling and foul." Because of the large numbers of people who flocked to hear these performances, the missionaries had to rebuild the chapel at Ahmadnagar twice. After the second renovation, when the original chapel had doubled in size, it was "still too crowded for all to fit."[79]

The Role of Women and Women's Issues in Hindu Reform

As songs about the saintliness and miracles of Jesus appealed to many Hindus, and missionary criticism of the caste system fed the longstanding Maratha tradition of iconoclastic piety, the missionary concepts of Republican Motherhood provided a basis on which many Hindu leaders in Maharashtra conceptualized modern reform. Missionary emphasis on the religious aspects of Republican Motherhood coincided nicely with the emphasis that Maratha reformers placed on the importance of religious life for social order. While contemporary reformers in Calcutta were more radical and revolutionary, and also more alienated from popular religious culture, religious leaders in Maharashtra assumed a prominent role in social reform. Thus while the Bengali reformer Vidyasaga disregarded religious authorities in his efforts to lift sanctions against widow remarriage and focused instead on obtaining government approval of it, the Maratha reformer Vishnu Shastri Pundit turned to the Shankaracharya of Karver and Sankeshwar, the highest religious authority in Maharashtra, to secure a similar reform. Similarly, Bengali reformers often relinquished their loyalty to ritual tradition while Maratha reformers did not. Thus Marathi reformers continued to practice the traditional Hindu marriage ceremony, even though they recognized that it had often been used to inculcate the very concepts of purity, caste, and women's subordination they criticized. While Bengali reformers repudiated the Hindu wedding ceremony and adopted the Brahmo Marriage Act, which was explicitly deistic and more egalitarian, Maratha reformers retained the traditional ceremony but interpreted it more liberally than before.[80]

The strong tradition of religious devotion and iconoclasm in Mahahrashtra also contributed to receptivity to American ideas about female education. The strong commitment to anchoring social change in Hindu religious tradition contributed to the strategy, embraced by Hindu elites from various parts of India, of justifying female education by invoking a tradition of female erudition that had flourished in ancient times. Advocates of increased equality for women pointed to passages in the ancient Vedic scriptures that identified women as teachers, administrators, and judges, and indicated that women had enjoyed the privilege of *upanayana* (sacred initiation), as well as the right to perform sacrifices. These and other passages were taken as evidence of a kind of golden age in ancient time in which religious life nurtured the learning and authority of women as well as men. Defenders of women's education argued that some of the hymns in the *Rig-Veda*, the oldest of Hindu scriptures, might have been composed by women, and pointed to passages in the Artharva Veda implying that women in ancient India were not deemed ready for marriage until they had studied the scriptures. Further evidence of learned women's status in the past came from the passage in the Brihadaranyaka Upanishad in which the female philosopher Gargi defeated Yajnavalkya in a contest of dialectics and forced him to plead, "O Gargi, do not ask me too much."[81]

Missionary arguments for women's literacy were appropriated by Marathas proud of a culture in which widow-burning and female infanticide were rarities, and the zenanas that were prevalent in the Punjab and Bengal did not exist. In the 1880s the Hindu scholar Anandabai Joshee contrasted the freedom that women enjoyed in Maharashtra with restrictions on their activities in Bengal. Because the Maratha-born Joshee traveled openly with her husband in Calcutta, the Bengalis assumed she was a prostitute. "There is so much of the zenana system here that a woman can scarcely stand in the presence of her relatives—much less before her husband," Joshee complained. "Her face is always veiled. She is not allowed to speak to any man—much less to laugh with him. Even the Baboos, who have spent years in England, will not drive here, with their wives, in open carriages."[82]

Among the Maratha reformers who figured importantly in the Hindu reform movements of the late nineteenth and early twentieth centuries were a number of prominent women—including Lakshmibai Tilak, Pandita Ramabai, Anandibai Karve, Parvati Athavale, and Leelabai Patwardhan.[83] Along with other Maratha leaders, these women were part of the religiously based reform movement centered in Poona, the traditional seat of religious learning in Maharashtra. Scholars at the Hindu College in Poona appropriated and recast western ideas in a Hindu context, and became leaders of a national movement for Hindu reform. Among the religious thinkers at Poona, a Hindu "school of thought developed with a constructive program for social and political advancement" that, as one historian put it, "dominated the course of the nationalist movement for several decades."[84]

The most well known of the women reformers based in Poona was Pandita Ramabai, who founded the Arya Mahila Samaj, a society to improve women's education, in the early 1880s. Although Ramabai converted to Christianity after a visit to the United States in the late 1880s, she had been educated by reformist teachers concerned to make female education part of Hindu tradition, and by the time she was twelve she could "recite twenty thousand Sanskrit verses by Heart." Branches of the Arya Mahila Samaj were established in various parts of Maharashtra, and they contributed to the region's leadership in the movement for national reform and freedom.[85]

Along with their British counterparts, American Protestant missionaries in Maharashtra contributed significantly but indirectly to the religiously based reform movements that made the Maharati people leaders in India's larger national independence movement. Concerns for women's education and for women's importance as contributors to the strength and betterment of society featured centrally in the reform movements that swept India in the nineteenth and early twentieth centuries, and these concerns carried tracings of American ideas about Republican Motherhood. These ideas became effective in India as their association with Protestant missionaries loosened and they were transmuted into Hindu thought.

While the improvements in women's lives associated with these Hindu reform movements cannot be denied, the transition to more modern expectations about education and married life also involved new dilemmas and pressures for women. The personal writings of Ramabai and other late-nineteenth- and early-twentieth-century Maratha women reformers reveal the emergence of these new difficulties. According to the historian Jyotsna Kapur, the reforms in women's education and marriage stimulated by missionaries led to "the recognition of a woman's individuality" but also weakened extended family ties and "made the husband the centre of the woman's world." The women reformers whose writings Kapur surveyed were actually more focused and dependent on their husbands than more conservative Hindu women, whose lives were more thoroughly intertwined with members of their extended families.[86] Wifely devotion may not have been less important in conservative Hinduism, but the familial context of that devotion was larger and more supportive. Thus while the concern for women's education expressed by the first American missionaries contributed to the development of an already-existing tradition of women's freedom in Maharashtra, missionary emphasis on the importance of companionate marriage and nuclear family life generated new problems of isolation and alienation for women whose traditional culture revolved around large joint families and a network of female companionship and domestic community.

American missionary women in Maharashtra touched off new appreciation of the individualities and capabilities of women and stimulated criticism of conventional restrictions against female education, even as they fostered new problems associated with individualism and nuclear family life. For good or ill, the first American missionary women in Maharashtra served as catalysts for Hindu reform, and as a result, their influence took a very different kind of direction from what they intended. Ironically, they contributed more to the development of modern Hinduism than to the growth of Christianity.

SIX

⚜

Mount Holyoke Missionaries
and Their Husbands in
Zululand and Natal

*I*n southeast Africa as well as in northwest Persia and Maharashtra, Mary
Lyon's students contributed to the formation of a western-educated elite who
led the way in social reform and pressed for a more egalitarian society. But
this African elite located itself differently with respect to both missionary and
traditional culture than either Nestorian Protestants or Hindu reformers. As
the racist structure of apartheid began to take shape, American-educated Africans in Natal developed an alternative culture deeply influenced by both missionary and traditional ideas, but more independent of missionary culture than
Nestorian Protestantism, and more distant from traditional culture than reformed Hinduism.

As a result of their hostility to Zulu culture, American missionaries failed to
live up to the egalitarian aspect of their theology and to the promise of Christian solidarity they preached. The consequences of this missionary behavior
was far more problematic in Africa than the consequences of similar behavior
in Maharashtra, where missionaries also failed to live up to the egalitarian
aspect of their theology, but where social change was less devastating, and
indigenous reformers were more able to control it. With their traditional life-
ways pressured both by powerful external forces and by internal change created
by their own leaders, the indigenous people of Zululand and Natal had a
much less solid cultural base from which to appropriate missionary ideas.
While Hindus found it relatively easy to exploit missionary ideas in order to
reform and revitalize their traditional culture, Africans in Natal and Zululand

found themselves in a situation at once more polarized and more tenuous. Forced both by missionaries and traditional leaders to choose between the two cultures, they found neither one really viable. Traditionalists found themselves caught up in destructive aspects of westernization in spite of their resistance to it, and converts to Christianity found that the social betterment promised by missionaries never materialized.

In addition to this dilemma, missionary insistence on the sharp conflict between Christian and traditional attitudes toward women was greater in Africa than in Persia or India. American women felt most distant from Zulu women, who were darkest, least fully clothed, and most different in their concepts of religious experience and divine reality, compared with Hindu women, who were similar in their commitment to pure love to God although different in physical appearance and forms of religious practice, or Nestorian women, who resembled American women more in their physical appearance and religious belief.

The heavy emphasis that American missionary women placed on the strangeness and inferior situation of their African counterparts led them to overlook underlying similarities between Zulu women and themselves. The American women failed to appreciate the common investment in women's maternal responsibilities that they shared with Zulu women. Disturbed by the custom of cattle exchange at marriage, and by the fact that Zulu women went about barebreasted, American women failed to see that bride price in Zulu culture involved men's recognition of women's value, or that the display of breasts was as much a sign of women's maternal office and social respectability as covering them up was in New England culture. Similarities involving respect for male authority and women's willingness to sacrifice themselves in the service of others also went unremarked and, most probably, unnoticed.

For Mary Lyon's students in southeast Africa, the failure to recognize these underlying commonalities not only involved simple lack of knowledge and insight, but also betrayal of the commitment to religious community nurtured at Mount Holyoke. Engagement in the reciprocity and mutuality of community was fundamental to Lyon's concept of benevolence and to the missionary vocations that concept inspired. Despite Lyon's express hope that the Mount Holyoke system would be replicated elsewhere, her students were unable to establish reciprocal relationships with nonwestern women, especially in Africa. This inability was partly a result of their theology, which was inclusive in its openness to all people but exclusive in its refusal to accommodate other beliefs. It was also a result of their religious experience, which involved a self-centered preoccupation with personal salvation and self-sacrifice that prevented missionaries from understanding some of the dilemmas that Africans faced.

In addition to the handicaps of theological exclusivism and religious self-preoccupation under which Lyon's students labored, early missionary alumnae of Mount Holyoke tended to operate from the assumption that social welfare for women required conformity to New England culture. In southeast Africa, where the critical intelligence of American missionary women was most needed, it was most compromised by this combination of theological, religious, and cultural imperialism. In a situation where their commitment to the welfare of others might have proved most beneficial, Lyon's students seemed completely unaware that they had relinquished the commitment to community that had been so important to their own development.

This failure helped free Protestant theology from missionary ownership and helped stimulate African Christians to develop systems of religious leadership on their own. But the process of independent growth was more difficult in Natal than in Maharashtra, where Hindu reformers were much more powerful and influential than mission-educated Africans. In southeast Africa, members of the reform culture that developed through missionary intervention were not better off without missionary cooperation. They really could have used missionary support.

Charlotte Grout's Exhibition of Power

In their inability to replicate reciprocity, sisterhood, and community in southeast Africa, Lyon's students contributed to a general failure of American will to confront and resist the racism that became institutionalized in that region. Harbingers of this failure can be found in the account of the first recorded encounter between the Zulu people and a Mount Holyoke alumna.

On a wagon trip into Zulu country to meet with King Mpande in May 1841, Charlotte Bailey Grout found herself the center of attention when she and her husband, Aldin, stopped at the kraal of one of the king's captains. Recalling the event in her journal, Charlotte wrote that the captain's wives, children, and soldiers gathered around the wagon to see her and Aldin "and to make remarks." She noted, "They were especially interested in looking at me and watching all my movements, as many of them probably never saw a white woman before." Certainly Charlotte was conscious of her skin. "As the sun was very hot, I took my gloves out of my pocket and put them on," she recalled. This roused the curiosity of her onlookers further: "At this they all wondered exceedingly and wished me to hold up my hands that they might see how they looked. The women then wished me to descend from the wagon that they might see me stand." After scrutinizing her more closely on the ground, they asked for snuff, a customary way of settling down for conversation. But this request Charlotte could not indulge; "I told them I never used snuff and thought it a bad thing." Thus refusing an opportunity to become more familiar on Zulu terms, the Grouts drank the milk the people provided and rode off.[1]

While Charlotte missed an opportunity to establish a friendly relationship with Zulu women, they may have interpreted her distance as a sign of her spiritual power. In addition to a certain hauteur in her demeanor toward them, she was traveling with her husband to meet with the king. Not only did she and her husband have access to Mpande, but Aldin also treated her with a greater show of solicitude than Zulu men usually treated their wives; at a subsequent stop a few days later, another of the king's captains "laughed outright" when he saw Charlotte take her husband's arm to walk over rough terrain, "remarking, that was a wonderful thing."[2]

Powerful women were not unknown in Zulu culture. The legendary character Uzembeni, for example, was a "great woman" who "devoured the men of the country where she lived." In an effort to get rid of her, some dogs chewed her "to powder" and tossed her in the river, but she came back to life.[3] In addition to such images of powerful women in folklore, women with spiritual powers were an important part of Zulu history and everyday Zulu life. Shaka, the warrior chief and founder of the Zulu state, became king as a result of his mother's boldness in confronting tradition and preparing him for power. And the great majority of Zulu diviners were women.[4]

Diviners helped people overcome illness and misfortune by interpreting the wishes of *amadlozi* (ancestral shades). Diviners were often used and were highly respected; husbands and fathers dared not stand in the way if the shades called one of their wives or daughters, and diviners could act more independently than other women and could make extraordinary demands. Female diviners had a degree of authority and autonomy that women often lacked in the patriarchal structure of Zulu society. But if a woman went too far in expressing ideas that conflicted with those associated with the shades of her husband's kraal, she could be suspected of witchcraft.[5] The loyalty of married women diviners in nineteenth-century Zulu society was especially questionable; the shades of a woman's own ancestors worked within her, not the shades of her husband's lineage, who were fed and cared for in the husband's kraal, where she lived. His ancestral shades protected him and other living members of the lineage, and it was easy to imagine that they might resent the intrusion of countervailing authorities.[6]

Charlotte may well have been interpreted in this religious context. The distinctiveness of her costume and manner suggested considerable potency; unlike the barebreasted and barefooted women who surrounded her, Charlotte was covered up except for her bonnet-shaded face. Her pale face may have been seen as a marker of spiritual power and her voluminous costume as a means of covering the spiritual danger associated with her skin. In Zulu culture, the color white was associated with the sanctity, power, and invisibility of the shades, as well as with the powers of the sky. Medicines, body paint, and the most highly prized cattle were often white, but white things were also ambivalent, potentially dangerous, and often covered up to prevent their drawing lightning.[7]

The African Context of American Involvement

King Mpande eventually came to suspect Charlotte and her husband of witchcraft, but he was initially attracted to the possibility that their spiritual powers would prove beneficial. Before the Grouts arrived, Mpande had "anxiously, earnestly, and repeatedly" requested "at least one missionary to dwell at his place,"[8] and when they appeared, he greeted them as welcome guests in his country, granting them permission to settle where they liked, hold religious services, and establish a school. Mpande hoped the Grouts would help him; he needed rain to make crops grow and ease recurrent periods of famine. He was also in a difficult political situation; during the previous reigns of his brothers Shaka and Dingan, thousands of refugees from Zululand had fled into the region south of the Tugela known to westerners as Natal, leaving Mpande with a weakened state and a much smaller army than his brothers had once controlled. These internal problems were linked to the external pressure exerted by the Europeans, who were converging on the ancestral lands of the Zulu royal household north of the Tugela River and south of Delagoa Bay, and establishing themselves in Natal.[9]

Mpande's need for protection and support made him more enthusiastic, at first, than his brother and predecessor Dingan had been about allowing Americans to settle in Zululand. In December 1835 or January 1836, Dingan had entertained Aldin Grout, along with two other American missionaries, George Champion and Newell Adams. The American men had left their wives in Algoa Bay and sailed to Port Natal, where they hired oxen and a wagon and traveled one hundred sixty miles northeast to the Zulu capital, hoping to receive Dingan's permission to open a school in his country. But the king refused. Francis Owen, a missionary representing the Church of England Mission Society, had already settled within distant sight of the king's kraal, and Dingan thought one missionary in his territory was enough. He advised the Americans to open their school in the area around Port Natal.[10]

Newell and Sarah Adams did establish a school eight miles west of Port Natal on the Mlazi river, and Newell and George Champion paid Dingan a second visit in 1836, during which he finally granted them permission to establish a mission in the Zulu homeland, ten miles north of the Tugela River, which the Champions occupied until forced to retreat to Port Natal the following year. Meanwhile, Aldin Grout's first wife, Hannah Davis, had died at Port Elizabeth in Algoa Bay soon after the Americans' first visit with Dingan, and he returned to New England, where he became engaged to Charlotte Bailey of Holden, Massachusetts, seven months after her matriculation in Mount Holyoke's first class. Aldin and Charlotte married in November 1838 and waited anxiously for the American Board to send them to Natal. But the officers of the board worried about the political instability of the region and vacillated over the question of whether or not to keep their Zulu mission open.[11]

As the Americans were making these initial forays into Zululand and Natal, the Zulu and neighboring tribes were in a state of considerable stress. Dingan had come to power in 1828 after participating in the assassination of his brother Shaka, whose conquests after 1816 had brought people from dozens of clans and chieftainships into a Zulu state. Ecological crises, caused by drought and competition for scarce resources, which led to famine, had contributed to Shaka's ability to exert unprecedented authority; so had the predatory incursions of European traders, in various parts of southeast Africa, seeking ivory, skins, and slaves. Expanding on a tradition of religious initiation and military ranking known as *ambutho*, Shaka created a system of loyalty to the state that built on but also compromised people's loyalties to particular clans commanded by lesser chiefs. Shaka's regiments of fierce, highly disciplined warriors intimidated and incorporated men from surrounding tribes, and he strained the traditional system of gender relationships by requiring men to serve in regiments, without marrying, until middle age. Under Shaka's rule, the Zulu presence was felt as far south and east as the borders of Cape Colony, where most of the Europeans in South Africa congregated, and as far north and west as the region around Delagoa Bay where, in 1817, the Portuguese had begun buying slaves and exporting them to Brazil.[12]

After Shaka's death in 1828, the Zulu monarchy continued to hold sway in southeast Africa, until Dingan ran afoul of the Voortrekkers, or Boers, farmers of primarily Dutch extraction who left Cape Colony when the British government there banned slavery, and invaded Natal in 1837 in a quest for free land and free African labor. In 1838 Dingan received a deputation of them at his kraal and signed a treaty yielding them land, but he surprised them afterward. After luring them to his hut with beer and dance, in the middle of the festivities, with words expressing his belief that the Europeans had magical powers and evil intentions, he ordered his men to "[k]ill ye the wizards." Leaving the heart and liver of the Dutch leader Peter Retief as a sign on the road, Dingan and his men then ambushed two Voortrekker encampments, killing many. The Voortrekkers retaliated and overpowered the Zulu with their superior weaponry, declaring their sovereignty from the Omphalos to the Mzimvubu Rivers and from the Kwahlamba or Drakensberg Mountains to the sea. To finish Dingan off, the Voortrekkers allied themselves with Mpande, who established an army of his own out of the ranks of his brother's army, defeated his remaining forces in a bloody battle, and sanctioned Dingan's assassination. In 1839 the Voortrekkers recognized Mpande as king of the Zulu nation and allowed him and those loyal to him to remain in Zulu country.[13]

In 1840, Mpande presided over a shocked and weakened Zulu state comprised of recruits, captives, and refugees from many different chieftainships, and dependent on the menacing authority of the Voortrekkers. The Zulu state was not completely broken, and many social customs remained intact, but the grief that people felt after having "lost thousands" in their last battle, while the Voortrekkers only "lost fifteen," was fresh. According to Aldin Grout, the Zulus were "afraid." Thankful that "their pride is now humbled," Aldin observed imperiously that "there may be a providence in causing this state of things." With great expectations of his own missionary triumphs, Aldin hoped the Zulu would now be accessible to Christian influence, and that his own preaching would lead to mass conversions.[14]

After securing the permission of the Voortrekkers, Aldin and Charlotte established a station on the eastern branch of the Mhlatusi River in Zulu country. Settling in a heavily populated area, within easy walking distance of no less than thirty-seven kraals, the Grouts found the people eager to make use of them and benefit from their skills. "Our school," Aldin wrote, "commenced before we had anything like a comfortable place for it." Because "[c]hildren for several days came about the place wishing to be taught," Charlotte told them that she would begin the school as soon as they assembled. The next day one hundred students arrived, from which she chose forty for her first class. Aldin was impressed by the people and initially optimistic about their conversion, mistaking their pragmatism for lack of a system of religious belief. "I think them the most interesting and promising people I know," he wrote. Although they practiced polygamy, which offended him, he saw "no system of idolatry to break down," and stealing was rare.[15]

On the other hand, Aldin realized that Mpande "would rather be rid of white men altogether," and that the people "do not yet understand or appreciate our objects." But the people did regard the Grouts as persons with potentially useful spiritual powers. "They came in large numbers upon the Sabbath," Aldin wrote after a drought in 1841, "and requested that I would pray to God for rain; which I did." In apparent response to Aldin's effort, the area around the mission station "had a good supply." Aldin and Charlotte "supposed that the whole country shared in the blessing," but as it turned out, Mpande's kraal and environing fields were still dry, and he sent one of his chiefs to ask if Aldin "could get more."[16]

Both the Grouts and the Zulus believed that the rain had been caused by divine intervention, but Aldin insisted on the fine point that God's power, not his own prayers, had caused the rain. He complained that the people attributed too much power to him: "After all that I can say to the contrary, they will have it that I am the author of the rains." Any similarity between his own prayers for rain and Zulu petitions for rain was lost on Aldin, who missed an opportunity to engage in one of the philosophical debates for which the Zulu were famous. Unable to see that his own behavior caused the Zulus to think that he was a self-important wizard, Aldin held up their perceptions of him as a sign of their ignorance. Thus he noted that some of the Zulus focused on his costume and its apparently powerful connection to the sky: "Upon a rainy Sabbath I put on my large loose coat, and some of the people asked if the rain did not come from my black coat."[17]

Although he did not see it clearly, Aldin had embarrassed the king and established himself as a threat to Mpande's power. In Zulu society, chiefs had priestly and magical responsibilities as well as social and political ones; the shades invested chiefs with powers of fertility, authority, and military prowess, and chiefs were expected to maintain a good communication with them. As the Zulu king, Mpande was chief among chiefs. The shades had invested his brothers Shaka and Dingan with more of their presence and power than other mortals, and if the shades worked in Mpande somewhat less effectively, that was his shame. Aldin's display of power had only compromised the king further and raised questions about the Grouts' intentions in establishing a mission in Zululand. Aldin's conviction that his missionary work was apolitical blinded him to the political effect of his behavior and to the reasons behind the king's growing displeasure.

Charlotte, too, seemed to be an agent of considerable power, and almost as insouciant toward the king's authority. Befitting a wife of great status in Zulu culture, she had a large hut built for herself and her husband, nearly tall enough for her to stand in upright. Her door was large enough to enter without much stooping, an obvious extravagance compared to the very low doors of most other Zulu huts. In addition to the prominence of her domestic situation, Charlotte had a skill with books that impressed even the king. Having heard him say repeatedly that "he did not think his people capable of learning to read," Charlotte boldly challenged him to an exercise that proved him wrong. "I took my pencil and paper & wrote such words as the king suggested," she recalled, and summoned one of her students to read the paper. "The king and his wives were utterly astonished and he told the boy to go out again & sent his servant to see that he was not sufficiently close to hear." When the procedure was successfully repeated, "[t]he king exclaimed 'I have been beaten today.'" Charlotte did not see that Mpande might have liked an opportunity to reciprocate with a demonstration of his own power; she remarked cheerfully, "Afterwards one of the little girls read in the same way, & he was equally pleased." But the king may have simulated pleasure, as Dingan had done in 1838 before he condemned the Dutch party led by Peter Retief to death as wizards. As Charlotte noted, Mpande was hardly won over: "Still he would not let one of his children come down and stop with us long enough to learn."[18]

The possibly dangerous and evil implications of reading and writing seem to have bothered the king. He and his wives may have understood Charlotte's ability to communicate with her students in writing as a magical ritual involving a principle of spiritual causation, much as later, in twentieth-century South Africa, healers sometimes rubbed the bodies of their patients with newspaper or other kinds of printed pages, believing that the writing on them had inherent power. Mpande may also have been suspicious of the objectification of reality in writing and reading, which proceeded under missionary supervision and lent a permanence to things that made them seem impervious to Zulu control.[19]

On the last day of February, just two days after Charlotte had beaten Mpande with her writing, she and Aldin took their leave of the king and returned to their own kraal. Mpande presented Aldin with a large ox and expressed his "regret" at their leaving, saying it had been "pleasant to talk together."[20] But this politeness only obscured the escalating tension. In September Aldin wrote that his "usefulness" had come to "an end the last of February," and that he and Charlotte had "feared for our lives" in the intervening months.

Worried that Mpande was displeased with them for taking up with the Grouts, the Zulus living near the Grouts and attending their classes and religious services had refused to meet with the king or to make any "plain statement" of their loyalty to him. Mpande became increasingly angry at this reluctance, which he interpreted as insubordination and defection. He ordered the execution of all the men, women, and children in three of the huts nearest the Grouts' at the mission station on the Mhlatusi river, as well as the execution of others believed to be especially friendly to the Grouts living in three huts at a slightly greater distance. When the king's soldiers carried out these orders in a surprise attack at dawn on July 25, 1842, the Grouts abandoned their station in Zulu country and fled to the Adams's station at Umlazi in Natal.[21]

Mpande laid the blame for the killings squarely on Aldin. "The missionary came to me, and I welcomed him, and allowed him to select a location where he pleased," Mpande told Newell Adams in 1843, when Adams traveled to Zululand to hear the king's side of the story. "But the people soon began to call themselves the people of the missionary, and refused to obey me," Mpande reported. "I had no authority over them—they cast off their allegiance to their king, and were of no use to me." According to the king, it was Aldin who created this intolerable situation and allowed it to escalate. "The missionary should have told the people in the beginning that he could not be their captain. I have been obliged to kill several of those people, and much mischief has resulted from the mission established there."[22]

This encounter with the Grouts kept Mpande leery of missionaries for the rest of his life. He refused to allow any missionaries to settle in Zulu country until 1850, when he fell ill and sent for the Norwegian physician-missionary Hans Schreuder, who had settled just beyond the border of Zululand in the hope of such opportunity. Schreuder cured Mpande with his medicines and, in return, received permission to establish a station in the area the Grouts had settled several years before. Schreuder and the other Norwegian missionaries who followed him established several stations in Zululand, although with only meager success in generating conversions. Mpande remained suspicious of missionaries, as did his son Cetshwayo, who shared the kingship with his father from 1856 to 1873, when he became full king.[23]

The Nature of American Influence

While Aldin and Charlotte temporarily retired to Cape Town and the American Board decided to close the American Zulu Mission, the British defeated the Voortrekkers and made Natal a British colony.[24] British troops took possession of Natal in 1842, and the following year, the British government issued a proclamation stating that the Voortrekkers would be allowed to continue to live in Natal only under the agreement that slavery and other legal distinctions based on color or place of origin were prohibited. This concern for the welfare of Africans impressed the Americans, who welcomed British government in Natal as a humane and stabilizing context for their own work. But the British takeover of Natal opened the door to a surge in British immigration and to the creation of a system of economic exploitation and dependence on British trade and industry. It also led to the establishment of a system of overwhelming legal discrimination that eventually eclipsed earlier British commitments to racial equality.[25]

When the British government took over Natal and banned slavery there, the American Board reopened its mission. For the next fifty years, missionaries representing the American Board allied themselves with the British government in Natal to an extent that alienated them from many of their students and parishioners and made them less sensitive than they otherwise might have been to the fundamental conflict emerging between the universalist message of their theology and the escalating racism of British policy. After Aldin and Charlotte's disastrous encounter with Mpande, the Americans gave up on their efforts to penetrate Zululand until the British conquered it and made it part of Natal in 1879. But they retained the name American Zulu Mission as an indicator of their special commitment to the Zulu people. The Americans concentrated their attention on Zulus who fled to Natal or emerged from hiding in Natal in the 1830s as refugees from the Zulu state or from the Voortrekkers.

Americans were the first and, for several decades, most dominant missionaries in Natal; in 1850 they had twelve stations, more than thirty missionaries, and a number of churches, schools, and books in the Zulu language to their credit. But beginning in 1841, when the English Wesleyan Methodist Society established stations in Durban (Port Natal) and Pietermaritzburg as part of a chain of mission stations extending from Cape Colony, the Americans acquired many competitors; according to the South African historian Du Plessis, "no other Mission has suffered as greatly as the American from the intrusion of other societies into its field." After Schreuder began a Norwegian mission in Natal in 1842, the Berlin Society established two stations in 1847 in response to a request from the British government. In the next decade, the Hanoverian Mission established stations in Natal, the Church of England made Natal a center of operations under Bishop Colenso, and the Roman Catholic Church began its first mission there. Still other mission societies were represented in the regions surrounding Natal, including Scottish, Moravian, Rhenish, French, and Dutch missionaries. No other region in the world of similar size in 1860 had such a plurality or saturation of Christian missions.[26]

This pattern continued through the late nineteenth century, to the point that, in 1903, one American missionary complained that "between the Tugela and Umvoti Rivers, a field twenty miles wide and fifty miles long, six mission societies have come in, and between our Umvoti station and Mapumulo, a distance of twenty-five miles, where our own out-station work joins hands, we find the Wesleyans, Salvation Army, Christian Alliance and Church of Norway, while these and other societies crowd us on all sides." To make matters worse for the successors of Aldin and Charlotte Grout, "new societies are still coming in, one even asking for one of our outstations, where we had a school building and regular work, to start a home station." Over and above this range of missionary enterprise, "The Church of England regards no other societies, but divides all Natal into districts, with a priest over each division."[27]

This complex, heterogeneous situation was complicated further by the occasional exchange of sites and personnel among different mission societies; for example, Bishop Colenso of the Church of England took over an American site on the Umlazi founded by Newell and Sarah Adams, and J. L. Dohne left the Berlin Society and later joined the American Board. In addition, the Africans who resided at mission stations or attended mission schools frequently moved from one mission environment to another, either because one station offered particular opportunities or conveniences that others did not, or because they were expelled by missionaries from one society and welcomed by the missionaries of another.[28]

The fluidity of African allegiance to western missions makes it difficult to isolate any unique effect that the Americans had in southeast Africa, but the most well-known historian of nineteenth-century Natal identifies education as the distinctive aspect of American missionary influence. "In one respect only," asserts Norman Etherington, "did the Americans particularly outshine their denominational rivals. Their high schools for boys and girls were much the finest educational institutions for Africans in Natal."[29]

The educational program of American Board missionaries in Natal did not elicit the same censure from the home office in Boston as that in western India, principally because missionaries were able to maintain a much stronger link between education and conversion in Natal than in Maharashtra. But while they were not censured for their educational efforts, American missionaries in Natal did not receive the level of support from the American Board that they wished. In one interchange with Rufus Anderson, missionary Lewis Grout (no relation to Aldin) argued that unless the American Board increased its spending on education in Natal, the young African men associated with the mission would be unprepared for decisionmaking, demoralized, and hindered from stepping into leadership roles.[30]

However short of the mark Lewis Grout and his African associates found them to be, the American schools in Natal did play important roles in the development of a new African elite. For many decades, the American-run Amanzimtoti Institute, established in 1853 and renamed Adams College in 1930 after becoming coeducational earlier in the twentieth century, was "a haven of comparative freedom" in southeast Africa, and functioned as one of the few places where Africans could receive a secondary school education, preparation for the ministry, or a college certificate in teaching.[31]

Amanzimtoti was the alma mater of Mvumbi Lutuli, the elected chief of the Christian Zulus at Mvoti from 1935 to 1952, and president of the African National Congress (ANC) from 1952 until he was killed, probably murdered, in 1967. Mvumbi Lutuli's uncle, Martin Lutuli, the son of one of Aldin and Charlotte Grout's first converts, was the first elected chief of the Christian Zulus at Mvoti. Mvumbi Lutuli entered the higher teacher's training course at Amanzimtoti in 1920 and subsequently became one of the first Africans appointed to the college staff. As the provincial president of the ANC in Natal in 1952, Lutuli's support of the ANC's Defiance Campaign led the South African government to dismiss him from his chieftainship. He responded to the government by publishing an essay, "The Road to Freedom Is via the Cross," which advocated nonviolence, asserted that all parties to apartheid were degraded, and predicted the coming of a shared society. While he was president-general of the ANC, the South African government often confined him to his rural home in Groutville. But he was allowed to travel to Oslo in 1961 to receive the Nobel Peace Prize, which one of the South African newspapers described as "an inexplicable pathological phenomenon."[32]

African women also led and participated in efforts to create a shared society in South Africa; through their involvement in labor strikes and civil disobedience, they contributed significantly to the pressure against the legal and economic system of apartheid. Among the women educated at Amanzimtoti, Sibusisiwe Makhanya was called "the outstanding Zulu woman of her generation" by an American biographer. Born in 1894, she attended the Girls' Seminary at Inanda, which was modeled after Mount Holyoke, before enrolling in the Teacher's College at Amanzimtoti. After graduating from Amanzimtoti, she returned to Inanda as a teacher. In 1919 she founded the Bantu Purity League to protect the safety and check the promiscuity of African girls. She received a scholarship from the Phelps-Stokes Fund in New York and attended a Quaker teacher-training school in South Carolina, but she resisted the ideology of accommodation to white supremacy, severed ties with Phelps-Stokes, and enrolled at Columbia Teacher's College along with other Africans disaffected with education in the American South. Returning to Natal in 1930, Makhanya organized a youth movement, a social center, and a school at Mbumbulu designed to adapt traditional customs to a western context. In the late 1930s she was a leader of the Zulu Society, founded to modernize the Zulu people while revitalizing traditional concerns for discipline and male authority.[33]

The westernized elite educated at Amanzimtoti came to function as a leadership alternative to the conservative chiefs, who were concerned with the preservation of tribal custom and their own tribal authority. And while many members of this new elite, like Sibusisiwe Makhanya, joined pride in tribal tradition to western ideas of social progress and reform, others were skeptical of tribal sovereignty and concepts of racial authenticity. The African anthropologist Absolom Vilakazi observed in 1965 that in Natal, especially, "there has not developed the theory of 'negritude' (or the glorification of the most typically African ways) or anything like it, such as has developed in French-speaking Africa, and which has been such an important ideology of nationalism there." Vilakazi argued that many in South Africa rejected this sort of theory as a form of "cultural primitivism" that would undermine their efforts to attain freedom and equality. Thus participants in a conference for African writers in 1959 dismissed the idea that they should confine themselves, or give any special veneration, to the Zulu language. "Again and again among Africans," wrote Vilakazi, "there has been a rejection of any attempt to isolate and insulate them from Western civilization, or even to divide them into tribal groups." The most well-known expression of this rejection of tribal conservatism was the ANC, which, according to Vilakazi, "was founded in 1912 to weld together the different African tribes and to fight not only for their rights but for their acceptance as full citizens of a west-oriented South African society."[34]

While Vilakazi may have somewhat overstated the degree to which the ANC and other progressive organizations distanced themselves from tribal culture, Zulu culture was newer, less popular, and more unstable than other traditional cultures in Africa, and Christian influence was more prevalent than elsewhere. As a manifestation of Christian influence that emphasized historical and social progress toward a harmonious society, American schools helped facilitate the progressivist vision of the African reformers in South Africa.[35]

Mount Holyoke Missionaries in Natal

Mount Holyoke alumnae played an important role in defining this commitment to social progress and in shaping the American focus on education in southeast Africa. Four women who studied with Mary Lyon worked in Natal, beginning with Charlotte Bailey Grout, who published at least one primer in the Zulu language and lived at Mvoti until returning with Aldin to the United States in 1870. In the late 1840s, three more alumnae of Mount Holyoke arrived in Natal—Lydia Bates Grout, Alvina Virtue Pixley Rood, and Abbie Temperance Linsley Wilder—all eager to teach African women and children to read, write, and adopt a Christian life.[36]

The activities of Lydia Bates Grout were especially well known, and her letters to her sister Nancy Bates Atkinson in Oregon offer accounts of interactions with African women that reveal her commitment to their educational and social progress. They also offer evidence of her inability to establish the kind of reciprocity with African women that she had shared with other women at Mount Holyoke. Because her initial commitment to missionary work had been shaped by a degree of concern for the abolition of slavery in the United States that was unusual at Mount Holyoke, the condescending attitude Lydia developed toward African women is especially significant.

Born in Springfield, Vermont, in 1818, the youngest of twelve children, Lydia was known for her "independence of thought and expression." This independence was encouraged by her father, who declared during her infancy that "he had governed eleven children and would let this one do as she pleased." Before attending Mount Holyoke, Lydia was an abolitionist, an anti-Mason, and a teetotaler who formed the idea of becoming a missionary while working as a governess to a slaveholding family in Maryland. She studied a single issue of the *Missionary Herald* over and over in Maryland, and she eventually received a subscription in return for the small donation she sent to the American Board. In 1843 she entered Mount Holyoke with the intention of becoming a missionary to Africa. Her classmate at Mount Holyoke, Sophia Spoford, recalled that for two years she and Lydia benefited from "the daily teaching of Mary Lyon." They "breathed the atmosphere of missions" at the seminary, and they attended a missionary prayer meeting on Sundays, "in which Africa and the Zulu mission were especially remembered." Another classmate remembered that Lydia "was one whom it was Miss Lyon's delight to have connected with the school." Lydia, in turn, "never failed to feel the marvelous, inspiring, uplifting momentum gained there." [37]

In 1847 Lydia and her husband, Lewis, established a mission station at the head of the Msunduzi River, an eastern branch of the Mhloti, thirty miles north of Port Natal. In her work at this station, Lydia became preoccupied with efforts to teach African women and girls how to sew New England–style clothes. She insisted that her students learn to sew in straight lines, even though this procedure was unpleasant for them, and even though she was aware that curved lines were omnipresent in Zulu material culture and fundamental to Zulu aesthetics. In a letter to her sister, she cited her agreement with the observation of a visiting artist that "the Zulus were constantly demonstrating the principle of a circle," noting that Zulu houses, fireplaces, cattle pens, kraal fences, baskets, and vessels for cooking, eating, and drinking were all circular. In addition, "[t]heir footpaths are constantly curving to the right and left even over level portions of the country." Lydia's insight into the prevalence of circular motifs in Zulu material culture did not prevent her from attributing the difficulty of cutting and sewing straight lines to the "extreme dullness" of her students. "When cutting they are constantly making larger or smaller curves and are sure to round every angle," she complained, expressing impatience with Zulu girls and women who "never will follow a pattern."[38]

While Lydia also taught her students to read, she seems to have focused more on teaching them sewing and western housekeeping skills than did early Mount Holyoke missionaries in other parts of the world. Fidelia Fiske taught her Nestorian students to sew, but this activity played a much less central role in her writings about her students than in Lydia Grout's letters to her sister. This greater emphasis on sewing and other household skills contributed to the emerging British policy of funneling African women into domestic labor.

Accounts of missionary women's interactons with their students are sparse at best, and many expressions of understanding and compassion may have gone unrecorded. But from accounts that do exist, Lydia never seems to have opened her heart to African girls as Fidelia Fiske did with her students in Persia, although she took interest in their intellectual progress. Thus she praised the cleverness of one girl, reporting that Utentormisa "[r]eads her own language fluently and has commenced learning English" and "irons, sews, washes, etc. remarkably well." She explained, however, "I have her do these things instead of nursing Anne" because she was hoping to find a Christian nurse and thereby "shield" her own daughter from "heathen influence." When Zulu women showed signs of conversion, she registered approval but not affection. Thus Lydia identified Utesa as "the best educated native woman connected with the mission," reporting that "She reads English fluently [and] is deeply interested in religion and some think she is a Christian," and that she was "very skillful in domestic work and keeps her house beautifully clean."[39]

Both Lydia and her husband were committed to western forms of knowledge, and both pursued a broad range of scientific interests. She studied plants, birds, ants, shells, stars, and especially geology in Africa. An accomplished artist who taught drawing after she returned to the United States in 1862, she sent two drawings and an essay describing the "[t]able lands and intervening Valleys in the vicinity of Natal" to Edward Hitchcock, the geologist president of Amherst with whom she had studied at Mount Holyoke; he incorporated them in his treatise on surface geology published by the Smithsonian in 1857.[40]

Lydia may also have made the sketches in her husband's book *Zulu-land* and provided much of the information in its botanical, biological, and geological chapters. Lewis published Zulu grammars as well as ethnographic, historical, and naturalist writings. In addition to *Zulu-land* in 1864, he published articles in the *American Orientalist* after returning to the United States in 1862, and he served as a member of the advisory council on African ethnology at the World Congress of the Columbian Exposition in 1893.

Although the Grouts were committed to sharing at least some aspects of their education, their scientific interest in Africa had the effect of distancing them from the people and cultural environment of Natal. The objectifying aspect of their intellectual work also fed the couple's tendency to imperiousness. At Msunduzi, Lewis was both respected and feared by the Africans drawn to the mission, who called him " 'Nkosi nkulu, a great king." Like the Zulu kings, he had a grand sense of largess and proprietary authority. During a famine he gave out food in exchange for work, employing the men in "laying out seven avenues . . . named after the hills of Rome." Lydia, too, was perceived as a kind of royalty. When she was ill, Zulu women gathered to "lean in silence over the gate" of the Grouts' house until Lewis appeared. "O our king," they asked, "how is it with our dear mother, the queen, today?"[41] Lydia often took charge at Msunduzi while Lewis was away traveling, and was noted for her capacious hospitality, to which her African servants no doubt contributed. She was known for "entertaining the entire mission (fifty in all) for a week at annual meeting, or distinguished visitors from the capital of the colony or English, Scotch & German missionaries, English officials and military men, travelers, hunters, philologists, and explorers."[42]

Alvina Virtue Pixley Rood cultivated a lower profile. She may have succeeded more than Lydia Grout in establishing empathetic relationships with African women, although she, too, was preoccupied with converting them to New England–style domesticity. Known for her patience and sweet temper, she "did much work in a quiet way," according to another American missionary woman in Natal. One of the Africans who knew her was reported to have declared that "Mrs. Rood was the best Christian I ever saw." Alvina arrived in Natal with her husband, David, in 1849, two years after Lydia and Lewis Grout. After studying the Zulu language with Charlotte Grout, Lydia Grout, and their husbands in Mvoti and Msunduzi, the Roods began a new station at Ifafa. In 1851, they took over the mission station at Amanzimtoti established by Newell and Sarah Adams, and from 1853 to 1857, David had charge of the boys' seminary at Amanzimtoti. At Ifafa, Amanzimtoti, and later at Mvoti, where the Roods moved after Aldin and Charlotte Grout's retirement in 1870, Alvina held weekly prayer meetings for women, taught the boys employed at the mission in the evenings, and brought girls to live in her house, often several at a time and, like other missionary women, taught her boarders to read, cook, and do housework in western style.[43]

Abbie Temperance Linsley Wilder was also perceived as an exemplary Christian, although her reputation as a disciplinarian set her apart from the gentle Alvina Rood and enabled her to assume some of the intimidating characteristics of certain legendary Zulu women. Some Zulu "women called her 'A nettle-plant,' Umbabazane—because they smarted so under her constant reproof for their delinquencies; the men 'A man'—Indoda—the highest compliment a Zulu can pay a woman." At Mtwalume, according to Mary W. Tyler Gray, one of the Zulu women was reported to have claimed, "I used to dread death, but Mrs. Wilder has taught me how to live and how to die." Apparently Abbie Wilder's belief in the necessity of submission coexisted with a powerful desire for dominance.

Abbie Wilder had arrived in Natal with her husband, Hyman, in 1849. She was inspired to become a missionary by the life story of Harriet Newell, America's first foreign missionary martyr, and she spent one year at Mount Holyoke as a middle-year student during Mary Lyon's last full year as seminary head in 1847–48. She and Hyman settled first at Mbilo and then more permanently at Mtwalume, seventy-five miles southwest of Port Natal, which they built into one of the largest missionary stations in Natal. Hyman "was fond of mechanical work of every kind" and encouraged Africans to become involved in sugar production, carpentry, silkworm raising, and other industries. According to Gray, one of American children in Natal who remembered him, "He was always restless and had many irons in the fire," but Abbie functioned as "a brake" on his "impetuosity." Thus she quashed a lion-hunting expedition, warning Hyman that the report of his demise during such an adventure would not read well in the *Missionary Herald.* Hyman was principal of Amanzimtoti Seminary from 1875 to 1877, and when he died after they returned to the United States that year, Abbie went back to Natal and spent the next ten years teaching at the Amanzimtoti Seminary and the Mzumbi Home, working with women and caring for the ill at Mtwalume, Mvoti, Mapumulo and Esidumbini.[44]

Other Mount Holyoke alumnae were sent to southeast Africa after Mary Lyon's death in 1849, and in recognition of the efforts that Mount Holyoke had inspired in American missionaries and their African students over the decades, the large residence hall at Adams College was named Mary Lyon House. Soon after their arrival in 1860, Laura Brainerd Nichols Bridgman (Mount Holyoke class of 1856) and her husband, Henry, founded the first boarding school for Zulu girls, which later became Inanda Female Seminary. Henry had this project in mind when he wrote Rufus Anderson in 1864 that the American missionaries in Natal had hopes of establishing a seminary for African Christian women "modeled after Mount Holyoke Seminary as much as the case will admit."[45]

The American Board also established missions in Cape Colony and Rhodesia. The Huguenot Seminary for European colonists at Wellington in Cape Colony was established as an officially designated Daughter School of Mount Holyoke in 1874, after a pastor of the Dutch Reformed Church read Hitchcock's *Life of Mary Lyon,* in a Dutch translation. Abbie P. Fergusen (Mount Holyoke class of 1856) and Anna E. Bliss (Mount Holyoke class of 1862) were the first teachers. Beginning in 1875, Hannah Juliette Gilson (Mount Holyoke class of 1868) taught for ten years in Stellenbosch, forty miles from Cape Town, where she founded the Bloemhof Seminary for girls of European heritage. In

1896, as an emissary of the Woman's Board of Missions, she became principal of the boarding school for colonists in Mt. Silinda, Rhodesia.[46]

While the missionary effort to make Mount Holyoke a model for African women was not without effect, it was complicated by a variety of factors. African suspicions that the Americans and the Africans they attracted were witches undermined missionary efforts to encourage African leadership, as did the Americans' failure to respect tribal culture, as well as the increasingly explicit racism of British imperialism, which Americans resisted, but not completely. In each of these problematic areas, the issues of sexuality and gender role differentiation figured prominently.

The Centrality of Women's Issues in Cultural Change

Lewis Grout reported that there were eighty to a hundred thousand Africans in Natal in 1847 and that they were "rapidly increasing in number both from the ordinary increase of families, and by immigration from neighboring tribes under despotic and cruel government." Lewis's own ebullience led him to report the most positive aspects of the Africans' situation: "By those who have come from abroad and by some of the natives who have always resided here, I sometimes hear this colony now called the 'Happy Country.'" He looked forward to even happier days, when African leaders would govern Natal, and the people would have abandoned heathenism and become a "new moral creation."[47]

As refugees from the Zulu state swelled the population of Natal in the 1840s, Africans flocked to nine mission stations the Americans established in the region—Mlazi, Amanzimtoti, Mvoti, Inanda, Ifumi, Msunduzi, Amahlongwa, Ifafa, and Mkambati. In 1850 thirteen families from the African Zulu mission resided in Natal, a record never matched or exceeded. Each American preacher attracted a hundred or more people to his sermons in the 1840s, and Newell Adams drew three to six hundred regularly between 1837 and 1847, when he moved to Amanzimtoti with two African assistants and continued to draw large crowds.[48]

But the crowds at missionary services dwindled in the 1850s as people learned how hostile the missionaries were to their tribal customs. As Lydia Grout reported in 1853, "So far as I know every church connected with this or other missions in Natal have been peculiarly tried the last years and we have recently learned that a similar defection has extended throughout the whole of So. Africa." This turn of events was the result of widespread recognition of missionary hostility to tribal custom. Thus when Lewis Grout met with a group of men living near his station at Msunduzi in 1852, their spokesman said, "teacher—white man—we black people do not like the news which you bring us. . . . You trouble us—you oppose our customs, you induce our children to abandon our practices, you break up our kraals and eat up our cattle, you will be the ruin of our tribe." The men threatened to leave the mission if Lewis did not stop troubling them, and Lewis responded by brandishing the prospect of God's anger and trying to frighten the men into submission, announcing that "one man had already left and he was bitten by a snake and died."[49]

Issues concerning the behavior and appearance of women were central to encounters between missionaries and traditionalists, and both sides insisted on the moral rightness of women's roles within their own culture. The missionaries regarded the treatment of women in Zulu society as the epitome of heathenism, and they held up missionary women, marriage, and family life as the epitome of Christianity. They never regarded the patriarchal aspect of missionary society as problematic or felt there was any point of comparison between it and the patriarchal structure of Zulu society. The Zulus, for their part, were aware that traditional marriage customs and women's responsibilities were essential to the structure of their society, and often resented missionary efforts to change them. Missionary hostility to Zulu marriage customs and attitudes toward women added significantly to Zulu apprehensions about missionary witchcraft. The Zulu king Cetshwayo was particularly adamant in objecting to missionary attitudes toward marriage and women's activities, complaining that missionaries would "bewitch" Zulu girls sent to their mission stations "so they never return to their fathers."[50]

While the liberal Anglican Bishop Colenso defended the practice of baptizing polygamists, the Americans insisted on defining admission to Christianity in terms of Protestant rules and sentiments about marriage. In the American struggle for souls, the relinquishment of traditional marriage customs was an absolute prerequisite for becoming a Christian, and conversion was represented by the exchange of tribal skirts, jewelry, and headpieces for dresses, suits, and hats just like the missionaries wore. Thus in her account of a wedding at which "[f]our couples were married in a Christian manner," Lydia Grout linked the clothes worn by the brides to their religious state. "They were all neatly dressed," Lydia reported. "The brides in new chintz frocks and capes and white aprons; and the two young brides had on straw bonnets while the others had turbans."[51]

But Zulus were no less offended by sexual promiscuity than American missionaries. Traditional Zulu custom imposed a standard of morality and sexual purity on men and women that insured women's respectability, provided a certain degree of safety, and established the basis for children's health and well-being. Sexual propriety and discipline were so obvious in traditional society that even missionaries acknowledged it. Aldin Grout observed that, with the exception of polygamy, which he viewed as a system of male licentiousness, "the Zulus have not their equal . . . for purity in any nation upon the globe, pagan or Christian."[52]

For Zulus, the sexual act was a religious event in which the husband did the shade's work by "working with his wife" to conceive a new offspring. As a twentieth-century traditionalist explained when asked if the shade were involved in the sex act, "[I]t is their [the shade's] work the man is doing when he is hot." When "he breathes slower after the work" that is a sign that "the shades have left him."[53] With the shades at work and the lineage and its future incarnation at stake, sex was a serious business, not to be taken lightly. Opportunities did exist for unmarried people to engage in sexual play, but this was supposed to stop short of coitus, and young women who became pregnant without the proper rituals of marriage were regarded as spoiled. The sympathy that missionaries extended to the numerous girls who ran away to mission stations seeking escape from prospective marriages arranged by their families offended many people's sense of religious propriety and gave the impression that the missionaries were immoral. The fact that sexual and marital rules characteristic of traditional culture were suspended at mission stations only added to the reputation of mission stations as dens of witchcraft.[54]

American missionaries interpreted the exchange of cattle at marriage as evidence that the Zulus treated women as chattel, purchased from their fathers and sold to the highest bidder at the time of marriage. Lewis Grout interpreted the Zulu explanation of how missionaries "eat up our cattle" in terms of slavery. "And as to our cattle," Lewis paraphrased the spokesman in his Protestant terms, "our girls and women are our cattle—but you teach that they are not cattle, and ought not to be sold for cattle, but to be taught and clothed and made servants of god, and not the slaves of men."[55]

While the Americans viewed the transfer of cattle from a prospective husband to the father of the bride as nothing more than a crass economic exchange, the Zulu custom of *lobolo* was in fact a complex ritual of fundamental religious and social importance in which the actual exchange of cattle, or *amabeka*, was only a part. The people regarded the amadlozi, or ancestral shades, as the real owners of cattle, and invested cattle and goats with spiritual significance. Their milk was imbued with the power of the shades, and only they could be sacrificed to the amadlozi in times of need or thanksgiving. The exchange of cattle in lobolo compensated the amadlozi of the bride's family for the loss of the bride's future children, who would now grow up as scions of the husband's amadlozi. The cattle belonged to the bride's mother in compensation for the pain she suffered in bringing her child into the world, and also served as an insurance policy, enabling her to establish a hut for herself when the time came for one of her husband's sons to become head of the lineage and its kraal.[56]

Ironically, the missionaries desire to liberate African women from the patriarchal oppression imposed by Zulu religion obscured the importance of women's roles in Zulu society and their traditionally sanctioned opportunities for authority. Missionary efforts to undermine lobolo threatened not only the structure of family and gender relations but also the customary means by which women obtained authority and status in a patriarchal society.[57]

While many African women resisted Christianity and asserted their loyalty to the complex ritual of lobolo, others were drawn to Christianity. The missionaries' first converts were often women, and Christianity continued to appeal to women in greater numbers than men. With women functioning as diviners in traditional society more often than men, the experience of a spiritual call was already an accepted means by which women transgressed conventional gender boundaries. Missionary belief in the importance of women as potential Christians and emissaries of Christian life may have appealed to some diviners, as it may have appealed to the "doctoress" who attended a missionary meeting at

Mvoti in 1847. If in some cases a call from the Christian God functioned similarly to a call from the shades, in other cases conversion may have seemed a welcome escape from the shades' demands and requirements, to which novices often responded only reluctantly because of the notorious difficulties of a diviner's life.[58]

At another level, in a society that was decidedly patriarchal, the gospel's egalitarian ring appealed especially to women. Although missionary society was also patriarchal, the language of Christian grace and redemption held forth a possibility of freedom of expression and gender equality that transcended missionary interpretation. According to Jean and John Comaroff, "the egalitarian rhetoric of the gospel" in all parts of southeast Africa "seems to have had a much greater and quicker impact on females than males."[59]

Young women escaping bad marriages or unwelcome marriage prospects fled to mission stations, as did women past childbearing, who were no longer regarded as wives. Violence was often a factor in the lives of the women who sought missionary protection. Lewis Grout described the case of a young woman who "had been purchased and put to hard labor in the field, but after enduring the oppression of her husband a few years," she took her children to another place. Her brother owned the cattle that had been exchanged at her lobolo. Angry at her behavior, which jeopardized his wealth, the brother "inflict[ed] severe blows upon her to induce her to return." The husband came and also heaped "much violence" on his wife, but he eventually "went home without her." A year and a half later, Lewis was convinced that such brutal treatment was not unusual. "I have seen the abject slavery in which the women and girls are held by their husbands and fathers," he wrote. "And I have seen them . . . driven like cattle."[60]

One of Lewis and Lydia Grout's first converts was a young woman from Mlazi who came to live with and work for the Grout family at Msunduzi. When her father arrived to demand her wages and "threatened" her, "she ran into the house and shut the door." The father "hid in the bushes" and then "pounced" on her when she went out, "dragging her towards home." Alerted by her cries, Lewis and Lydia interceded, but "he became more violent." The young woman pled with Lewis to save her, asserting that her father "would kill her" if he took her home. When Lewis extricated the young woman from her father's grip and allowed her to escape into his house, the man "threw himself on the ground in the most furious manner, wallowed in the dirt; beat his own head with clubs and stones, and continued several hours his raging and howling." He gave up and went home only after Lewis and Lydia treated him to a rendition of the hymn "Christ Our Hope."[61]

Missionary Influence on Gender Role Differentiation and Sexual Behavior

In addition to condemning violence against women, missionaries also criticized the division of labor in Zulu society, especially the relegation of physical labor to women. According to Lewis, while "the men make baskets and mats, prepare the ground for digging and planting, store the grain when harvested, take care of their cattle, hunt, visit, and go out to war if called," the work of women was both more tedious and arduous. "The women dig, plant and weed the field, harvest the crops, bring wood and water, cook the food and take care of their children." In addition, "women carry all the burdens to be transported, and make the floors of earth to their huts." In Lewis's view, these occupations marked the "extreme degradation" of women in Zulu society, and proved that the "proper dignity and provence of women are utterly disregarded."[62]

From the Americans' perspective, the "province" of women was closely tied to the home. Although missionary women were also teachers with considerable authority and influence beyond their own domestic circle, there was tacit agreement among the Americans in Natal that women were principally responsible for rearing children and managing well-ordered households. In the late nineteenth and early twentieth centuries, as the radicalism of missionary millennialism faded, and the role missionaries expected women to play in Christian society became more bourgeois, the identification of women's religious and domestic life became increasingly explicit. Thus in the 1920s Clara Bridgman praised young African Christian couples intent on "founding comfortable and happy homes where the man earns the money and his wife keeps the home and really tries to bring up the children."[63]

Vilakazi noted that among Christian Zulus in the mid–twentieth century, men did the weeding if they were home, and lighter tasks were assigned to women, while traditionalists still considered farming women's work. One could often find women in traditional families "standing in the field and breaking the soil with hoes while the men" who were not away from home working "sit at home," Vilakazi remarked disapprovingly, "drinking beer." Vilakazi also noted that Christian women were often expected to seek work outside the home, while traditionalist women were not. As teachers, nurses, domestics, and factory workers, Christian women supported their families, often as single mothers and heads of households, while traditional women tried to preserve the old customs of gender role differentiation.[64]

In certain respects, the *kholwa* (believers), as African Christians were called, were a new kind of tribe, with missionaries functioning as chiefs in the first decades of Christianization, and African leaders gradually taking over authority. Thus Vilakazi observed that "the Church has taken the place of the kinship group for most Christians, and its systems of dependence which support the individual are as important for the Christian as the kinship systems of reciprocity and mutuality to the traditionalists." But at the same time, the reciprocity and mutuality of traditionalist culture reinforced kinship ties in ways that Protestant individualism did not,[65] and the breakdown of traditional culture encouraged by American missionaries had disastrous effects.

While the Zulus had once been renowned for their universal restraint from casual or unsanctioned sex, by the early twentieth century sexual promiscuity had become a problem that concerned missionaries, African Christians, and traditionalists. Premarital pregnancies rose sharply with the decline of sex-based initiation groups, which instructed young people in the rituals of proper sexual activity, and with the breakdown of patriarchal supervision as mining and other forms of industry drew men away from their homes.

At Groutville during Pentecost in 1912, missionaries pressed the older women associated with the church to exert greater control over their daughters and end the custom of premarital sexual play. Thus began the *isililo* (mother's prayer association), which became an important part of twentieth-century African Christianity. In 1919 Sibusisiwe Makhanya, the Zulu woman leader who had been schooled by Americans at Inanda, founded the Bantu Purity League for the purpose of controlling the premarital sexuality of young women and encouraging older women to adjust to the breakdown of patriarchal authority. Makhanya hoped the league would enable mothers to assume greater control over their daughters and take charge of their sexual education, which had traditionally been managed by female initiation groups and paternal relatives.[66]

Ironically, the missionaries' simplistic view of lobolo became reified in government policy and contributed to women's loss of status, protection, and respect. When the British government in Natal and Zululand became involved in legislating the process of lobolo, they adopted laws that followed the missionaries' interpretation of that rite as a simple economic exchange of women for cattle. While the Americans would have preferred the government to outlaw lobolo, their profane conception of it became institutionalized, with the effect of undermining the advantages that African women had derived from its religious associations.

The Entrenchment of Separate Communities and the Violation of Christian Fellowship

British lobolo laws were an outgrowth of policies instituted by Theopholis Shepstone, the British diplomatic agent to native tribes and secretary for native affairs in Natal between 1845 and 1875. The son of an English Methodist missionary on the Cape frontier, Shepstone operated as a kind of king of the Africans in Natal, allowing tribal chiefs to continue to govern in matters of local concern but inserting his authority above theirs and requiring them to implement his policies of taxation, welfare, and wage labor. Shepstone would have preferred to govern the Africans more directly, and at first he protested the mandate of the Royal Instructions to preserve customary law, arguing that African chiefs were notoriously ruthless and despotic and that, in any case, at least half the African population in Natal lived without chiefs as a result of the dislocations that had occurred since Shaka's time. But Shepstone settled down to superintend reservations created for Africans, and he constructed a system of taxation and labor recruitment that built on and exploited the earlier tribute system commanded by the Zulu kings. He facilitated the establishment of an economic system that controlled African labor and demanded material surplus from the Africans' precapitalist farming and hunting economy. He also created an elaborate legal machinery that made it difficult for Africans to purchase

land, become self-employed, and achieve exemption from his system of taxation, recruitment, and economic management. As the first in southeast Africa
to implement a legalized system of racial segregation, and as the engineer
of legal and economic policies bolstering this segregation, Shepstone laid the
foundations for the system of apartheid that became the law of the land
throughout South Africa in 1948, under the government ruled by the Afrikaner
descendants of the Voortrekkers.[67]

Shepstone's policies put an end to many of the hard-won successes that
some African Christians had begun to reap. In the 1850s the kholwa had begun
to buy land, accumulate surplus property, and engage in industrial and entrepreneurial activities. After Aldin Grout obtained startup funds for an experimental sugar cane plantation in 1859, the Christian men at Mvoti eagerly
joined the venture, and in four years they succeeded in making an annual
profit of seventeen hundred American dollars. This project inspired the men
at the American stations of Amanzimtoti and Ifumi to start similar ventures.
David Rood, the missionary at Amanzimtoti, called the enterprise at his station
a "triumph of Christianity and civilization which the most skeptical cannot
gainsay. Men with black skins who a few years ago were naked boys," Rood
wrote, "are now competing with the white man in manufacturing sugar in a
steam mill of their own from canes of their own cultivation and without any
superintendence in the work."[68]

Beginning in 1856, the British government had allocated five to twelve
thousand-acre tracts of land where Africans worked under missionary supervision. When the government began to levy taxes on these so-called mission
reserves, and relied on missionaries to collect the taxes, Africans working the
lands began to regard missionaries as government agents. American missionaries had naively thought the reserve system would protect African Christians
from government mistreatment, and they had imagined that African farmers
and entrepreneurs would eventually buy up the land. Unwilling to be identified with these repressive taxation policies, the missionaries found their responsibilities to the government "more and more onerous," and they were initially
relieved when the government took over the Reserves at the turn of the twentieth century. But they became distraught when the government established laws
making it impossible for Africans to purchase land.[69]

In 1879 the British invaded Zululand, which they considered an obstacle to
political federation and increased economic production, and made it a British
colony dependent on the government of Natal. After the war, as the labor
recruitment policies of the British government drew Africans from Zululand
and Natal to mines and cities in increasing numbers, and as a system of prole-
tarianism developed in which Africans were low-paid workers in an increasingly industrialized capitalist society, British officials began to look more favorably on Cetshwayo and other members of the Zulu royal family. Exploiting
the influence that the Zulu monarchy had on many people, the British came
to see Zulu culture as an important but permanently primitive subculture. At
the same time, the ethnographic term *Bantu* came to be used as the blanket
term for all the indigenous peoples in southeast Africa, with the exception of

the San (Bushmen), and came to denote a primitive group increasingly removed from economic and political power. American missionaries like Frederick Bridgman, who played a leading role in establishing the Bantu Men's Social Centre, accepted the stereotypical Bantu label, even as they worked to introduce discussion groups and recreational activities transplanted from American culture.[70]

In his work as a philologist, Lewis Grout contributed to the acceptance of the kind of racist thinking that led to the Bantu concept. He recognized similarities among various dialects in southern Africa and concluded that all the indigenous people south of the equator, except the San, were members of the Zingian race, and descendants of Ham and his first son, Cush, who settled in the Near East, perhaps on the Euphrates river, and migrated first to Egypt and then to southern Africa. Distinguishing the Zingians from "the real negro of the Soudan," Lewis concluded that the Zingians were "more robust, taller, of a lighter color, with hair less woolly, with a nose more elevated, of a much greater facial angle, a higher forehead, and altogether of a more intelligent, Caucasian look, than their Nigritian neighbors of the Ethiopic or Negro stamp."[71]

The Americans caught up in this pseudoscientific process of racial stereotyping failed to see any conflict between it and the universalism of their theology. Ultimately, Lewis believed, even the sons of Ham were descended from Adam and Eve, and there was one human nature beneath physical, historical, and geographic diversity. But his unquestioning acceptance of a racial approach to ethnography contributed to the objectification of the African population and to the belief underlying Shepstone's policies that black and white people were fundamentally different.

The efforts that missionary women made to teach Africans to read and write contributed both to the cementing of belief in African inferiority and to the development of new forms of African leadership. In their emphasis on a common Zulu language, which they reduced to writing and taught to both Zulu and other African people in Natal, missionaries exerted considerable pressure on the oral cultures of southeast Africa, in which modes of perception and traditional authority were collectively rooted. While these cultures were already disrupted to a great extent by the massive dislocations that had occurred in southeast Africa since 1820, missionaries facilitated the further breakdown of traditional communities.

Charlotte Grout's primer in the Zulu language encouraged Africans to think of their own language and themselves with a new kind of distance, and helped make it possible for them to see African culture as a thing that could be criticized, reformed, or abandoned. As Jean and John Comaroff suggest in a recent study of the Tswana people northwest of Natal, the objectifying process inherent in reading and writing was closely linked to the process of conversion. These skills encouraged a mental process of objectification that focused in a new way on the self. As taught by missionaries, reading and writing encouraged people to think of the "I" as an entity distinct from a kinship network, and contributed in the most fundamental way to missionary efforts to encourage people to take personal responsibility for their own sins and for the scrutiny of their own intentions apart from their extended families and communities.

The process of objectifying the self also led to a new kind of distinction between the intentional self and the material world around it. This distinction challenged the Zulu tendency to see lightning, snakes, and other natural phenomena as inherently spiritual realities. It also worked against the traditional Zulu concern to maintain a harmonious relationship between the living community of Zulu people and the surrounding world from which they drew their economic and spiritual well-being. According to the Comaroffs, Protestants of the Reformed tradition "went as far as to regard the entire physical world as providentially-given so that ordinary mortals might use its resources to redeem their innate sinfulness."[72] But if Protestant theology drew people away from their traditional regard for the spiritual dimensions of nature, it could also lead them to question the belief that oppressive social structures were grounded in nature.

The objectifying processes associated with reading, writing, and conversion could be liberating, as the missionaries believed that they were, and enable people to see their own situation with new critical distance.[73] But missionaries complicated this liberating aspect of Protestant conversion and western education with racist thinking and behavior. Even though their theology presumed an underlying human nature out of which both Africans and westerners emerged, missionaries perceived and treated Africans as the Other in their everyday life. Unwritten missionary rules against interracial friendships, mingling, and eating accumulated in the course of the 1850s and '60s, and led to increasing concern among African Christians about the gap between the inclusivism of Christian theology and the exclusivism of missionary behavior. Such rules were sufficiently entrenched at Inanda by 1869 that Africans there praised an American woman new to the mission who sat down to eat with them, and told her that "their best and wisest men have said that the missionaries do not know them; they keep at too great a distance."[74]

Just as the process of objectification associated with conversion and literacy could function to stereotype as well as to liberate, so the otherworldly message preached by missionaries could function both to draw attention away from concerns for social injustice and to fuel those concerns. The American Board's official insistence on the primacy of conversion involved a prominent dimension of otherworldliness that mitigated against consistent concern for social justice and allowed missionaries to see themselves as apolitical agents of God, despite the dramatic political effects of their religious actions, and despite their accommodation of British policies of racial segregation.[75] Yet it was precisely this other worldly dimension that allowed Africans to embrace Christianity as a basis of spiritual authority that was independent of both racist government policy and the hypocritical behavior of missionaries. Thus in the late 1860s, Christian faith in a transcendent God and in the promise of divine redemption played a crucial role in encouraging the African Christians at Mvoti to criticize Aldin Grout and his paternalistic authority. Similarly, the desire to fully express his evangelical faith as a missionary pastor led Mbiana Ngidi to break away from American control and from American willingness to accommodate Christianity to racist practice and ideology. The missionaries "did not mingle with them nor love them," Ngidi claimed in 1869, and "taught the people not to respect black people, so they could not manage the stations." As proof of the missionaries' hypocrisy and betrayal of the Christian gospel, Ngidi reported "that while in the pulpit the missionaries said 'dear friends and brethren.' However, as soon as they came out of the pulpit they would not call them that because they were black, but despised them."[76]

Only when the Americans lacked sufficient manpower of their own to expand their missionary enterprise in Natal in the 1870s did they establish the Native Home Missionary Society and appoint Ngidi and Benjamin Hawes the first African Christian missionaries in Natal. The African Christians living on American mission stations enthusiastically supported the society, and their work as members led to increasingly bold efforts to interpret the Christian gospel apart from missionary control. In 1875 an independent missionary movement founded and led by African Christians, called Unzondelelo, emerged at the Methodist station of Edendale, and beginning in the 1880s independent churches composed of African Christians separated from missionary institutions. Thus in 1897, soon after Joseph Booth launched the Africa for Africans movement in Natal, two of the preachers ordained by American missionaries established the Zulu Congregational Church.[77]

In the wake of this development, new African churches sprung up spontaneously, without any prior allegiance to mission churches, and they incorporated traditional forms of African expression that missionaries disapproved of, including divination and belief in witchcraft. The existence of these indigenous churches demonstrated the attractiveness and power of Christian ideas, as well as African distrust of missionaries and allegiance to traditional forms of religious culture.[78]

While American educational ventures contributed significantly to the emergence of a new African leadership, the dependent relationships that American missionaries established with Africans worked against the development of a shared society. Missionary efforts to define a social distance between themselves and the converts contributed to distrust of the United States among African peoples in the twentieth century. In antebellum New England, missionary vocations had been inspired by the Edwardsean concept of God's work of redemption as the construction of universal social harmony. Especially at Mount Holyoke, where Mary Lyon systematically endeavored to bring this concept to reality in the everyday workings of her seminary, commitment to community played a fundamental role in the development of missionary interest. This commitment to community at Mount Holyoke also established continuity between the moral values and cultural stability of the New England past and the new opportunities and challenges associated with industrialization. But Lyon's students in Natal failed to see any underlying commonality between their situation and the Zulu concern for cultural continuity in the midst of social change, much as they failed to see any underlying commonality between their own investment in Republican Motherhood and the Zulu investment in women's maternal productivity and social responsibility.

Missionaries failed to follow through on their commitment to community because they focused on the obvious differences between their own cultural expectations and those of the Zulus. Given the emphasis on both community and self-criticism at Mount Holyoke, one might have hoped Lyon's students would have taken the lead in establishing reciprocity in their relationships with Africans and broken out of the religious imperialism of the missionary agenda. But the critical and ethical thinking of these otherwise capable women was undermined by the authoritarian character of their religious ideology and by a preoccupation with self-sacrifice that both disguised and legitimated their desire for dominance over other women. Thus Lydia Grout, one of Lyon's most independent-minded and intellectually gifted students, became imperious in Africa, and lost sight of the religious community, reciprocity, and affectionate mutuality that had inspired her career.

Conclusion

*T*his book has considered Mary Lyon and her missionary students as representatives of significant but often unrecognized tendencies in nineteenth-century American life and thought. These tendencies include the coinciding popularity of New Divinity theology and the ideology of Republican Motherhood, and the resulting synthesis of the former's emphasis on disinterested benevolence and criticism of social elitism with the latter's commitment to advancing women's education and assertion of the necessity of women's moral responsibilities to society. In the minds of New Divinity women, God's work of redemption required the social elevation and intellectual development of women around the world, and their belief in this work motivated them to considerable effort at self-development and activism in behalf of other women.

The lives of Mary Lyon and her students also represent the stresses faced by many early-nineteenth-century New Englanders, especially women. Living in the midst of the decline of self-sufficient village-based culture and the emergence of a national economy born of new forms of industry and transportation, Lyon and her students sought to capitalize on the entrepreneurial expansiveness of their era without relinquishing the social stability, moral purposiveness, and communal feeling associated with traditional New England culture. At the same time, they struggled with depression and often crippling feelings of guilt and inadequacy. The processes of conversion and missionary commitment framed these internal struggles and encouraged increased self-control and unstinting efforts of self-sacrifice. The book argues that this constellation of emotional, social, and intellectual forces drove Lyon's students to devote themselves to missionary careers and shaped their interactions with nonwestern women.

In addition to their role in this book as representatives of an important subculture within antebellum New England, Lyon's missionary students also stand as representatives of the early dissemination of American culture in three regions of the nonwestern world. The book argues that antebellum New England women exerted significant impact on the lives of nonwestern women and figured importantly in the early exportation of American culture to the Middle East, India, and Africa. It also argues that the effect of missionary efforts was quite different from what missionaries intended. In Persia, American missionary efforts to reform Nestorian culture led to the decline of that culture; in Maharashtra, American missionary efforts to promote female literacy contributed to a revitalization of Hinduism; and in Natal, American missionary education helped establish an African Christian elite that rebelled against mission churches. Thanks to the competing power of traditional cultures, and the creative use to which the people of those cultures put the ideas that missionaries introduced, missionaries' failure to realize their intentions was not without positive outcome. Missionary intervention contributed to the creation of new cultures formed from elements of both traditional and missionary cultures, and, in each case, the degree to which missionaries failed to control a new culture was directly tied with that culture's success. In Maharashtra especially, missionaries' failure to control religious reform meant that their most socially beneficial ideas passed rather easily to native ownership. In contrast, missionaries exerted much more control over the development of a reformed Nestorian culture, but that culture was weak, and eventually disappeared.

In southeast Africa, the issue of control was quite clearly linked to the inability of missionaries to actualize the commitment to Christian community that they preached. In Natal, African Christians had to wrest control of Christian theology and church governance from missionaries in order to save them from the pollution of racist interpretation. A similar failure of missionary intelligence and ethical insight occurred in Maharashtra, where missionaries paid little respect to Hindu traditions of religious knowledge and piety, and in Persia, where American women established condescending relationships to Nestorian women. These moral and intellectual failures can be attributed partly to the inexperience of American missionaries and to their distrust of people different from them—a type of distrust they shared with most peoples of the world—and partly to the aggressively authoritarian quality of New Divinity theology. This theology drove Americans out of the isolation of their own traditional culture into commitment to the well-being of people in other cultures, but it also fueled missionary hostility to non-Protestant religions, and it fostered a pernicious form of self-righteousness that was hidden from its proponents, who condemned self-righteousness in themselves when they saw it.

Early-nineteenth-century American missionaries left no evidence of being aware of the tension between the religious elitism of their theology, which allowed no room for competing truths, and their religious commitment to benevolence, which involved a trenchant moral critique of elitism and prompted important social reforms. As we have seen, Samuel Hopkins defined belief in the inferior humanity of Africans as un-Christian, and he argued that no one who condoned slave ownership could attain salvation. Although the theology of Jonathan Edwards, on which Hopkins's views were based, did not spell out an explicit agenda for social reform, his concept of true virtue presumed that genuine love of God produced intelligent concern for the welfare of others.

Mary Lyon's students were, in some respects, in an ideal position to comprehend and act on this aspect of New Divinity thought, and this book has presented some evidence that they did, in fact, actualize their commitment to the welfare of others more easily than their male counterparts. Like other antebellum missionary women, Lyon's students carried forward a Puritan tradition of female piety in which their socialization as wives and mothers emphasized the same qualities of affection, humility, self-criticism, and responsibility to others that defined Christian sanctity. As a result of this coincidence of religious and gender role expectations, New England women were positioned to exemplify and be recognized as exemplary Christians more often than men.

If this legacy of female piety placed Lyon's students in a better position than their husbands to develop theological notions of true virtue and benevolence into an ethic of genuine service, it also hampered them from becoming aware of how their humility and benevolence failed. The insistence on self-sacrifice that characterized their theology undermined their capacity for self-criticism and self-understanding, even though they prized these virtues, pursued them energetically, and believed them to be essential to their ability to establish ethical relationships with others. Their insistence on self-sacrifice, which grew out of a centuries-old tradition of Christian self-mortification, received new impetus in New Divinity thought as a means of enabling concern for others. But the New Divinity preoccupation with self-sacrifice also functioned to focus attention on the self, while paralyzing the self-confidence requisite for pursuing the logic of benevolence beyond its conventional association with the patriarchal authority and alleged superiority of New England culture.

Concern for self-sacrifice skewed missionary thinking, making it possible for missionaries to overlook the arrogance involved in their disdain for other beliefs and to overlook the conflict between this disdain and their commitment to benevolence. The religious and cultural imperialism permitted by their preoccupation with self-denial also prevented missionary women from seeing the underlying commonalities between their own lives and the lives of nonwestern women. Despite being prepared for such insight by the advanced education and deliberate cultivation of sisterhood at Mount Holyoke, Lyon's students in Persia, India, and Africa failed to see that they shared with nonwestern women a belief in maternal responsibility for maintaining religious tradition and cultural stability, and a loyalty to male authority as an essential aspect of religious tradition and cultural stability.

Lyon's students and other American missionary women also failed to apprehend that both they and nonwestern women were caught up in powerful, and to some extent similar, forces of social change. These forces threatened social stability and the survival of traditional religious cultures, but they also led to the creation of new religious cultures that involved new opportunities for women through education, teaching, and social influence, and new opportunities for philanthropic service that wedded traditional forms of mutual aid with new and more systematic commitments to human rights and social welfare. The failure of Lyon's students to recognize any similarity in the forces of social change that engaged them and other women contributed to a superiority complex in American women and helped create a legacy of problematic relationships between American and nonwestern peoples that still persists. But at the same time, the concept of benevolence introduced by American missionaries carried salutary impulses to which important elements in today's global consciousness can be traced.

In antebellum New England, the investment in self-sacrifice enabled women to justify advances in their own education and new forms of public activism. In an era of social change and individual stress, this investment functioned as a flawed but perhaps necessary bridge that women built to carry themselves and other women toward greater individuation and achievement. One measure of the success of this bridge may be the willingness of many women today, including some of those involved in missionary work, to criticize and disown it. But whether or not this bridge of self-sacrifice deserves burning, it played a crucial role in the development of women's education and American philanthropy, and it occupies a historic place in the development of American culture.

The antebellum preoccupation with self-sacrifice also highlights the enormity of the psychological struggle involved in women's efforts to improve their own lives and those of other women. If advancing women's education and welfare had been easier, heroic efforts of self-sacrifice would not have been required as justification. And if antebellum women had been less committed to this advancement, their willingness to subject themselves to the rigors of self-sacrifice would not have been so intense.

In its link to a social structure grounded in male authority, and in its loyalty to an ideal of religious community and social harmony, the investment in self-sacrifice also helped establish an underlying common ground between antebellum missionary women and their nonwestern contemporaries. Although missionary women were largely unaware of its contours, this common ground was an important basis of the new cultures formed in nonwestern regions in response to missionary intervention. In this respect, nineteenth-century women in New England, Persia, India, and Africa had more in common with one another than with feminists today, whose commitment to women's social and personal development is more straightforward and whose loyalty to cultural traditions based on male authority is more tenuous, if not completely broken.

Analysis of women's ties to traditional cultures dominated by men is worthy of the most serious consideration. Analysis of the social impact of feminist critiques of male authority in various parts of the world also needs to be pursued. And the role of religion in relation to women's education in various parts of the world also needs to be more fully understood.

At a time when numerous government and nongovernment agencies are becoming increasingly aware of women's roles in maintaining cultural stability and in effecting cultural change, and at a time when intervention aimed at empowering impoverished women is increasingly a target of philanthropic interest, the historical study of missionary efforts to elevate women is especially instructive. As this book has attempted to show, Mary Lyon and her students provide lessons about the pitfalls of self-sacrificial intervention in behalf of women. They are equally instructive in demonstrating correlations between women's education and empowerment, and in demonstrating the necessity of defining these goods in terms of community.

Notes

Introduction

1. Clifton Jackson Phillips, *Protestant America and the Pagan World: The First Half Century of the American Board of Commissioners for Foreign Missions, 1810–1860* (Cambridge: Harvard University Press, 1969), 20–31; quotation from 28.

2. Leonard Woods, *Sermon Preached at Haverhill, (Mass.) in Remembrance of Mrs. Harriet Newell, Wife of the Rev. Samuel Newell, Missionary to India. Who Died at the Isle of France, Nov. 30, 1812, Aged 19 Years. To Which are Added Memoirs of Her Life,* 3rd ed. (Boston: Samuel T. Armstrong, 1814), 11.

3. Elizabeth Alden Green, *Mary Lyon and Mount Holyoke: Opening the Gates* (Hanover, N.H.: University Press of New England, 1979; reprint 1983), 264; Edward Hitchcock, ed., *The Power of Christian Benevolence Illustrated in the Life and Labors of Mary Lyon* (Northampton: Hopkins, Bridgman, 1852), 346.

4. For an important study of late-nineteenth-century American women missionaries, see Jane Hunter, *The Gospel of Gentility: American Women Missionaries in Turn-of-the-Century China* (New Haven: Yale University Press, 1984).

5. R. Pierce Beaver, *All Loves Excelling: American Protestant Women in World Mission* (Grand Rapids, Mich.: William B. Eerdmans, 1968), 11, 118.

Chapter One

1. Linda K. Kerber, *Women of the Republic: Intellect and Ideology in Revolutionary America* (Chapel Hill: University of North Carolina Press, 1980), 35–113, 269–288.

2. Gerda Lerner, *The Grimké Sisters from South Carolina: Pioneers for Woman's*

Rights and Abolition (New York: Schocken, 1967; reprint 1971), 164–166, 169, 233; Ann Braude, *Radical Spirits: Spiritualism and Women's Rights in Nineteenth-Century America* (Boston: Beacon Press, 1989), 63, 82–96. For discussion of changing relationships between gender and public space during the nineteenth century, see Mary P. Ryan, *Women in Public: Between Banners and Ballots, 1825–1880* (Baltimore: Johns Hopkins University Press, 1990).

3. Benjamin Rush, "Thoughts Upon Female Education," quoted in Kerber, *Women of the Republic*, 229.

4. Kerber, *Women of the Republic*, 204; Barbara J. Berg, *The Remembered Gate: Origins of American Feminism: The Woman and the City, 1800–1860* (New York: Oxford University Press, 1978).

5. Quoted in Edward Hitchcock, ed., *The Power of Christian Benevolence Illustrated In the Life and Labors of Mary Lyon* (Northampton: Hopkins, Bridgman, 1852), 243–245; see also Elizabeth Alden Green, *Mary Lyon and Mount Holyoke: Opening the Gates* (Hanover, N.H.: University Press of New England, 1979; reprint 1983), 367 n. 64.

6. Kerber, *Women of the Republic*, 110.

7. Mary Lyon, quoted in Hitchcock, *Power of Christian Benevolence*, 172.

8. See Kerber, *Women of the Republic*, 35–67.

9. Cotton Mather, *Ornaments for the Daughters of Zion or the Character and Happiness of a Vertuous Woman* (Cambridge, Mass.: 1692), 48, 3–4. See Amanda Porterfield, *Female Piety in Puritan New England: The Emergence of Religious Humanism* (New York: Oxford University Press, 1992).

10. Gerald F. Moran, "Sisters in Christ: Women and the Church in Seventeenth-Century New England," and Mary Maples Dunn, "Saints and Sisters: Congregational and Quaker Women in the Early Colonial Period," in *Women in American Religion*, ed. Janet Wilson James (Philadelphia: University of Pennsylvania Press, 1980), 48–53, 36–37.

11. Jon Butler, "Enthusiasm Described and Decried: The Great Awakening as Interpretive Fiction," *Journal of American History* 69 (1982), 305–325.

12. During this period, New England ministers divided over questions of free will and self-interest; the New Divinity followers of Jonathan Edwards rejected these as incompatible with true virtue, while liberal ministers interpreted them more acceptingly.

13. Joseph A. Conforti, *Samuel Hopkins and the New Divinity Movement: Calvinism, the Congregational Ministry, and Reform in New England between the Great Awakenings* (Grand Rapids, Mich.: William B. Eerdmans, 1981), 35.

14. Ibid., 9, 18–20, 26–30, 55, 75, 94, 119–120.

15. Ibid., 128–129, 153–154.

16. Ibid., 102–105.

17. Clifton Jackson Phillips, *Protestant America and the Pagan World: The First Half Century of the American Board of Commissioners for Foreign Missions, 1810–1860* (Cambridge: Harvard University Press, 1969), 1–31; Matthew Mayhew, *A Brief Narrative of the Success which the gospel hath had, among the Indians of Martha's Vineyard* (Boston, 1694); Edward Winslow, ed., *Glorious Progress of the Gospel amongst the Indians in New England* (London: 1649).

18. C. C. Goen, "Jonathan Edwards: A New Departure in Eschatology," *Church History* 28 (1959), 25–40; John F. Wilson, "History, Redemption, and the Millennium," in *Jonathan Edwards and the American Experience*, ed. Nathan O. Hatch and Harry S. Stout (New York: Oxford University Press, 1988), 131–141, especially 132.

19. Conforti, *Samuel Hopkins*, 158.

20. The missionaries' lack of appreciation for foreign religions and cultures was offensive to cosmopolitan liberals and did not go unchallenged. In 1844, Elizabeth Sanders was critical of American foreign missions, and pointed to the virtues of Chinese civilization, arguing that the people of China were, on the whole, more moral than the people of America. And Herman Melville satirized missionaries and celebrated the vitality of the South Sea Islanders in his novels *Omoo* and *Typee*. But missionaries played a powerful role in reporting on "heathen savagery" and emphasizing America's moral obligation to reform the world. See Elizabeth Sanders, *Tracts on Missions* (Salem: 1844), 4–5; Phillips, *Protestant America and the Pagan World*, 278.

21. As Rufus Anderson, the influential secretary of the American Board, wrote, "It is for the female missionary to search out and collect the young children for [mission] schools, and to shed a softening, subduing influence over their dispositions and manners, and impress religious truth . . . upon their hearts and consciences." Foreign women who sought schooling "should [also] be to a considerable extent under the presiding influence of the female members of the mission." Finally, and most important for Anderson, "The heathen should have an opportunity of seeing christian families," which only the presence of missionary wives and mothers could provide. Since the "domestic constitution among them is dreadfully disordered," Anderson believed, a certain order must be brought to family life if Christianity was to take hold. This reorganization of families "require[d] example as well as precept." Anderson concluded that "the christian wife, mother, husband, father, family must all be found in all our missions to pagan and Mohammedan countries." See Rufus Anderson, *To Advance the Gospel: Selections from the Writings of Rufus Anderson*, ed. R. Pierce Beaver (Grand Rapids, Mich.: William B. Eerdmans, 1967), 211–213.

22. Phillips, *Protestant America and the Pagan World*, 105–106 and 125; 88–132. See also Rufus Anderson, *A Heathen Nation Evangelized: History of the Sandwich Islands Mission* (Boston: Congregational Publishing Society, 1870); Mary Zwiep, *Pilgrim Path: The First Company of Women Missionaries to Hawaii* (Madison: University of Wisconsin Press, 1991).

23. Jane Hunter, *The Gospel of Gentility: American Women Missionaries in Turn-of-the-Century China* (New Haven: Yale University Press, 1984), xiii.

24. R. Pierce Beaver, *All Loves Excelling: American Protestant Women in World Mission* (Grand Rapids, Mich.: William B. Eerdmans, 1968), 71. The American Board was founded in 1810 by Congregationalists, and joined by Presbyterians in 1812. In the course of the nineteenth century, American mission societies were also founded or expanded by Baptists, Presbyterians, Methodists, Quakers, and other religious groups. But in the first five decades of the nineteenth century, no other mission society in America rivaled the American Board in popular support or scope of outreach, or functioned so fully as an outlet for the enthusiasm of antebellum religious enthusiasm. See Phillips, *Protestant America and the Pagan World*, 1–31.

25. Anonymous author, quoted in Anderson, *To Advance the Gospel*, 217.

26. Lucy (Lyon) Lord to her mother, quoted in *Memoir of Mrs. Lucy T. Lord of the Chinese Baptist Mission*, with an introduction by William Dean (Philadelphia: American Baptist Publication Society, 1854), 208.

27. In 1860, partly in retaliation for a statement published by Rufus Anderson expressing reservations about the appropriateness of sending out single women as missionaries, women who had supported the American Board in the past established their own independent board to assist single women missionaries. The establishment of this and other independent mission societies by and for women in the 1860s and 1870s marked

an important expansion both in women's participation in foreign mission work and in their public visibility. From then until World War I, the American missionary work force was predominantly female and consisted increasingly of single women. By 1890, 60 percent of all American missionaries were women. (See Hunter, *Gospel of Gentility*, xiii.) In R. Pierce Beaver's analysis, the reabsorption of these female societies under male-dominated boards in the twentieth century sapped an important source of vitality for American Protestant churches. Twentieth-century girls were not "brought up in the mission" as their mothers were, and "have not the challenge of vocation constantly before them." Writing in 1968, Beaver reported that women who remained involved in mission work "believe that women have less and less of a place of genuine influence and participation in administrative offices, board membership, and policy-making." *All Loves Excelling*, 200–202.

28. Lori Ginzberg, *Women and the Work of Benevolence: Morality, Politics, and Class in the Nineteenth-Century United States* (New Haven: Yale University Press, 1990); Hunter, *Gospel of Gentility*; Patricia R. Hill, *The World Their Household: The American Women's Foreign Missionary Movement and Cultural Transformation, 1870–1920* (Ann Arbor: University of Michigan Press, 1985).

29. R. Pierce Beaver stressed the tendency of late-nineteenth- and early-twentieth-century missionary work to be "built upon a celibate order of life." Beaver noted "dozens of instances" in the late nineteenth and early twentieth centuries "when young women were practically accused of being unfaithful to Christ as well as to the [women's mission] society because of marriage. Yet," Beaver also observed, "the bond of love and fellowship was far more intimate between the single women on the field and the women who supported them at home than between the missionaries of the general boards and the churches." *All Loves Excelling*, 179–180.

30. Hitchcock, *Power of Benevolence*, 228–229.

31. See Kathryn Kish Sklar, *Catharine Beecher: A Study in American Domesticity* (New Haven: Yale University Press, 1973), 159–161. For discussion of this missionary attachment to Victorian domesticity, see Hunter, *Gospel of Gentility*, 128–173.

32. Catharine Beecher, quoted in Hunter, *Gospel of Gentility*, xiii; Hill, *The World Their Household*, 28–34, 40–41, 88, 96.

33. Sklar, *Catharine Beecher*, 32, 38.

34. Joseph Haroutunian, *From Piety to Moralism: The Passing of the New England Theology* (New York: Henry Holt, 1932). An earlier historiographic tradition recognized the vitality of the Puritan tradition in the Republican and antebellum eras. In 1907 Frank H. Foster argued that Samuel Hopkins and other disciples of Jonathan Edwards "took the initiative in the greatest forward movement of American Christianity in all its formative years. In foreign missions, in home missions, in the founding of theological seminaries, in the planting of colleges, in revivals, in denominational co-operation, Congregationalism, . . . took the unquestioned lead among American churches." Frank H. Foster, *A Genetic History of the New England Theology* (Chicago: University of Chicago Press, 1907), 3–4.

Some scholars question the decline of Calvinist thought by suggesting that its initial influence has been greatly exaggerated. Jon Butler and David D. Hall have demonstrated the great extent to which occult phenomena and magical thinking have occupied people's religious imaginations since the seventeenth century. These scholars question the influence attributed to Puritan theology by Perry Miller and the intellectual historians who followed him, as do social historians Gerald F. Moran and Maris A. Vinovskis, who see theology as secondary to and derivative of social behavior. While Butler and Hall argue that Calvinist theology has always competed with and often been overshadowed in the popular mind by other forms of thought, even in seventeenth-century New England, Moran and Vinovskis argue that the Puritan family developed and even thrived in the course of New England history, and suggest that its decline is a myth perpetuated by scholars who take Puritan jeremiads too literally. See Jon Butler, *Awash in a Sea of Faith: Christianizing the American People* (Cambridge: Harvard University Press, 1990); David D. Hall, ed., *Witch-Hunting in Seventeenth-Century New England: A Documentary History, 1638–1692* (Boston: Northeastern University Press, 1991); Gerald F. Moran and Maris A. Vinovskis, *Religion, Family, and the Life Course: Explorations in the Social History of Early America* (Ann Arbor: University of Michigan Press, 1992).

35. Sidney E. Mead, *Nathaniel William Taylor, 1786–1858: A Connecticut Liberal* (Chicago: University of Chicago Press, 1942); Sklar, *Catharine Beecher,* 140–148, 187–195, 244–246.

36. Ann Douglas, *The Feminization of American Culture* (New York: Avon Books, 1977). See also Elizabeth White, "Sentimental Heresies: Rethinking *The Feminization of American Culture,*" *Intellectual History Newsletter* 15 (1993), 23–31.

37. Ryan, *Women in Public,* 173. See also Mary P. Ryan, *Cradle of the Middle Class: The Family in Oneida County, New York, 1790–1865* (Cambridge: Cambridge University Press, 1981); Carol Smith-Rosenberg, *Disorderly Conduct: Visions of Gender in Victorian America* (New York: Oxford University Press, 1985); Ruth Bloch, "Untangling the Roots of Modern Sex Roles: A Survey of Four Centuries of Change," *Signs: Journal of Women in Culture and Society* 4:2 (Winter 1978), 237–252.

38. See Braude, *Radical Spirits,* 6. See also Catherine L. Albanese, *Nature Religion in America: From the Algonkian Indians to the New Age* (Chicago: University of Chicago Press, 1989); William L. Andrews, *Sisters of the Spirit: Three Black Women's Autobiographies of the Nineteenth Century* (Bloomington: Indiana University Press, 1986). For recent studies that explore the ambiguity of gender reform in alternative religious movements in the antebellum era, see Linda A. Mercadante, *Gender, Doctrine and God: The Shakers and Contemporary Theology* (Nashville: Abingdon Press, 1990); Stephen J. Stein, *The Shaker Experience in America* (New Haven: Yale University Press, 1992); Wendy E. Chmielewski, Louis J. Kern, and Marilyn Klee-Hartzell, eds., *Women in Spiritual and Communitarian Societies in the United States* (Syracuse: Syracuse University Press, 1993).

39. In her comparison of conversion narratives from the first and second Great Awakenings, Barbara Leslie Epstein showed that many New England women persisted in identifying with the uncompromising Calvinist picture of themselves as innately sinful creatures, despite the option of a more Arminian alternative that allowed them to think of sin more as a regrettable act to be forgiven than as an inherent deformity. Although she does not judge it favorably, Epstein demonstrates women's loyalty to Calvinism. See Barbara Leslie Epstein, *The Politics of Domesticity: Women, Evangelism, and Temperance in the Nineteenth Century* (Middletown, Conn.: Wesleyan University Press, 1981).

40. Joseph A. Conforti, "Mary Lyon, the Founding of Mount Holyoke College, and the Cultural Revival of Jonathan Edwards," *Religion and American Culture: A Journal of Interpretation* 3:1 (Winter 1993), 69–89, quotation from 75. See also Conforti, *Samuel Hopkins.*

41. Kathryn Kish Sklar, "The Founding of Mount Holyoke College," in *Women of America: A History,* ed. Carol Ruth Berkin and Mary Beth Norton (Boston: Houghton Mifflin, 1979), 177–201; Green, *Mary Lyon,* 337–338. See also Conforti, "Mary Lyon," 69–70.

42. Anne Firor Scott, "What, Then, Is the American: This New Woman?" *Journal of American History* 65 (December 1978), 679–703; Anne Firor Scott, "The Ever Widening Circle: The Diffusion of Feminist Values from the Troy Female Seminary, 1822–1872," *History of Education Quarterly* 19 (Spring 1979), 3–25.

43. Linda K. Kerber, *Women of the Republic: Intellect and Ideology in Revolutionary America* (Chapel Hill: University of North Carolina Pres, 1980); Linda K. Kerber, "Daughters of Columbia: Educating Women for the Republic, 1787–1805," in *The Hofstadter Aegis: A Memorial*, ed. Stanley Elkins and Eric Mckitrick (New York: Alfred A. Knopf, 1974), 36–59. See also Mary Kelley, " 'Vindicating the Equality of Female Intellect': Women and Authority in the Early Republic," *Prospects* 17 (1992), 1–27; Nina Baym, "Between Enlightenment and Victorian: Toward a Narrative of American Women Writers Writing History," *Critical Inquiry* 18 (Autumn 1991), 22–42; Nina Baym, "Women and the Republic: Emma Willard's Rhetoric of History," *American Quarterly* 43:1 (March 1991), 1–23. Baym challenges an uncomplicated view of Willard as "a proto-liberal and a feminist foremother," arguing that "she simultaneously submerged and advanced the cause of women by placing it within the framework of national and even universal destiny"; "Women and the Republic," 18–19.

44. One example of this failure to appreciate the importance of women within New England culture and the recognition they received as exemplars of Puritan virtue is Ruth Bloch's argument that seventeenth- and eighteenth-century Puritans regarded virtue as a masculine trait. But Edwards and earlier Puritan writers often equated virtue with piety, which they regarded both as accessible to women and, in some writings, closely associated with female imagery and women's capacities for humility and suffering. See Ruth H. Bloch, "The Gendered Meanings of Virtue in Revolutionary America," *Signs: Journal of Women in Culture and Society* 13:1 (January 1987), 37–58; Jonathan Edwards, *The Nature of True Virtue* (Ann Arbor: University of Michigan Press, 1960). See also Porterfield, *Female Piety in Puritan New England*, 6–9, 153.

45. Valerie Saiving, "The Human Situation: A Feminine View," in *Womanspirit Rising: A Feminist Reader in Religion*, ed. Carol P. Christ and Judith Plaskow (New York: Harper & Row, 1979), 25–42; quotations from 37.

46. At one end of the spectrum of feminist theology, some women have given up Christianity altogether because of what they see as its systematic denial of women's power and authority. Some radical feminists have identified themselves as neopagans and called women to the spiritual power of the earth and its rhythms and affinities with their own bodies. See, for example, Mary Daly, *Pure Lust: Elemental Feminist Theology* (Boston: Beacon Press, 1984); Mary Daly, *Outercourse: The Bedazzling Voyage* (San Francisco: Harper & Row, 1992); Starhawk, *The Spiral Dance: A Rebirth of the Ancient Religion of the Great Goddess* (San Francisco: Harper & Row, 1979); Starhawk, *Truth or Dare: Encounters with Power, Authority, and Mystery* (San Francisco: Harper & Row, 1987). At the other end of the spectrum, more reform-minded feminist theologians foster inclusive language about God and women's religious leadership. See Rosemary Radford Ruether, *Sexism and God-Talk: Toward a Feminist Theology* (Boston: Beacon Press, 1983); Rebecca S. Chopp, *The Power to Speak: Feminism, Language and God* (New York: Crossroad, 1991); Sharon D. Welch, *Communities of Resistance and Solidarity: A Feminist Theology of Liberation* (Maryknoll, New York: Orbis Books, 1985); Carter Heyward, *Touching Our Strength: The Erotic as Power and the Love of God* (San Francisco: Harper & Row, 1989).

47. Jacquelyn Grant, *White Women's Christ and Black Women's Jesus: Feminist Christology and Womanist Response* (Atlanta: Scholar's Press, 1989), 212, 214. To a considerable extent, Jewish feminists have followed Christian feminists in their criticism of

theological concepts that encourage women's submissiveness. See for example, Judith Plaskow, *Standing Again at Sinai: Judaism from a Feminist Perspective* (San Francisco: Harper & Row, 1990). But Jewish feminists have also criticized Christian feminists both for the anti-Semitism involved in celebrating Christ as a feminist who represented an alternative to the misogyny of first-century Judaism, and for failing to appreciate the importance of traditional religious community for many women, especially Jewish women. See Susannah Heschel, "Anti-Judaism in Christian Feminist Theology," *Tikkun: A Bimonthly Jewish Critique of Politics, Culture, and Society* 5:3 (May/June 1990), 25–28, 95–97; Susannah Heschel, "The Feminist Confrontation with Judaism," in *Judaism in the Modern World*, ed. Alan L. Berger (New York: New York University Press, 1994).

48. For discussion of the piety and activism of late-nineteenth-century African-American women missionaries, see Evelyn Brooks Higginbotham, *Righteous Discontent: The Women's Movement in the Black Baptist Church, 1880–1920* (Cambridge: Harvard University Press, 1993).

Chapter Two

1. Mary Lyon to Hannah White, February 26, 1834, Mary Lyon Collection, Series A, Sub-series 1, Correspondence, Mount Holyoke College Archives.

2. David F. Allmendinger, "Mount Holyoke Students Encounter the Need for Life Planning, 1837–1850," *History of Education Quarterly* 19:1 (Spring 1979), 27–43. For discussion of economic and social change in this era, see Charles Sellers, *The Market Revolution: Jacksonian America, 1815–1846* (New York: Oxford University Press, 1991).

3. Kathryn Kish Sklar, "The Founding of Mount Holyoke College," in *Women of America: A History*, ed. Carol Ruth Berkin and Mary Beth Norton (Boston: Houghton Mifflin, 1979), 177–201; quotation from 181.

4. Ibid., 179–181; quotation from 181. For demographic statistics on literacy in New England, see Kenneth A. Lockridge, *Literacy in Colonial New England: An Enquiry into the Social Context of Literacy in the Early Modern West* (New York: W.W. Norton, 1974). For evidence supporting higher levels of female literacy in the eighteenth century, see Gerald F. Moran and Maris A. Vinovskis, "The Great Care of Godly Parents: Early Childhood in Puritan New England," in *Religion, Family, and the Life Course: Explorations in the Social History of Early America* (Ann Arbor: University of Michigan, 1992), 109–139. Moran and Vinovskis emphasize the importance of home schooling in New England Puritan culture.

5. Mary Lyon, *General View of the Principles and Design of the Mount Holyoke Female Seminary* (Boston: Perkins & Marvin), 1837.

6. Edward Hitchcock, *The Power of Christian Benevolence Illustrated in the Life and Labors of Mary Lyon* (Northampton: Hopkins, Bridgman, 1852), 11.

7. Joseph Emerson, quoted in Ralph Emerson, *Life of Rev. Joseph Emerson, Pastor of the Third Congregational Church in Beverly, Ms. and Subsequently Principal of a Female Seminary* (Boston: Crocker and Brewster, 1834), 248.

8. Mary Lyon to Zilpah Grant, March 1, 1833, Mary Lyon Collection, Mount Holyoke College Archives, quoted in Hitchcock, *Power of Benevolence*, 178.

9. See Allmendinger, "Mount Holyoke Students Encounter the Need for Life Planning," for statistical analysis of the family backgrounds of Mount Holyoke students.

10. Lawrence Foster, *Religion and Sexuality: The Shakers, the Mormons, and the Oneida Community* (Urbana: University of Chicago Press, 1984), 117–118; Robert S.

152 Notes

Fogarty, "Oneida: A Utopian Search for Security," *Labor History* 14 (Spring 1973), 216, 219; George Wallingford Noyes, *The Religious Experience of John Humphrey Noyes* (New York: Macmillan, 1923), 291. For discussion of women's roles in nineteenth-century religious communities, see Wendy E. Chmielewski et al., eds., *Women in Spiritual and Communitarian Societies in the United States* (Syracuse: Syracuse University Press, 1993).

11. Noyes, *Religious Experience*, 45–46, 53, 115, 291.

12. C. C. Goen, "Jonathan Edwards: A New Departure in Eschatology," *Church History* 28 (1959), 25–40; John F. Wilson, "History, Redemption, and the Millennium," in *Jonathan Edwards and the American Experience*, ed. Nathan O. Hatch and Harry S. Stout (New York: Oxford University Press, 1988), 131–141.

13. As Patricia Tracy shows, Edwards was more successful in the revival of 1735 than in the Great Awakening of 1740–41. Moreover, conflict over his authority and right to establish communal consensus plagued him throughout his tenure at Northampton and led to his ouster in 1750. See Patricia J. Tracy, *Jonathan Edwards: Pastor* (New York: Hill and Wang, 1979).

14. Mary Lyon, *Female Education. Tendencies of the Principles Embraced, and the System Adopted in the Mount Holyoke Female Seminary* (South Hadley, Mass.(?), 1839), 6–7. In her study of the seminary's early years, Lisa Drakeman noted that the concept of family was central to the organization of Mount Holyoke. See Lisa Natale Drakeman, "Seminary Sisters: Mount Holyoke's First Students, 1837–1849" (Ph.D. diss., Princeton University, 1988). Drakeman also suggested similarities between Mount Holyoke and Shaker communities.

15. Mary Lyon to Theron Baldwin, July 12, 1838, Mary Lyon Collection, Series A, Sub-series 1, Correspondence, Mount Holyoke College Archives. This letter may have been composed in part by the assistant principal, Eunice Caldwell. All subsequent correspondence cited from Mary Lyon is located in this collection and quoted with permission of Mount Holyoke College.

16. Lyon, *General View*, 4–5.

17. Lyon to Baldwin, July 12, 1838, Mary Lyon Collection.

18. Bernard Bailyn, *The Ideological Origins of the American Revolution* (Cambridge: Harvard University Press, 1967); Gordon S. Wood, *The Radicalism of the American Revolution* (New York: Alfred A. Knopf, 1992); Nathan O. Hatch, *The Democratization of American Christianity* (New Haven: Yale University Press, 1989).

19. Thomas Bender, *Community and Social Change in America* (Baltimore: Johns Hopkins University Press, 1978; reprint 1982), 2–43, quotation from 17–18.

20. Ibid., 87; see also 48–49.

21. Lyon to Baldwin, July 12, 1838, Mary Lyon Collection.

22. In 1838 Lucy Goodale demonstrated "the excellent design and arrangement" of the seminary building by drawing a floor plan of its domestic department; Elizabeth Alden Green, *Mary Lyon and Mt. Holyoke: Opening the Gates* (Hanover, N.H.: University Press of New England, 1979; reprint 1983), 183. For a contrasting interpretation of Mary Lyon's relation to modernity, and of the socioeconomic implications of Edwardsean theology, see Joseph A. Conforti, "Mary Lyon, the Founding of Mount Holyoke College, and the Cultural Revival of Jonathan Edwards," *Religion and American Culture: A Journal of Interpretation* 3:1 (Winter 1993); Mark Valeri, "The Economic Thought of Jonathan Edwards," *Church History* 60:1 (March 1991), 37–54.

23. Lyon to Baldwin, July 12, 1838, Mary Lyon Collection.

24. Quoted in Louise Porter Thomas, *Seminary Militant* (Portland, Me.: 1937), 14.

25. Mary Lyon, *Prospectus of Mount Holyoke Female Seminary* (Boston: Perkins & Marvin, 1837), 8.

26. Mary Lyon to R. C. Galbraith, June 1842, Mary Lyon Collection, Series A, Sub-series 1, Correspondence.

27. Lyon to Baldwin, July 12, 1838, Mary Lyon Collection.

28. Lyon, *Female Education*, 10–14.

29. Mary Lyon, "To the Friends and Patrons of Ipswich Female Seminary," 1834, quoted in Hitchcock, *Power of Christian Benevolence*, 187–188.

30. Mary Lyon to Miss C. E. Beecher, July 1, 1836, quoted in Hitchcock, *Power of Christian Benevolence*, 228.

31. Mary Lyon, *Mount Holyoke Female Seminary* (South Hadley, Mass.: M. Lyon, 1835). Known by the title *The character of young ladies*.

32. Lyon, *General View*, 8.

33. Ibid.

34. Nancy Everett to her uncle, South Hadley, November 26, 1837, quoted in Green, *Mary Lyon*, 176.

35. Hitchcock, *Power of Christian Benevolence*, 347; Fidelia Fiske to Mary Whitman, March 13, 1843, Fidelia Fiske Papers, Series A, Correspondence, Mount Holyoke College Archives.

36. Green, *Mary Lyon*, 37–38.

37. Green, *Mary Lyon*, 220–221.

38. Hitchcock, *Power of Christian Benevolence*, 11, 16–17.

39. Mary Lyon to Pamela Burr, August 10, 1837, Mary Lyon Collection, Series A, Sub-series 1, Correspondence.

40. Isaac Watts, *The Improvement of the Mind; or, A Supplement to the Art of Logic. Containing A Variety of Remarks and Rules for the Attainment and Communication of Useful Knowledge In Religion, in the Sciences, and in Common Life*, ed. Joseph Emerson (Baltimore: Bayly & Burns, 1832; reprint 1845), quotations from 32, 6, 12.

41. Green, *Mary Lyon*, 221; Thomas, *Seminary Militant*, 19, 28.

42. Joseph Butler, *The Analogy of Religion, Natural and Revealed to the Constitution and Course of Nature* (New York: Robert Carter, 1736; reprint 1845), 1–73.

43. Thomas, *Seminary Militant*, 20.

44. Emerson, 154. In 1818, the year he opened the Ladies Seminary in Byfield, Emerson published a series of lectures on the millennium, largely based on Jonathan Edwards's *History of the Work of Redemption*.

45. Fidelia Fiske, *Recollections of Mary Lyon, with Selections from Her Instruction to the Pupils at Mt. Holyoke Female Seminary* (Boston: American Tract Society, 1866), 93, quotation from 104. For a discussion of Lyon's relation to Edwards, to which this chapter is much indebted, see Conforti, "Mary Lyon," 69–90.

46. Mary Lyon to Hannah White, February 26, 1834; Mary Lyon to Sarah Brigham, August 25, 1834, Mary Lyon Collection, Series A, Sub-series 1, Correspondence.

47. Mary Lyon to Zilpah P. Grant, October 9, 1836; Mary Lyon, *Dear Madam* (South Hadley, Mass.: M. Lyon, 1836).

48. Hitchcock, *Power of Christian Benevolence*, 201, 311.

49. Jonathan Edwards, A *History of the Work of Redemption; Comprising an Outline of Church History* (Boston: American Tract Society, 1774; reprint n.d.), 15, 18; quotation from 22.

50. Edwards, *Work of Redemption*, 128.

51. Ibid., 474, 479.

52. See Ann Braude, *Radical Spirits: Spiritualism and Women's Rights in Nineteenth-Century America* (Boston: Beacon Press, 1989).

53. Lyon, *Dear Madam*.

Chapter Three

1. See Marcel Mauss, *The Gift: The Form and Reason for Exchange in Archaic Societies* (1925; reprint, trans. W.D. Halls, New York: W.W. Norton, 1990); Michael P. Moody, *Pass It On: Serial Reciprocity as a Principle of Philanthropy*, Essays on Philanthropy, no. 13 (Indianapolis: Indiana University Center on Philanthropy, 1994).

2. Hooker laid out his strategy for curing Joanna Drake's self-pity in *The Poor Doubting Christian Drawn Unto Christ* (London: 1629). See also Jasper Hartwell, *The Firebrand taken out of the Fire. Or, the Wonderful History, Case, and Cure of Mis Drake* (London: 1654); George Huntston Williams, "Called by the Name, Leave Us Not: The Case of Mrs. Joan Drake, a Formative Episode in the Pastoral Career of Thomas Hooker in England," *Harvard Library Bulletin* 26:2 (April 1968), 278–303. Jonathan Edwards advanced a similar line of interpretation in his concern to distinguish true signs of conversion from feelings and behaviors that could be mistaken for grace. Like Hooker, Edwards studied the conversions of particular women, and he held up his wife's effort to unmask self-love as example of evangelical humility. See Jonathan Edwards, *Some Thoughts Concerning the Present Revival of Religion in New England* (1742) in *The Great Awakening*, ed. Clarence C. Goen, vol. 4 of *The Works of Jonathan Edwards* (New Haven: Yale University Press, 1972), 331–341.

3. "Emily Dickinson to Abiah Root, 29 January, 1850," and "Emily Dickinson to Austin Dickinson, 16 November, 1851," *The Letters of Emily Dickinson*, ed. Thomas H. Johnson (2 vols.; Cambridge, Mass.: Harvard University Press, 1958), 1, 89 and 158.

4. Edward Hitchcock, ed., *The Power of Christian Benevolence Illustrated in the Life and Labors of Mary Lyon* (Northampton: Hopkins, Bridgman, 1852), 8, 11, 15; quotation from p. 15. This volume prints many letters from the *Mary Lyon Collection*, housed in the Mount Holyoke College Archives.

5. Mary Lyon to her sister Rosina, July 30, 1821; Mary Lyon to Hannah White, July 2, 1824; Mary Lyon to Eunice Caldwell, February 21, 1825; Mary Lyon to her mother, September 25, 1825; Mary Lyon to her mother, May 20, 1826, quoted in Hitchcock, *Power of Christian Benevolence*, 23, 37, 41, 45, 47.

6. Mary Lyon to her sister Freelove, August 22, 1827; Mary Lyon to Zilpah Grant, December 10, 1827, quoted in Hitchcock, *Power of Christian Benevolence*, 53–56.

7. Mary Lyon, letter to Zilpah Grant, quoted in Hitchcock, *Power of Christian Benevolence*, 131.

8. In response to Grant's objection about the low salaries she proposed, Lyon wrote: "[M]ay it not be expedient that those who first enter the field of laborer should receive as a reward so little of 'filthy lucre,' that they may be able to commend themselves to every man's conscience, even to those whose minds are narrow, and whose hearts are not much enlarged by Christian philanthropy." Mary Lyon to Zilpah Grant, May 6, 1834, quoted in Hitchcock, *Power of Christian Benevolence*, 194.

9. Mary Lyon to Zilpah Grant, February 2, 1829, December 21, 1829, and October 6, 1832; *Power of Christian Benevolence*, 68, 74, 86.

10. Mary Lyon, November 9, 1832, quoted in Hitchcock, *Power of Christian Benevolence*, 87. Edwards argued that emotional or religious excitement was not a certain sign of grace, and that the person who had grace evidenced emotional balance. See Jona-

than Edwards, *A Treatise Concerning Religious Affections* (1746), ed. John E. Smith, vol. 2 of *The Works of Jonathan Edwards* (New Haven: Yale University Press, 1959), 127–131, 365–76.

11. Teachers quoted in *Power of Christian Benevolence*, p. 89; Nancy Everett to her uncle, November 26, 1837, quoted in Elizabeth Alden Green, *Mary Lyon and Mount Holyoke: Opening the Gates* (Hanover, N.H.: University Press of New England, 1979; reprint 1983), 176.

12. Hitchcock, *Power of Christian Benevolence*, 203; Mary Lyon to Zilpah Grant, March 8, 1841; Mary Lyon to Mrs. Miron Winslow, quoted in Hitchcock, *Power of Christian Benevolence*, 394, 412–413.

13. Quotations from Hitchcock, *Power of Christian Benevolence*, 424–425; Rebecca Fiske to Fidelia Fiske, March 5, 1849, cited in Green, *Mary Lyon*, 310; and Fidelia Fiske, Mount Holyoke Journal Letters, letter of March 9, 1849.

14. James D. Knowles, *Memoir of Ann H. Judson, Missionary to Burmah* (Boston: Gould, Kendall, and Lincoln, 1850), 42–43; Ralph Emerson, *Life of Rev. Joseph Emerson, Pastor of the Third Congregational Church in Beverly, Ms. and Subsequently Principal of a Female Seminary* (Boston: Crocker and Brewster, 1834).

15. Knowles, *Memoir*, 44–45. For discussion of the ironic tendency in the Puritan tradition to which Hasseltine and Lyon were heir, see Sacvan Bercovitch, *The Puritan Origins of the American Self* (New Haven: Yale University Press, 1975).

16. Knowles, *Memoir*, 162–163.

17. Lydia Maria Child, *Good Wives* (Boston: 1833), 246; Joan Jacobs Brumberg, *Mission for Life: The Story of the Family of Adoniram Judson, the Dramatic Events of the First American Foreign Mission, and the Course of Evangelical Religion in the Nineteenth Century* (New York: Free Press, 1980), 15–16.

18. Knowles, *Memoir*, 23. Nancy Hasseltine was born and raised in the Congregational Church, but followed her husband in joining a Baptist church in Calcutta. When news of the Judsons' rejection of infant baptism and their withdrawal from the Congregationalist-dominated American Board reached New England in 1812, members of the fledgling board, which Adoniram had helped to found, reacted with astonishment and anger.

19. Nancy Judson, quoted in Knowles, *Memoir*, 180.

20. See "The Martyrdom of Perpetua," trans. Rosemary Rader, in *A Lost Tradition: Women Writers of the Early Church*, eds. Patricia Wilson-Kastner et al. (Washington, D.C.: University Press of America, 1981).

21. Caroline Walker Bynum, *Holy Feast and Holy Fast: The Religious Significance of Food to Medieval Women* (Berkeley: University of California Press, 1987), quotation from 155.

22. Anne Bradstreet, "Meditations Diuine and morall," meditation no. 38, in *The Complete Works of Anne Bradstreet*, ed. Joseph R. McElrath, Jr., and Alan P. Robb (Boston: Twayne, 1981), 200; see also Amanda Porterfield, *Female Piety in Puritan New England: The Emergence of Religious Humanism* (New York: Oxford University Press, 1992), especially 124–127.

23. Mary Rowlandson, "Narrative of the Captivity of Mrs. Mary Rowlandson" (1682), in *Narratives of the Indian Wars, 1675–1699*, ed. Charles H. Lincoln (1913; reprint, New York: Barnes & Noble, 1966), 107–299; see also Mitchell Robert Breitwieser, *American Puritanism and the Defense of Mourning: Religion, Grief, and Ethnology in Mary White Rowlandson's Captivity Narrative* (Madison: University of Wisconsin Press, 1990).

24. For discussions of the antebellum novel, see Herbert Ross Brown, *The Sentimental Novel in America, 1789–1860* (1940; New York: Octagon, 1975); Helen Papashvily, *All the Happy Endings* (New York: Harper & Row, 1956). Mary Lyon regretted the influence of novels, which she thought of as trash, on the minds of women.

25. Knowles, *Memoir*, 180–181.

26. Knowles, *Memoir*, 36.

27. "Oh that my soul were *holy, as he is holy!*" Brainerd wrote in February 1744, as he struggled to demonstrate the Christian gospel to Native Americans in Kaunaumeek, west of Stockbridge. "O methinks I could bear any sufferings; but how can I bear to grieve and dishonour this blessed God." Brainerd longed to "give up myself to him, so as never more to attempt to be my own, or to have any will or affections that are not perfectly conformed to him!" Jonathan Edwards, *Memoirs of the Rev. David Brainerd; Missionary to the Indians on the Borders of New-York, New-Jersey, and Pennsylvania: Chiefly Taken from his own Diary,* ed. Sereno Edwards Dwight (New Haven: S. Converse, 1822), 29, 135. See also Edwards, *Religious Affections,* 376–383.

28. Edwards, *Memoirs of Brainerd,* 30–31.

29. Knowles, *Memoir,* 16–19, 29–31.

30. Lucy Lyon, Mount Holyoke Journal Letters, letter of July 13, 1843.

31. Fidelia Fiske to Abigail Moore, July 19, 1843, Fidelia Fiske Papers, Series A, Correspondence, Mount Holyoke College Archives; see also Louise Porter Thomas, *Seminary Militant* (Portland, Me.: 1937), 31–32.

32. Mary Lyon to Mrs. Banister, March 8, 1843, quoted in Hitchcock, *Power of Christian Benevolence,* 339.

33. Mary Lyon to Mrs. Banister, March 20, 1843, quoted in Hitchcock, *Power of Christian Benevolence,* 341.

34. Mount Holyoke Journal Letters, letter of February 27–August 7, 1843, p. 2.

35. In the fall of 1847, when Emily Dickinson entered Mount Holyoke, this organizational plan was well established. See Mount Holyoke Journal Letters, letter of October 2, 1847; see also Jay Leyda, ed., *The Years and Hours of Emily Dickinson* (New Haven: Yale University Press, 1960), 1:123.

36. Mary Lyon to Mrs. Banister, March 20, 1843, quoted in Hitchcock, *Power of Christian Benevolence,* 342.

37. Lydia Pomeroy to her mother, March 30, 1843, quoted in Green, *Mary Lyon,* 245.

38. Fidelia Fiske quoted in Thomas, *Seminary Militant,* 31; Mary Lyon, quoted in Green, *Mary Lyon,* 262.

39. R. Pierce Beaver, *All Loves Excelling: American Protestant Women in World Mission* (Grand Rapids, Mich.: William B. Eerdmans, 1968).

40. Fidelia Fiske to Abigail Moore, March 21, 1843, Fidelia Fiske Papers, Series A, Correspondence.

41. Mount Holyoke Journal Letters, 1843–1891, No. 4, March 2, 1844, 3. In January 1847 the seminary began to receive copies of the *Missionary Herald* by express mail, as soon as it came off the press.

42. Mount Holyoke Journal Letters, letter of August 4, 1843.

43. Mary Lyon, quoted in Green, *Mary Lyon,* 252.

44. Mary Lyon, quoted in Green, *Mary Lyon,* 254.

45. Susan Tolman, Mount Holyoke Journal Letters, letter of February 2, 1846.

46. Lucy Lyon, Mount Holyoke Journal Letters, letters of August 28, 1843, July 22, 1844, May 18, 1845, July 23, 1845.

47. Lucy Lyon, Mount Holyoke Journal Letters, June 7, 1843, 5.

48. Lucy Lyon, Mount Holyoke Journal Letters, letter of March 13, 1844, and Susan Tolman, Mount Holyoke Journal Letters, letter of November 18, 1846.

49. Nancy Judson, quoted in Knowles, *Memoir*, 78.

50. For discussion of the centrality of this imagery about other women for later American women missionaries, see Joan Jacobs Brumberg, "The Ethnological Mirror: American Evangelical Women and Their Heathen Sisters, 1870–1910," in *Women and the Structure of Society: Selected Research from the Fifth Berkshire Conference on the History of Women*, ed. Barbara J. Harris and JoAnn K. McNamara (Durham: Duke University Press, 1984), 108–128; see also Leslie A. Fleming, "A New Humanity: American Missionaries' Ideals for Women in North India, 1870–1930," in *Western Women and Imperialism: Complicity and Resistance*, ed. Nupur Chaudhuri and Margaret Strobel (Bloomington: Indiana University Press, 1992), 191–206; Barbara Fassler, "The Role of Women in the India Mission, 1819–1880," in *Piety and Patriotism: Bicentennial Studies of the Reformed Church in America, 1776–1976*, ed. James W. Van Hoeven (Grand Rapids, Mich.: William B. Eerdmans, 1976), 149–191.

Chapter Four

1. Fidelia Fiske to Abigail Moore, July 19, 1843, Fidelia Fiske Papers, Series A, Correspondence, Mount Holyoke College Archives. "The Holyoke of Oroomiah," Fiske wrote just six weeks after her arrival, "breathes not yet. But I hope that bone is coming to bone, and that these dry bones will soon be covered with flesh."

2. Thomas Laurie, *Woman and Her Savior in Persia* (Boston: Gould and Lincoln, 1863), 223–224. Laurie's *Woman and the Gospel in Persia* (Chicago: Women's Presbyterian Board of Missions of the Northwest, 1887) is, to a large extent, an abridgment of the former volume. Also see Fidelia Fiske Biographical File and Notes by Anna Edwards, "The Nestorians (Account of F. Fiske and Fiske Sem)," Mount Holyoke College Archives.

3. Fidelia Fiske to Mary Whitman, March 13, 1843, Fidelia Fiske Papers, Series A, Correspondence.

4. See Justin Perkins, *A Residence of Eight Years in Persia, Among the Nestorian Christians; with Notices of the Muhammedans* (Andover, Mass.: Allen, Morrill & Wardwell, 1843), 172–176.

5. Laurie, *Woman and Her Savior*, 57; Laurie, *Woman and the Gospel*, 12.

6. Laurie, *Woman and the Gospel*, 51–52.

7. Ibid., 58, 68.

8. Fidelia Fiske to Abigail Moore, July 19, 1843, Fidelia Fiske Papers, Series A, correspondence; Laurie, *Woman and Her Savior*, 65, 69.

9. Lucy Lyon, Mount Holyoke Journal Letters, Letter of August 18, 1845, Mount Holyoke College Archives.

10. Quoted in Laurie, *Woman and Her Savior*, 69–70.

11. Perkins, *Residence in Persia*, 234–41; quotation from 235. Lucy Lyon also recalled the story about Americans being married on railroads in a letter to Fidelia Fiske: Mount Holyoke Journal Letters, Letter of October 24, 1845.

12. Quoted in Laurie, *Woman and Her Savior*, 291.

13. When pressed by the missionaries to account for the habit of prevarication in their daughters, Nestorian parents pointed to the prevalence of lying in their culture, which they explained was the only way Nestorians could succeed in business. Laurie, *Woman and Her Savior*, 61.

14. Quoted in Laurie, *Woman and Her Savior*, 120–121.

15. "Letter from Mr. Stocking, March 3, 1850," *Missionary Herald* 46 (1850), 241.

16. "Mr. Stocking's Report on Fisk's School in Oroomiah, February 21, 1845," *Missionary Herald* 41 (1845), 232–233.

17. Fidelia Fiske, quoted in Laurie, *Woman and Her Savior*, 64.

18. Quoted in Laurie, *Woman and Her Savior*, 224.

19. John Joseph, *The Nestorians and Their Muslim Neighbors: A Study of Western Influence on Their Relations* (Princeton: Princeton University Press, 1961), 71–73.

20. Student compositions and letters are published in Laurie, *Woman and Her Savior*; for reference to the flow of literary expression after the revival of 1846, see p. 244. For students who came to the seminary from the mountain villages, where a different dialect of Aramaic, influenced by Kurdish, was spoken, the work of learning to read in the Urmiyah dialect must have contributed to the initial difficulty of writing. See Joseph, *Nestorians*, 75.

21. Asahel Grant, quoted in Joseph, *Nestorians*, 65.

22. Joseph, *Nestorians*, 115–122.

23. Quoted in Laurie, *Woman and Her Savior*, 248–251.

24. Perkins, *Residence in Persia*, 20.

25. Quotation from Laurie, *Woman and Her Savior*, 162, 165; George Stocking, Letter from Persia, Autumn 1851, in *Missionary Herald* 48 (1852), 70; and Laurie, *Woman and Her Savior*, 271.

26. Joseph, *Nestorians*, 1–39, quotation from 23–24.

27. See E. A. Livingstone, ed., *The Concise Oxford Dictionary of the Christian Church* (New York: Oxford University Press, 1977), 354–355, 510, 258, 104. The name *Nestorian* was not always embraced by the people it identified. Justin Perkins reports a conversation with the bishop Mar Yohanan, who "objected to my calling him and his people *Nestorians*. I asked him what I should call them, and he answered, *Chaldeans*." When Perkins queried Yohanan about the usage of Chaldean to refer to Nestorians converted to Roman Catholicism, the bishop replied, "[S]hall a few Catholic converts from our people arrogate to themselves the name of the whole nation?" Perkins went on to note other names for the Nestorians, commonly translated as *Syrian* and *Assyrian*: "The people usually call themselves, *Syrianee*, and less often, *Nuzranee*, for the purpose of designating both their religion and their nation." Perkins, *Residence in Persia*, 175.

28. Joseph, *Nestorians*, 1–39, especially 23–24. See also Julius Richter, *A History of Protestant Missions in the Near East* (New York: AMS Press, 1910), 279–317.

29. Eli Smith and H. G. O. Dwight, quoted in Perkins, *Residence in Persia*, 26–27. See also Robert E. Speer and Russell Carter, *Report on India and Persia of the Deputation sent by the Board of Foreign Missions of the Presbyterian Church in the U.S.A. To Visit These Fields in 1921–1922* (New York: Presbyterian Missions Board, 1922), 315–576; Richter, *Protestant Missions in the Near East*, 294–317; P. E. Shaw, *American Contacts with the Eastern Churches, 1820–1870* (Chicago: American Society of Church History, 1937), 71–108. The biggest threat the first American missionaries perceived was the threat of a resurgence of Roman Catholic missions to the Nestorians. "Had we not come to their rescue," wrote Justin Perkins (22), "the incessant working of the artful machinations of the Jesuit emissaries . . . would, in time, have gradually obliterated the Nestorians and transferred the last man of them to the Romish standard." Perkins's concern about the incursions of Rome so impressed Mary Lyon that, as Lucy Lyon wrote Fidelia Fiske, "The senior class have all been writing on Popery for the last two months. . . . Miss Lyon was chiefly induced to give them this subject from a suggestion of Mr. Perkins last year." Mount Holyoke Journal Letters, letter of October 24, 1845.

30. Joseph, *Nestorians*, 63–67.

31. Richard Merrill Schwartz, *The Structure of Christian-Muslim Relations in Contemporary Iran*, Occasional Papers in Anthropology, no. 13 (Halifax, Nova Scotia: Saint Mary's University, 1985), 41–55; also see Laurie, *Woman and Her Savior*, 14. In Schwartz's argument, American influence actually created tension between previously peaceful Muslims and Christian Nestorians. But the writings of missionaries, which Schwartz does not reference, describe tensions already in place. For example, Schwartz does not mention Kurdish raids before 1843. But Fidelia Fiske, who arrived in Urmiyah in 1843, reported in the summer of 1835, "the Koords overran Gawar, taking from the poor people their flocks, burning, in some villages, almost every house, and reducing the people to great extremities." Missionaries of the A.B.C.F.M., *Nestorian Biography: Being Sketches of Pious Nestorians, Who Have Died at Oroomiah, Persia* (Boston: Massachusetts Sabbath School Society, 1857), 27.

32. Schwartz, *Structure of Christian-Muslim Relations*, 77–78.

33. Laurie, *Woman and Her Savior*, 18–19.

34. Schwartz, *Structure of Christian-Muslim Relations*, 50; see also 77–80.

35. Ibid., 17–19.

36. Fidelia Fiske, quoted in Laurie, *Woman and Her Savior*, 20–21. See also *Nestorian Biography*, 25–26.

37. Tajol-Saltaneh, quoted in Sima Bahar, "A Historical Background to the Women's Movement in Iran," in *Women of Iran: The Conflict with Fundamentalist Islam*, ed. Farah Azari (London: Ithaca Press, 1983), 171.

38. See Schwartz, *Structure of Christian-Muslim Relations*, 77–80.

39. Abraham Yelelson, *United States–Persian Diplomatic Relations, 1883–1921* (New Brunswick: Rutgers University Press, 1956), especially 23–26.

40. Joseph, *Nestorians*, 127–37.

41. Joseph L. Grabill, *Protestant Diplomacy and the Near East: Missionary Influence on American Policy, 1810–1927* (Minneapolis: University of Minnesota Press, 1971), 135–185, 292–293.

42. Robert E. Speer, "The Need and Destitution of Persia," in Speer and Carter, *Report on India and Persia*, 371.

Chapter Five

1. Keshari N. Sahay, "The Christian Movement in India: A Historical Perspective," in *Christianity and Social Change in India* (New Delhi: Inter-India Publications, 1986), 15–52, especially 15–20; quotation from 15.

2. Ibid., quotation from 20.

3. *Minutes of the General Meeting of the American Missionaries of the Bombay Presidency, Held at Ahmednuggur, December, 1854* (Bombay: American Mission Press, 1855), 56. A second group of American Board missionaries arrived in Ceylon in 1816, and their station became a base for the establishment of a mission in Madura in 1835.

4. Clifton Jackson Phillips, *Protestant America and the Pagan World: The First Half Century of the American Board of Commissioners for Foreign Missions, 1810–1860* (Cambridge: Harvard University Press, 1969), 32–56; *Memorial Papers of the American Marathi Mission, 1813–1881* (Bombay: Education Society's Press, 1882), ix–xi (hereafter cited as *Memorial Papers of the AMM*); R.V. Modak, "History of the Native Churches Connected with the Marathi Mission, and Especially Those in the Ahmednagar Districts, for the Last Fifty Years," *Memorial Papers of the AMM*, 11; quotation from *Minutes of the General Meeting*, 57. The Bombay and Ahmadnagar missions separated in 1841, and then rejoined as one mission in 1860.

5. Charles H. Heimsath, *Indian Nationalism and Hindu Social Reform* (Princeton: Princeton University Press, 1964), 51–53; quotations from 53.

6. Quoted in Heimsath, *Indian Nationalism*, 52.

7. William Hazen, *A Century in India: A Historical Sketch of the Marathi Mission of the American Board of Commissioners for Foreign Missions From 1813 to 1913* (Bombay: American Marathi Mission, 1913), 1–5; quotations from "Harriet Newell's Religious Concerns and Call to Serve," Letters and Papers of the American Board of Commissioners for Foreign Missions, Houghton Library (hereafter cited as Letters and Papers of the ABCFM).

8. The eclectic culture and multiethnic population of Maharashtra was an important factor in this accommodationism. In Bombay, forty different languages were spoken at mid-century; enclaves of Arabs, Egyptians, Jews, and Iranians had long existed in the Koncan; and trade with the Dutch and Portuguese had existed for centuries. Although not so cosmopolitan, the western part of Maharashtra was also ethnically complex. In ancient times this western part, known as the Desha or Deccan, was colonized by peoples of different cultures and complexions. Migrations from the north, south, and east continued, while a distinctive culture developed around two sources of Maharashtra identity and pride, military prowess and religious devotion.

9. Abby Allen, x-Class of 1845, Biographical File, Mount Holyoke College Archives; *Missionary Herald* 49 (1853), 23–24.

10. Samuel B. Fairbank to Mrs. Bowen, Bombay, August 25, 1852, Letters and Papers of the ABCFM, Houghton Library.

11. Abigail Burgess to Samuel Fairbank, Satara, August 23, 1853, Letters and Papers of the ABCFM. Samuel Fairbank to Mr. Kimball, August 25, 1952, Abby Allen, x-Class of 1845, Correspondence. Fairbank to Bowen, Bombay, August 25, 1852, Letters and Papers of the ABCFM.

12. Caroline Healey Dall, *The Life of Dr. Anandabai Joshee, A Kinswoman of Pundita Ramabai* (Boston: Roberts Brothers, 1888), 64–69.

13. Fairbank to Bowen, Bombay, August 25, 1852, Letters and Papers of the ABCFM.

14. George Bowen, quoted in ibid. Haripunt was an honorific name designating Hari's role as teacher.

15. Jonathan Edwards, "A Dissertation Concerning the End for which God Created the World," *Works of President Edwards*, ed. Sereno E. Dwight (New York: S. Converse, 1829–1830), 3:82–84; Jonathan Edwards, *A Treatise Concerning Religious Affections* (1746), ed. John E. Smith, vol. 2 of *The Works of Jonathan Edwards* (New Haven: Yale University Press, 1959), 191–461.

16. Along with a few other liberal intellectuals in America in the 1840s, Emerson was attracted to Hinduism and Buddhism, and found encouragements for his own idealism in what he read about them. But his understanding was not always accurate; he wrongly identified the Bhagavad Gita, for example, as a "much renowned book of Buddhism." Quoted in Thomas A. Tweed, *The American Encounter with Buddhism, 1844–1912: Victorian Culture and the Limits of Dissent* (Bloomington: Indiana University Press, 1992), xviii.

17. George Bowen, quoted in Speer, *George Bowen*, 56. See also 44.

18. The Mundaka Upanishad portrays *Brahman* as an imperishable flame from which all reality derives: "[A]s from a fire, blazing, sparks like fire issue forth by the thousands, so many kinds of beings issue forth from the imperishable and they return to it. . . . From him are born life, breath and mind, all the sense organs, also space, air, light, water and earth, the support of all. Fire is his head, his eyes are the sun and the moon, the regions are his ears, the revealed *Vedas* are his speech, air is his life

breath and his heart is the universe. Out of his feet the earth is born, indeed he is the soul of all beings." Quoted in Klaus K. Klostermaier, A *Survey of Hinduism* (Albany: State University of New York Press, 1989), 200.

19. For example, there were gurus and saints who worshiped and identified with the mother goddess Devi, or Shakti, and represented her to their followers through their own presence and influence. Further discussion of worshipers of the mother goddess Devi, or Shakti, in Maharashtra follows later. See also Klostermaier, *Survey of Hinduism*, 272–276.

20. Quoted in Klostermaier, *Survey of Hinduism*, 20.

21. George Bowen, quoted in Speer, *George Bowen*, ix, 161; also see 149–193. In a less hostile atmosphere, he sat on the beach in Bombay for ten weeks or more in the winter of 1849, "where the Parsees assemble to worship the sea and the setting sun," accompanied by a Brahman converted to the Scotch Free Church, who joined him in debating representatives of various non-Christian religions. A Parsee teacher was the principal combatant, but he was joined "occasionally" by Hindu, Muslim, and Jewish "interlocutors." These beach debates drew as many as two hundred auditors, who listened, standing around the debaters, "till 2 hours after dark." "On one occasion," Bowen reported in a letter to the American Board in Boston, "a Roman Catholic priest participated. Thomas Paine has also acted a considerable part, along with Voltaire and other infidel writers, with whose works or arguments the educated Parsees and Hindoos are surprisingly familiar." "Letter from Mr. Bowen, written December 15, 1949," *Missionary Herald* 46 (1850), 176–177.

22. S. B. Fairbank, "A Historical Sketch of the Evangelistic Work Done By the Ahmednagar Branch of the Marathi Mission of the ABCFM in the Half Century, Closing with this Year of 1881," *Memorial Papers of the AMM*, 50.

23. *Dynanodya* 4:12 (June 16; 1845); *Dynanodya* 2:10 (October 1843); *Dynanodya* 3:8 (August 1844).

24. Royal Wilder quoted in Henry Ballantine, "Report of the Ahmednagar station for 1847," Letters and Papers of the ABCFM; "Letter from Mr. Wilder, February 12, 1848," *Missionary Herald* 44 (1848), 233; Henry Ballantine, "Annual Report from the Ahmednagar Mission for 1848," *Missionary Herald* 45 (1849), 267.

25. "Letter from Mr. Hazen, September 24, 1953," *Missionary Herald* 50 (1854), 28.

26. *Missionary Herald* 45 (1849), 176.

27. Anandabai Joshee, quoted in Dall, *Life of Dr. Anandabai Joshee*, 51.

28. Henry J. Bruce, "The Literary Work of the American Marathi Mission, 1813–1881," *Memorial Papers of the AMM*, 118; Julia Ballantine Greenwood, *Rev. Henry Ballantine: In Memorium*, Letters and Papers of the ABCFM, 12. See also R. V. Modak's *Sermon on the Death of Mrs. E. D. Ballantine* (Bombay: Bombay Tract Society, 1874).

29. *Missionary Herald* 38 (1842), 460; "Letter from Henry Ballantine, August 23, 1842," *Missionary Herald* 39 (1843), 20–21.

30. "Letter from Mrs. Wilder," *Dayspring* (June 1857), reprinted in Royal G. Wilder, *Mission Schools in India of the American Board of Commissioners for Foreign Missions* (New York: A. D. F. Randolph, 1861), 253–256.

31. List of Mount Holyoke Missionaries Who Went to India from the Classes of 1838 to 1935, Mount Holyoke College, Missions/Missionaries File: India, Mount Holyoke College Archives; *One Hundred Year Biographical Directory* (South Hadley: Alumnae Association of Mount Holyoke College, 1937); *Memorial Papers of the AMM*, ix–xi; Charlotte Dennett Staelin, "The Influence of Missions on Women's Education in India: The American Marathi Mission in Ahmadnagar, 1830–1930" (Ph.D. diss., University of Michigan, 1977), 283.

32. Lyon had funded Moore's schooling in Ipswich before Mount Holyoke was founded, and chose her to be one of three teaching assistants during Mount Holyoke's first year of operation. In 1838 Moore became a full-time teacher at Mount Holyoke, instructing a range of classes in history, botany, logic, physics, and French. In 1842 she assumed additional administrative duties as assistant principal, and was highly respected for her organizational competence. See Elizabeth Alden Green, *Mary Lyon and Mount Holyoke: Opening the Gates* (Hanover, N.H. : University Press of New England, 1979), 98.

33. Henry Ballantine, "Death of Mrs. Burgess," *Missionary Herald* 49 (1853), 252; "Report from Ahmednuggur," *Missionary Herald* 47 (1851), 269; "Letter from Ebenezer Burgess, February 14, 1852," *Missionary Herald* 48 (1852), 156; Abigail Moore Papers, series C, Biographical Material, Mount Holyoke College Archives. By William's account, the death of his own wife, Lucy, had a significant effect on the women of Satara: " 'And who will now teach us?' said the women who came to look upon the face of Mrs. Wood, cold in death." But "God sent them another teacher," William added, in reference to Abby Burgess. After Lucy died in Satara in 1851, Abby treated William and his children as her own family and assumed responsibility for the girls' schools that Lucy had supervised. Abby worked with girls and women in Satara, and often "visited them in their homes." William Wood, "Death of Mrs. Burgess, May 4, 1853," *Missionary Herald*, 49 (1853), 251.

34. In 1857 Farrar addressed Banister as "My dear very dear Mrs. Banister" in a letter acknowledging her "influence" and "example." Cynthia Farrar to Mrs. Banister, January 30, 1857, Zilpah P. Grant Banister Papers, Series A, Sub-series 2, Correspondence, Mount Holyoke College Archives; Lemuel Bissell, "History of the Educational Operations of the American Marathi Mission from its Commencement to 1881," *Memorial Papers of the ABCFM*, 62.

35. Sarah Hume, quoted in Staelin, "Influence of Missions on Women's Education in India," 78–79; "Report from Henry Ballantine and Allen Hazen," *Missionary Herald*, 49 (1853), 173.

36. Lemuel Bissell, "History of the Educational Operations of the American Marathi Mission," 64–65; Hollis Read, "The American Mission," *Memorial Papers of the AMM*, 8; Staelin, "Influence of Missions on Women's Education in India," 45. Abby Burgess took charge in 1849 when Ballantine visited the United States. Ballantine resumed her position in 1852 and remained until 1865, when Martha Hazen, previously second in command, took over.

37. Read, "The American Mission," 8; "Letter from Mr. Munger, October 15, 1839," *Missionary Herald* 36 (1840), 275.

38. "Letter from Robert Hume, Bombay, June 25, 1850," *Missionary Herald* 46 (1850), 369–370; "Report from Ahmednuggur," 269–270; "Report from Mr. Hume in Bombay, May 19, 1854," *Missionary Herald* 50 (1854), 275.

39. Modak, "History of the Native Churches," 11.

40. Modak, "History of the Native Churches," 36–37. Hari had come from Satara to teach the Hindu girls under Elizabeth Ballantine's supervision. When he become involved in the conversion process, he had difficulty convincing his mother that this involvement was appropriate. When he told her that the Hindu gods were not gods, and "should not be worshiped," his mother responded by "abus[ing] him." As a result "he had no pleasure in going home, for he could find no peace while there." His brother Narayan stepped into the dispute by abducting Hari's wife, Radhabai, who still lived with her mother-in-law according to Hindu custom. But when Radhabai arrived in Ahmadnagar, she insisted on living apart from Hari and cooking her own meals,

informing him that she wished to keep her caste. When a British magistrate intervened and asked her whether she wanted to return to her mother-in-law, she responded by saying, "I do not wish to leave my husband and go away." She defended herself to her mother-in-law by explaining, "I intended to say that I wished to go to my mother-in-law and live, but how the contrary answer came out of my mouth, I do not know. I am sorry for it. What shall I do?" After the magistrate determined that it was too late to change her mind again, Radhabai eventually became more confident in following the path her husband had taken. She was baptized in 1841, and she was still living in 1881, after Hari's death, doing "Bible woman's work" in Bombay. Modak, "History of the Native Churches," 28–29.

When Hari went through the process of conversion, Narayan became preoccupied with the question of whether Hinduism was true, and he determined, presumably under missionary guidance, that there was no evidence in its favor. But Narayan's wife took his mother's part, hiding her eight-year-old son before the magistrate could deliver him to his father, and declaring that "she would give him nothing to eat, unless he performed idol worship." "Report from Henry Ballantine," *Missionary Herald* 36 (1840), 263–273.

41. "Letter from Royal Wilder, February 11, 1850," *Missionary Herald* 46 (1850), 275–279. In another incident in 1853, Vishnupunt Bhaskar Karmarkar, a teacher from Poona brought to Ahmadnagar to teach at a Hindu girl's school, was in the process of converting to Christianity when his mother tried to bring him home with the device of a message saying she was sick and dying. Anticipating an ambush but not wishing to deny his mother's wish, Vishnupunt brought along two missionaries and two native Christians, who stationed themselves at the back door of the house with a cart. After Vishnupunt's male relatives "started beating" them, the Christians escaped and alerted the British, who warned the mother that she would be committing a civil offense if she attempted to "carry . . . off" her son. Modak, "History of the Native Churches," 28–30, 36.

42. Staelin, "Influence of Missions on Women's Education in India," 141, 232, 265, 268, 140; quotations from 268 and 140.

43. Henry Ballantine to Rufus Anderson, Ahmednagar, November 9, 1848, Letters and Papers of the ABCFM.

44. In numerous writings and speeches, Royal Wilder claimed that Anderson had manipulated this major revision in the Marathi mission policy against the will of the missionaries in the field. And it is true that in the minutes of the meetings between the deputation and the missionaries, reports on various aspects of missionary policy were rejected until they coincided with board policy. But in response to Wilder's claims, several missionaries denied that they were coerced against their wills. Thus Henry Ballantine wrote, "While we have often been blamed by others for having yielded our views to the Deputation, we have always thought that we were right in yielding to what appeared to us to be right views and sound common sense." Henry Ballantine to Dr. Wallace, Ahmednagar, February 18, 1862, Case of the Rev. Royal G. Wilder of India, Letters and Papers of the ABCFM. See also Wilder, *Mission Schools in India*; *Minutes of the General Meeting*.

45. William R. Hutchison, *Errand to the World: American Protestant Thought and Foreign Missions* (Chicago: University of Chicago Press, 1987), 77–90.

46. Rufus Anderson, *An Address, Delivered in South Hadley, Mass., July 24, 1839, at the Second Anniversary of the Mount Holyoke Female Seminary* (Boston: Perkins & Marvin, 1839), 6.

47. In Anderson's words, "On no part of the missionary operations in Bombay did the blessing of God seem to rest so much as upon Mrs. Hume's boarding school for

girls." Anderson noted that eleven of her students had been baptized, "several of whom were in stations of usefulness." Quoted in Bissell, "History of the Educational Operations of the AMM," 67.

48. Cynthia Farrar to Mrs. Anderson, December 29, 1854, Letters and Papers of the ABCFM.

49. In a note to him while they were both in Ahmadnagar, Jane Wilder wrote, "I will call for you at the usual time for a drive." Eliza J. Wilder to Rufus Anderson, December 26, 1854, Letters and Papers of the ABCFM. On January 25, 1855, the deputation wrote Royal Wilder that a "concession" had been made for the continuation of girls' schools in Kolhapur, "reluctantly granted by Dr. Anderson to the earnestly expressed wishes of Mrs. Wilder." The concession was granted "for an indefinite period," and it was also understood that "as a matter of Mission policy, schools for girls should not be maintained in India without maintaining at the same time schools for boys." Case of the Rev. Royal G. Wilder of India, Letters and Papers of the ABCFM, sealed documents consulted and quoted by permission of United Church of Christ headquarters, Cincinnati. See also Rufus Anderson to Hon. William Strong, December 20, 1862, Letters and Papers of the ABCFM.

50. "Report on the Case of the Rev. R. G. Wilder," Henry Ballantine to Royal G. Wilder, May 26, 1859, Sendol Munger to Rufus Anderson, January 22, 1857, all in Case of the Rev. Royal G. Wilder, Letters and Papers of the ABCFM.

51. "Report from John Aiken, Linus Child, Henry Hill, Boston, January 31, 1860," Case of the Rev. Royal G. Wilder, Letters and Papers of the ABCFM.

52. Royal G. Wilder, "Deterioration of Missionaries: Executive Domination," the *Missionary Review* 6(1883), 261–266, preserved in Case of the Rev. Royal G. Wilder, Letters and Papers of the ABCFM.

53. Copied extract of letter from Allen Hazen, July 26, 1883, Case of the Rev. Royal G. Wilder, Letters and Papers of the ABCFM. Hazen's letter was written after Wilder published a book attacking the policies of the American Board, and seems to have been preserved for the purpose of casting discredit on Wilder's character.

54. Samuel Fairbank to Rev. G. W. Wood, D.D., Ahmednuggur, February 22, 1862, Case of the Rev. Royal G. Wilder, Letters and Papers of the ABCFM. See also Wilder, *Mission Schools in India.*

55. Hanry Ballantine, "Death of Mrs. Burgess," 251–252; William Wood, quoted in Green, *Mary Lyon,* 382 n.1.

56. Wood, quoted in "Death of Mrs. Burgess."

57. This missionary withdrawal from women's education coincided both with increasing interest among Hindus in promoting it, and with the British government's Educational Despatch of 1854, which gave official support to the education of girls as a principal means of improving human welfare.

58. Sushil Madhava Pathak, *American Missionaries and Hinduism: A Study of Their Contacts from 1813 to 1910* (Delhi: Munshiram Monoharlal, 1967), 61.

59. Heimsath, *Indian Nationalism,* 47–48.

60. Quotations from "an Elpinstone Scholar" in "Discussions in Bombay" in *Dyanodaya* 2:4 (April 1843); from Krishna Shastree in "Discussions in Bombay," *Dyanodaya* 3:11 (November 1844); and from Pestonjee Manockjee in "Discussion of Christian Scriptures," *Dyanodaya* 4:21 (November 1845).

61. Henry J. Bruce, "Literary Work of the American Marathi Mission," 107–108. (The most important articles were printed in English and Marathi until 1867, when English was dropped.)

62. *Dynanodya* 3:6 (June 1844) and 4:5 (March 1845).

63. Modak, "History of the Native Churches," 27.

64. Ibid., 35.

65. According to the *Dynanodya*, this sect was popular both in the Koncan and in the Deccan. "Secret Religious Societies Among Hindus," *Dynanodya* 2:8 (August 1843); Klostermaier, *Survey of Hinduism*, 261.

66. Ann Grodzins Gold, written communication, March 1994, Syracuse, New York.

67. Hazen, *Century in India*, 37; also see *Memorial Papers of the AMM*, 36; and Henry Ballantine, "Report of the Ahmednagar Mission for 1844," January 28, 1845, Letters and Papers of the ABCFM

68. Henry Ballantine, "Mr. Ballantine's Tour Among the Mahars," *Missionary Herald* 39 (1843), 265.

69. Hazen, *Century in India*, 37.

70. *Minutes of the General Meeting*, 74; Datoo Vaman Potdar, "Mind of Maharashtra," *Journal of the University of Poona* 9 (1958), 57–64, especially 61; C. A. Kincaid and Rao Bahadur D. B. Parasnis, *A History of the Maratha People* (Delhi: S. Chand, 1968), 105–108.

Although Mahatma Ghandi was born in Gujarat, he lived in Maharashtra during some of his life, and he is recognized by M. P. Mangudkar as an exemplar of "Liberal Thought in Maharashtra," *Journal of the University of Poona* 9 (1958), 77–86, especially 80–81.

71. Kincaid and Parasnis, *History of the Maratha People*, 103–108.

72. Henry Ballantine, "Report of the Ahmednagar Station for 1847," April 12, 1848, Letters and Papers of the ABCFM.

73. Govind Sakharam Sardesai, "Maharashtra Dharma—The Ideal of the Marathas," in *The Main Currents of Maratha History* (Patna: Patna University, 1926), 1–29; Heimsath, *Indian Nationalism*, 9–106. See also Potdar, "Mind of Maharashtra," 61–62.

74. *Dynanodya* 2:6 (1843) and 4:25 (1845). The bhakti tradition in Hinduism originated in South India in ancient times and interacted with Islam in northern India over the course of several centuries after Islam was introduced in the eighth century.

75. *Memorial Papers of the AMM*, 1–4; quotation from p.1. The Americans were more adamant in their hostility to caste than Muslims had ever been, and this hostility had the result of making Christianity completely unacceptable to most members of the higher castes. While the Americans insisted on remaining outside the caste system and made relinquishment of caste a condition of baptism for their converts, Muslims were integrated into the caste system "only a little below" the Brahmans and Kunabis (cultivators) and "far higher" than the Mahars and Mangs, who were outcastes.

76. Modak, *History of the Native Churches*, 27. According to the *Missionary Herald*, the procedure for accepting Hindu men as converts to Islam included purification through a "dose of physic" and ten days of intensive instruction. If everyone involved in the process agreed that the candidate was sufficiently prepared, circumcision was performed, followed by a feast. The convert's debts were paid off, and a "wife obtained if necessary." *Missionary Herald* 44 (1848), 307.

77. Stanley A. Wolpert, *A New History of India* (New York: Oxford University Press, 1977), 244–249.

78. As Marutiraw R. Sangale complained in 1881, the "habit of dependence upon the mission has spread to all the villages [and] destroyed the last vestiges of an independent spirit. Hence we see to-day so few Christian people in Government employ, and

very few have entered upon any secular occupation." Overlooking the racist policies of the British operative in the selection of government personnel, Sangale blamed the American missionary policy, instituted in 1854, of discouraging the study of English. He also pointed to the harmful effects of the paternalism exercised by the early missionaries, who had made "every arrangement for the Christians and their children," leaving them "little liberty to choose their own occupation." Marutiraw R. Sangale, "Abstract of an Address on Those Who Became Christians in Connection with a Mission, But are Now Independent of it," trans. from Marathi, *Memorial Papers of the AMM*, 38–39.

79. Quotations from Modak, "History of the Native Churches," 20–21; and Bruce, "Literary Work of the American Marathi Mission," 125.

80. Heimsath, *Indian Nationalism*, 98–99, 86–87. The Maratha tradition of religious iconoclasm led reformers away from laying the blame for the corruptions of their society on the false religion perpetuated by Brahmanic priests, as many Bengali reformers did. According to the Marathi reformer Mahadev Govind Ranade, the reasons for India's three-thousand-year decline were more various: "isolation, submission to outward force or power more than to the voice of inward conscience, perception of fictitious differences between men, . . . passive acquiescence in civil wrong doing, and a general indifference to secular well-being, almost bordering on fatalism." Ranade, quoted in Heimsath, *Indian Nationalism*, 19.

81. S. P. Agrawal and F. C. Aggarwal, *Women's Education in India: Historical Review, Present Status and Perspective Plan with Statistical Indicators and Index to Scholarly Writings in Indian Educational Journals since Independence* (New Delhi: Concept Publishing Company, 1992), 13–21; quotation from 19. Also see Lakshmi Raghuramaiah, "Emergence of Modern Indian Womanhood," *Encyclopedia of Women in India*, ed. B. K. Vahshishta (New Delhi: Praveen Encyclopedia Publications, 1976), 70–74.

82. Dall, *Life of Dr. Anandabai Joshee*, 38.

83. Jyotsna Kapur, "Putting Herself into the Picture: Women's Accounts of the Social Reform Campaign in Maharashtra, Mid–nineteenth to Early Twentieth Centuries," *Manushi* 56 (1990), 28–37.

84. Kenneth Ballhatchet, *Social Policy and Social Change in Western India, 1817–1830* (London: Oxford University Press, 1957), 250; Heimsath, *Indian Nationalism*, 16–17.

85. Manmohan Kaur, *The Role of Women in the Freedom Movement, 1857–1947* (Delhi: Sterling, 1968), 86–89; quotation from 86.

86. Kapur, "Putting Herself into the Picture," 37.

Chapter Six

1. "Extracts from Mrs. Grout's Journal, Journey from Natal to the Zulu Country," May 19, 1841, Letters and Papers of the American Board of Commissioners for Foreign Missions, Houghton Library (hereafter cited as Letters and Papers of the ABCFM).

2. Ibid. According to Charlotte, the captain went on to say that "our people are great rascals to treat their women as they do." But given the novelty of the Grouts' interaction and the importance attached to very different forms of conjugal behavior in Zulu culture, it is possible that Charlotte's word "rascal" was a mistranslation, and that the captain thought the Grouts' behavior both astonishing ("wonderful") and amusing (he "laughed outright").

3. Henry Callaway, *Nursery Tales, Traditions, and Histories of the Zulus, in Their Own Words, with a Translation into English, and Notes*, vol. 1 (London: Trubner, 1868), 47–54, quotations from 47, 54.

4. Axel-Ivar Berglund, *Zulu Thought-Patterns and Symbolism* (Bloomington: Indiana University Press, 1976; reprint 1989), 188. Berglund found sixty-eight diviners in the 1970s, sixty-one of whom were women. In 1917 an earlier ethnographer found that 90 percent of diviners were women. See A. T. Bryant, "The Zulu Cult of the Dead," *Man* 17 (1917), 140–145.

5. Berglund, *Zulu Thought-Patterns*, 120–122, 270–272, 307–308. Because the defining element of witchcraft was anger, all women had reason to suppress that emotion, even if their husbands and in-laws treated them badly.

6. Ibid., 139. In the twentieth century, women diviners came to be called by their husband's shades as well as the shades of their own ancestors. This new flexibility may have been a response to the extended absences from home that the South African labor system imposed on African men, and the need for women to step in and preserve the religious life of the home by maintaining communication with the husband's shades.

7. Ibid., 136–150, 51–52, 90.

8. Aldin Grout to Rufus Anderson, Umlazi, July 14, 1840, Letters and Papers of the ABCFM.

9. Bartholomew Diaz named this region north of the Mzimkudu and south of the Tugela, between the Kwahlemba or Drakensburg mountains and the sea, the Tierra de Natal, or land of the Nativity, when he landed there on Christmas Day 1497. See Lewis Grout, *Zulu-Land; or, Life Among the Zulu-Kafirs of Natal and Zulu-Land, South Africa* (Philadelphia: Presbyterian Publication Committee, 1864), 18–25.

10. Ibid. See also Johannes Du Plessis, *A History of Christian Missions in South Africa* (Cape Town: C. Struik, 1911; reprint 1965), especially 219–232. Also in 1835, Daniel Lindley, Alexander E. Wilson, and Hyam L. Venable rode inland north and west of Cape Town and settled among the Moselekatse's people in Grinqualand as representatives of the American Board until the Voortrekker invasion two years later drove them to Port Natal.

11. Grout, *Zulu-land*, 201–204; Aldin Grout, *Missionary Herald* 36 (1840), 19; Charlotte Bailey, x-Class of 1838, Biographical File, Mount Holyoke College Archives. Charlotte entered Mount Holyoke in October 1837, its first year. She stayed there only a few months. In April 1838 Aldin wrote to Rufus Anderson from Charlotte's home town of Holden. In May, he wrote, "I expect that Miss Charlotte Bailey of Holden will accompany me to Africa as my companion." (Aldin Grout to Rufus Anderson, May 25, 1838, Letters and Papers of the ABCFM.)

12. Elizabeth A. Eldredge, "Sources of Conflict in Southern Africa, c. 1800–30: The 'Mfecane' Reconsidered," *Journal of African History* 33 (1992), 1–35; James Gump, "Origins of the Zulu Kingdom," *Historian* 50:4 (August 1988), 521–534; Julian Cobbing, "The Mfecane as Alibi: Thoughts on Dithakong and Mbolompo," *Journal of African History* 29 (1988), 487–519; Jeff Guy, "Ecological Factors in the Rise of Shaka and the Zulu Kingdom," in *Economy and Society in Pre-Industrial South Africa*, ed. Shula Marks and Anthony Atmore (London: Longman, 1980), 265–289. Eldredge contests Cobbing's argument that Shaka's *Mfecane* (crushing) is only a myth used to justify apartheid. Although she agrees that tribal activity in southeast Africa during Shaka's rule was more complicated than has been acknowledged, she points to African testimony to Shaka's power and reign of terror as evidence that the Mfecane was a historical reality. She also contests Cobbing's claim that destabilization resulting from the slave trade at Delagoa Bay was an important factor in the situation *leading* to Shaka's rise to power. But she does not dispute the existence of slave trade at Delagoa Bay after 1817, thus she leaves room for the idea that refugees from slave raids may have contributed to Shaka's army after 1817, and that European menace was a factor in Shaka's rule.

Eldredge agrees with Guy that environmental stress played a role in Shaka's rise to power, but disagrees with Guy's emphasis on overgrazing and overpopulation as the causes of this stress. Eldredge's view is that droughts increased competition over agricultural resources and over access to new forms and levels of trade.

13. Grout, *Zulu-land*, 68–78, 201–212.

14. "Aldin Grout to Rufus Anderson," July 14, 1840, Letters and Papers of the ABCFM; see also Newell Adams, "Letter from Umlazi" and "General Letter from the Missionaries at Umlazi," *Missionary Herald* 37 (1841), 36–38.

15. Aldin Grout, "Letters from Aldin Grout, October and November 1841," *Missionary Herald*, 38 (1842), 338–339; see also Grout, *Zulu-land*, 210–211.

16. "Letters from Aldin Grout" 339–340.

17. Ibid.

18. "Mrs. Grout's Journal," February 26, 1842.

19. See Jean and John Comaroff, *Of Revelation and Revolution: Christianity, Colonialism, and Consciousness in South Africa* (Chicago: University of Chicago Press, 1991); Jean Comaroff, *Body of Power, Spirit of Resistance: The Culture and History of a South African People* (Chicago: University of Chicago Press, 1985).

20. "Mrs. Grout's Journal," March 1, 1842.

21. "Letter from Mr. Grout, Umlazi, September 16, 1842," *Missionary Herald* 39 (1843), 77–78; Grout, *Zulu-land*, 211.

22. Newell Adams to Rufus Anderson, May 30, 1843, Letters and Papers of the ABCFM, quoted in Norman Etherington, *Preachers, Peasants, and Politics in Southeast Africa, 1835–1880: African Christian Communities in Natal, Pondoland, and Zululand* (London: Royal Historical Society, 1978), 75.

23. Du Plessis, *History of Christian Missions*, 382–384; Etherington, *Preachers, Peasants, and Politics*, 76–83.

24. The Grouts stopped in Cape Town on what they thought would be their way back to America, but British evangelicals there urged them to return to Natal and raise funds to support their missionary work. The Grouts had returned to Natal as missionary agents of the British government when the American Board reopened their mission and renewed their appointment. See Grout, *Zulu-land*, 213–214; "Letters from Mr. Grout" and untitled note, *Missionary Herald* 40 (1844), 181–183, 286.

25. Grout, *Zulu-land*, 90–93; Charles Ballard, "Traders, Trekkers and Colonists," in *Natal and Zululand from Earliest Times to 1910: A New History*, ed. Andrew Duminy and Bill Guest (Petermaritzburg, Sourth Africa: University of Natal Press, 1989), 116–145.

26. Du Plessis, *History of Christian Missions*, 306; see also Grout, *Zulu-land*, 238–253.

27. "South African Deputaton Papers," quoted in Du Plessis, *History of Christian Missions*, 306.

28. Grout, *Zulu-land*, 217–218; Du Plessis, *History of Christian Missions*, 217–218; Etherington, *Preachers, Peasants, and Politicians*, 106–107.

29. Etherington, *Preachers, Peasants, and Politicians*, 29. Etherington cautions against overstating the influence of the Americans and their schools on government policy in Natal, because American policies were "often atypical" and the size of American congregations was generally not large; 29 n. 1.

30. Lewis Grout to Rufus Anderson, September 15, 1851, Letters and Papers of the ABCFM.

31. Sylvia Vietzen, "Fabian Transplant," quoted in Shula Marks, ed., *Not Either an Experimental Doll: The Separate Worlds of Three South African Women* (Bloomington: Indiana University Press, 1987), 19.

32. Thomas Karis and Gwendolen M. Carter, eds., *From Protest to Challenge: A Documentary History of African Politics in South Africa 1882–1964*, vol. 4, *Political Profiles 1882–1964* (Stanford: Hoover Institution Press, 1977), 60–63. At Amanzimtoti, Lutuli met Z. K. Matthews, who was appointed principal of the high school in 1925 and became the most distinguished intellectual in South Africa. In 1930 Matthews was the first African to receive a law degree in South Africa, before pursuing a master's degree at Yale and studying anthropology under Bronislaw Malinowski at the London School of Economics. After returning to South Africa in 1935, he became involved in the ANC and later became the secretary of the Africa division of the World Council of Churches, the ambassador to the United States, and the chief United Nations representative of Botswana.

33. Myrtle Trowbridge, unpublished biography of Sibusisiwe Makhanya, Marks, *Not Either an Experimental Doll*, 31; see also 23, 31–37.

34. Absolom Vilakazi, *Zulu Transformations: A Study of the Dynamics of Social Change* (Pietermaritzburg, South Africa: University of Natal Press, 1965), 143–144.

35. Compare Du Plessis, *History of Christian Missions*, 261.

36. A decade later, in 1857, Louisa Healy Pixley (Mount Holyoke class of 1857) and her husband, Stephen, settled at Amahlongwa on the Umlazi and rebuilt the station first established by Newell and Sarah Adams. Louisa Healy, x-Class of 1857, Biographical File, Mount Holyoke College Archives. Stephen may have been the brother of Alvina Pixley Rood, who arrived in Natal in 1847.

37. Lydia Bates, Class of 1846, Biographical File, Mount Holyoke College Archives; Letters From Miss S.S and Mrs. M.A.C., Classmates of Mrs. Grout, quoted in Lewis Grout, *A Memorial Sketch of the Life and Character of Mrs. Lydia B. Grout, Who Died in West Brattleboro, Vermont, April 27, 1897* (Brattleboro, Vt.: Phoenix Job Printing Office, 1897), 17.

38. Lydia Bates Grout to Nancy Bates Atkinson, July 31, 1851, Papers of George A. Atkinson, Oregon History Center, Portland Ore. Thanks to Chris Lowe for discovering Lydia Grout's letters and to Gabriele B. Sperling for transcribing them.

39. Lydia Bates Grout to Nancy Bates Atkinson, November 20, 1847, Papers of George A. Atkinson.

40. Lydia Bates, Biographical File; Edward Hitchcock, "On the Erosions of the Earth's Surface, Especially by Rivers," pt. 2 of *Illustrations of Surface Geology*, Smithsonian Contributions to Knowledge, vol. 9 (Washington: Smithsonian Institution, 1857), 120–121 and 155, plate 9, figs. 1, 2.

41. Lydia Bates, Biographical File; Carles W. Kilbon, "Rev. Lewis Grout, D.D.," undated article, Mount Holyoke College Archives; Grout, *Memorial Sketch*, 13.

42. Ibid., 6.

43. Alvina V. Pixley, x-Class of 1849, Biographical File, Mount Holyoke College Archives.

44. Mary W. Tyler Gray, *Stories of the Early American Missionaries in South Africa* (Johannesburg: By the author, 1935), 58; Abby T. Linsley, x-Class of 1849, Biographical File, Mount Holyoke College Archives.

45. Laura B. Nichols, Class of 1856, Biographical File; Fidelia Phelps, x-Class of 1885, Biographical File, Mount Holyoke College Archives; Mary Lyon House pictured in Marks, *Not Either an Experimental Doll*, following 107; Henry Bridgman to Rufus Anderson, quoted in Etherington, *Preachers, Peasants, and Politics*, 28. Fidelia Phelps served as principal of the Inanda Seminary from 1884 to 1930.

46. Hannah J. Gilson, class of 1868, Biographical File, Mount Holyoke College Archives; Sarah D. Stow, *History of Mount Holyoke Seminary, South Hadley, Mass.*

During Its First Half Century, 1837–1887 (South Hadley: Mount Holyoke Seminary, 1887), 340–342.

47. Lewis Grout to Rufus Anderson, April 16, 1847, Letters and Papers of the ABCFM.

48. James Dexter Taylor, *The American Board Mission in South Africa. A Sketch of Seventy-Five Years* (Durban, South Africa: John Singleton & Sons, 1911), 9; Daniel Lindley, Aldin Grout, and Newton Adams to Rufus Anderson, August 22, 1837, Letters and Papers of the ABCFM; Etherington, *Preachers, Peasants, and Politicians*, 47–48. While the Americans defined their work primarily in terms of the Zulus, many of the residents and visitors at mission stations were, from the beginning, members of a variety of groups. The Zulus themselves were an ethnically complex nation including Ndelus, Ngcobos, Mdlulis, Mthembus, Mthiyanes, and other lineages. Refugees from, or members of, the Qadi, Nyuswa, and other groups never incorporated in the Zulu state also lived in Natal and became involved in missionary activities. For a partial list of families in Natal and Zululand, see Vilakazi, *Zulu Transformations*, 139. Among the families Vilakazi discussed in 1965, the Qadi and Nyuswa comprised primarily traditionalists, although both included a contingent of Christians. The other families just listed above were prominent Christians.

49. Lydia Bates Grout to Nancy Bates Atkinson, May 3, 1853, Papers of George A. Atkinson. Lewis Grout, "A Report of the Umsunluzi Mission Station for the year ending September 1852," Letters and Papers of the ABCFM.

50. Cetshwayo to S. M. Samuelson, Samuelson's Quarterly Report, quoted in Etherington, *Preachers, Peasants, and Politicians*, 81; see also 96, 103–104.

51. Lydia Bates Grout to Nancy Bates Atkinson, July 31, 1851, Papers of George A. Atkinson.

52. "Aldin Grout to Rufus Anderson, November 7, 1841," 339–340.

53. Berglund, *Zulu Thought-Patterns*, 85.

54. Etherington, *Preachers, Peasants, and Politicians*, 96–99.

55. Grout, "A Report of the Umsunduzi Mission Station for September 1852."

56. H. C. Lugg, "The Practice of Lobolo in Natal," *African Studies* 4:1 (March 1945), 23–27; M. D. W. Jeffreys, "Lobolo Is Child-Price," *African Studies* 10:4 (December 1951), 145–184.

57. At several points in time, British missionaries found that African women led the resistance against them. For reference to African women's resistance to missionary work, see Etherington, *Preachers, Peasants, and Politicians*, 61–62.

58. Lewis Grout to Rufus Anderson, Umvoti, May 18, 1847, Letters and Papers of the ABCFM; Etherington, *Preachers, Peasants, and Politicians*, 96–97; Berglund, *Zulu Thought Patterns*, 136–138.

59. Comaroff and Comaroff, *Of Revelation*, 240.

60. Grout to Anderson, Umvoti, April 16, 1847, Letters and Papers of the ABCFM; Lewis Grout to Rufus Anderson, Umsunduzi, November 21, 1848, Letters and Papers of the ABCFM.

61. Lewis Grout, "Umsunduzi Mission Station Annual Report, September, 1848," Letters and Papers of the ABCFM.

62. Grout to Anderson, Umvoti, April 16, 1847, Letters and Papers of the ABCFM.

63. Clara Bridgmen, quoted in Deborah Gaitskell, " 'Wailing for Purity': Prayer Unions, African Mothers, and Adolescent Daughters 1912–1940," in *Industrialization and Social Change in South Africa: Africa Class Formation, Culture and Consciousness 1870–1930*, ed. Shula Marks and Richard Rathbone (London: Longman, 1982), 339.

64. Vilakazi, *Zulu Transformations*, 138–139.

65. Vilakazi, *Zulu Transformations*, 102 and 139, quotation from 102.

66. Gaitskell, " 'Wailing for Purity,' " 338–357.

67. Shula Marks, "Natal, the Zulu Royal Family and the Ideology of Segregation," *Journal of Southern African Studies* 4:2 (April 1978), 172–194; Norman Etherington, "The 'Shepstone System' in the Colony of Natal and beyond the Borders," in Duminy and Guest, *Natal and Zululand*, 170–192; Etherington, *Preachers, Peasants, and Politicians*, 6–23; Jeff Guy, "The Destruction and Reconstruction of Zulu Society," in Marks and Rathbone, *Industrialization and Social Change in South Africa*, 167–194.

68. David Rood, quoted in Taylor, *American Board Mission*, 51; see also 50–53. Judson Smith, *A History of the American Board Missions in Africa* (Boston: American Board of Commissioners for Foreign Missions, 1905), 24.

69. Taylor, *American Board Mission*, 50–53, quotation from 51; Judson Smith, *A History of the American Board Missions in Africa* (Boston: ABCFM, 1905), 24.

70. Guy, "The Destruction and Reconstruction of Zulu Society" in Marks and Rathbone, *Industrialization and Social Change*, Shula Marks, "Natal, the Zulu Royal Family and the Ideology of Segregation," and Tim Couzens, " 'Moralizing Leisure Time': The Transatlantic Connection and Black Johannesburg 1918–1936," in Marks and Rathbone, *Industrialization and Social Change*, 314–337. In the twentieth century, scholars classified all the tribes in southeastern Africa, with the exception of the San (Bushmen) and the Khoisan (Hottentots) as Nguni, emphasizing, as nineteenth-century missionaries did, the common linguistic and cultural characteristics of these groups. In 1986 John Wright wrote, "The word 'Nguni' is today commonly used by academics as a collective term for the black peoples who historically have inhabited the eastern regions of southern Africa from Swaziland through Zululand, Natal, the Transkei and the Ciskei to the eastern Cape. These people," Wright continues, "are conventionally distinguished by language and culture from the Thonga peoples of the interior plateau to the west and north-west. Use of the Nguni in this extended sense is now so well entrenched in the literature on southern African ethnography, linguistics, and history as probably to make the term irremovable, but it is important to note that it is only within the last half-century that this usage has become current." John Wright, "Politics, Ideology, and the Invention of the 'Nguni,' " in *Resistance and Ideology in Settler Societies*, Southern African Studies, 4, ed. Tom Lodge (Johannesburg: Raven Press, 1986), 96–111, quotations from 96.

71. Grout, *Zulu-land*, 59–67, quotation from 66–67.

72. Comaroff and Comaroff, *Of Revelation and Revolution*, 62–65, quotation from 65. The Comaroffs overlook the alternative forms of objectification in African culture, and mistakenly link objectification itself with western culture.

73. In twentieth-century Latin America, Marxist-Christian educators linked the experience of liberation to a somewhat similar process of teaching people to draw pictures of their environment. See Paulo Friere, *Pedagogy of the Oppressed*, trans. Myra Bergman Ramos (New York: Herder and Herder, 1968).

74. Katherine Lloyd to N. G. Clark, quoted in Etherington, *Preachers, Peasants, and Politicians*, 150. In 1846, one of the first Zulus converted by Americans had marked her baptism and profession of faith by sitting down with Newell and Sarah Adams to celebrate the Lord's Supper. But such intimate expressions of Christian community had disappeared twenty years later. See Grout, *Zulu-land*, 215

75. Although opposed to slavery, Mary Lyon was troubled by the agitation over abolitionism at meetings of the American Board in the United States. See also Elizabeth Alden Green, *Mary Lyon and Mount Holyoke: Opening the Gates* (Hanover, N.H.: University Press of New England, 1979; reprint 1983), 205. Lyon allied herself with the

views upheld in William Ellery Channing's *Slavery and Emancipation*; Channing argued that "The word ABOLITIONIST in its true meaning . . . is a name of honorable import," but that it had become "restricted" to "enthusiasts" who acted "as if no evil existed but that which they opposed, and as if no guilt could be compared with that of countenancing or upholding it." (1836; reprint, New York: Negro Universities Press, 1968), chapter 7, 5th page.

76. Mbiana Ngidi, quoted in Etherington, *Preachers, Peasants, and Politicians*, 150.

77. Taylor, *American Board Mission*, 29–30.

78. Ibid., 152–156; Bengt G. M. Sundkler, *Bantu Prophets in South Africa* (London: Oxford University Press, 1948; reprint 1961), 297, 301.

Index

Adams, Hannah, 14
Adams, John Quincy, 20
Adams, Newell, 116, 120, 121, 126, 128
Adams, Sarah, 116, 126
Adams College. *See* Amanzimtoti
    Institute
Africa, 112–38, 140
African Americans, 17, 27
African Christians, 137, 140
African National Congress (ANC), 122,
    123
Ahmadnagar (India), 88, 89, 97, 98, 101,
    102, 107
Allen, Abby. *See* Fairbank, Abby Allen
Allmendinger, David, 30
amabeka (exchange of cattle), 130
amadlozi (ancestral shades), 115, 129, 130
Amanzimtoti Institute, 122, 123, 126, 127
ambutho tradition, 117
American Board of Commissioners for
    Foreign Missions, 5, 19, 20, 21, 54,
    63, 64, 65, 80, 86, 89, 97, 100, 101–2,
    120, 121, 122, 127, 136
American Indians, 17, 18

Analogy of Religion (Butler), 43
ANC. *See* African National Congress
Anderson, Rufus, 65, 99–101, 102, 103, 122,
    127, 147n. 21, 163n. 44, 164n. 49
Anthony, Susanna, 17
apartheid, 112, 134
Arthur, Chester A., 85
Arya Mahila Samaj society, 110
Athavale, Parvati, 110
Atkinson, Nancy Bates, 124
Avery, Caroline, 64
Avery, Mary, 64

Bailyn, Bernard, 36, 37
Ballantine, Elizabeth, 95, 96
Ballantine, Henry, 94, 96, 97, 101, 102,
    106
Banister, Mrs. William B. *See* Grant,
    Zilpah (Polly)
Bantu people, 134–35
Bantu Purity League, 123, 133
Barton, James L., 85, 86
Beaver, R. Pierce, 7, 148n. 29
Beecher, Catharine, 22–23, 24, 39

Bender, Thomas, 37
benevolence, 32, 38, 39, 46, 48, 49, 52,
    113, 139, 141, 142. *See also*
    disinterested benevolence
Benjamin, Samuel G. W., 85
Berlin Society, 121
bhakti tradition, 90, 105, 107, 108
Bible, 69, 70, 104
Bliss, Anna E., 127
Bloemhof Seminary, 127–28
boarding schools, 29
Boers. *See* Voortrekkers
Bombay (India), 89, 98, 103
Bombay Presidency. *See* Maharashtra
    (India)
Booth, Joseph, 137
Bowen, George, 92–94, 100, 161n. 21
Bradstreet, Anne, 58
Brahmanism, 89, 98–99, 104–5, 160n. 18
Brainerd, David, 17, 60–61, 156n. 27
Brethren, The, 34
Bridgman, Clara, 132
Bridgman, Frederick, 135
Bridgman, Henry, 127
Bridgman, Laura Brainerd Nichols, 127
Brigham, Sarah, 45
British missionaries, 7, 19, 88, 89
Buchanan, Claudius, 55
Burgess, Abigail. *See* Moore, Abigail
Burgess, Ebenezer, 91, 95, 97, 101, 102
Burgess, Mary Grant, 96, 102
Burma, 55–56, 57
Butler, Jon, 148n. 34
Butler, Joseph, 43
Bynum, Caroline Walker, 58

Caldwell, Eunice, 51
Calvin, John, 58
Calvinism, 24, 25, 148n. 34
Cape Colony, 117, 127
caste system, 104, 106, 109, 165n. 75
Catholic Church, 39–41, 121, 158n. 29
cattle, 130
Cetshwayo, King, 120, 129, 134
Champion, George, 116
Chandravarkar, N. G., 90
Child, Lydia Maria, 56
Christianity
    in Africa, 129, 130, 136–37
    in India, 88–90, 104, 108

    See also conversion; New Divinity
        thought; *specific denominations*
Church of England, 121
Colenso, Bishop, 121, 129
Comaroff, Jean and John, 131, 135, 136
community, 35–37
Conforti, Joseph A., 25
Congregational Church, 51, 56
conversion, 154n. 2
    in Africa, 130–31
    Brahman, 99, 105
    of Hindus, 100, 104
    to Islam, 107–8
    Lyon's, 50–54
    missionaries as exemplars, 49–50
    precedents for at Mount Holyoke, 54–
        62
    and reading and writing, 135, 136

Davis, Hannah, 116
Dawes, R. R., 85
Dayspring, 96
Dean, William, 65
death, 72–73
De Nobili, Robert, 301
Dickinson, Emily, 50
Dingan, King, 116, 117, 118, 119
disinterested benevolence, 11–12, 14, 16,
    17, 18, 23
diviners, 115
Dohne, J. L., 121
domesticity, 22, 23
Douglas, Ann, 24
Drake, Joanna, 50
Du Plessis (historian), 121
Durkheim, Emil, 36
Dwight, H. G. O, 80, 86
Dynanodya, 104

East India Company, 89
Eaton, Amos, 42
education
    in Africa, 122–23
    and Hinduism, 104
    and religion, 14
    See also teaching; women, education
        of
Edwards, Jonathan, 17, 18, 24, 25, 34, 39,
    44–46, 51, 56, 60–61, 67, 70, 80, 93,
    141, 154n. 2

Eliot, John, 18
Elphinstone, Monstuart, 103–4
Elphinstone Institute, 103, 104
Emerson, Joseph, 16, 17, 26, 31–32, 42, 43, 44, 51, 54
Emerson, Ralph Waldo, 93
Emmons, Nathaniel, 16, 17
emotionalism, 73
employment, 30
Epstein, Barbara Leslie, 149n. 39
Etherington, Norman, 122
Everett, Nancy, 40–41

Fairbank, Abby Allen, 91–93, 96, 102
Fairbank, Samuel, 91, 96, 102
family life, 34, 35, 147n. 21
   patriarchal, 88, 131
Farrar, Cynthia, 97, 100–101
female piety, 4, 5–6, 88, 90–91, 141
Female Seminary (Urmiyah), 68–72, 75, 76, 78
feminism, 26–28, 150nn. 46–47
Feminization of American Culture, The (Douglas), 24
Fergusen, Abbie P., 127
Fisk, Pliny, 62, 64
Fiske, Fidelia, 41, 44, 67, 68–76, 78, 83, 91, 125
Fiske seminary. *See* Female Seminary (Urmiyah)
Fogarty, Robert S., 34
foreign missionary work, 140
   American, 7, 19–21, 80–86, 134, 140, 147n. 20
   British, 7, 19
   Lyon's nurturing of, 62–65
   and New Divinity thought, 19–20
   as New England endeavor, 4–5
   women's role, 5, 7, 148n. 27
   zeal at Mount Holyoke, 62–65
   See also specific geographic locations; specific missionaries
Foster, Frank H., 148n. 34
Foster, Lawrence, 34
free will, 24

Gemeinshaft and Gesellschaft (Tonnies), 36
gender roles, 23, 24–25, 82–84, 131–32, 141
Getell, Richard G., 3

Gilson, Hannah Juliette, 127–28
Gospel of Gentility, The (Hunter), 23
Grant, Asahel, 69, 75, 76, 81
Grant, Jacquelyn, 27
Grant, Judith, 69–70
Grant, Mary. *See* Burgess, Mary Grant
Grant, Zilpah (Polly), 14, 26, 45, 51, 52, 63
Gray, Mary W. Tyler, 127
Great Awakening (1740–42), 16
Great Awakening (second), 4
Green, Elizabeth Alden, 25
Grimké, Sarah and Angelina, 13
Grout, Aldin, 114–21, 124, 129, 134, 136
Grout, Charlotte Bailey, 114–21, 124, 126
Grout, Lewis, 122, 124–26, 128, 130, 131, 132
Grout, Lydia Bates, 124–26, 128, 129, 131, 138

Hadewijch, Beguine, 57
Hall, David D., 148n. 34
Hanoverian Mission, 121
Haroutunian, Joseph, 24
Hasseltine, Nancy. *See* Judson, Ann Hasseltine
Hatch, Nathan O., 36
Hawaiian Islands, 20
Hawes, Benjamin, 137
Hazen, Allen, 97, 101, 102
Hazen, Martha, 95, 96–97
Hill, Patricia R., 23
Hindu College (Poona), 110
Hinduism, 87–111, 140
History of the Work of Redemption (Edwards), 44–45, 56, 67, 70
Hitchcock, Edward, 41, 42, 102, 125
Home Missionary, 64
Hopkins, Samuel, 11, 17–18, 25, 56, 141, 148n. 34
Hubbell, Eliza, 64
Huguenot Seminary, 127
Hume, Hannah, 100
Hume, Robert, 94, 98
Hume, Sarah, 97
humility, 6, 49, 82–83, 141
Hunter, Jane, 23
Hutchinson, Anne, 15

iconoclasm, 87, 91, 103–7, 109, 166n. 80
imperialism, 19–21, 88

Improvement of the Mind (Watts), 43
Inanda Female Seminary, 123, 127
India, 7, 18, 19, 66, 87–111
    Christianity in, 88–90
    decline, 166n. 80
intellectual mastery, 50
Ipswich Female Seminary, 52
Iran. *See* Persia
Islam. *See* Muslims

Jesus Christ, 107, 108
Jnaneshwar, 106
Joseph, John, 79
Joshee, Anandabai, 96, 110
Judson, Adoniram, 54, 57
Judson, Ann Hasseltine, 22, 54–61, 66, 67

Kamehamehan, King, 20
Kapur, Jyotsna, 110
Karve, Anandibai, 110
Kerber, Linda K., 11, 26
Khiste, Hari Ramchandra, 91, 92, 99,
    162–63n.40
Khiste, Narayan, 99, 162–63n. 40
kholwa (believers), 132, 134
kirtans, 108
Knowles, James D., 56
Krishna, 106, 107, 108
Kurds, 81, 85, 159n. 31

labor-saving devices, 37–38
Ladies Seminary at Byfield, 31–32
literacy, 30, 140. *See also* education;
    women, education of
lobolo (ritual), 130, 133
Lutuli, Martin, 122
Lutuli, Mvumbi, 122
Lyon, Lucy, 62, 65–66, 71
Lyon, Mary
    and Beecher, 23
    on Catholic Church, 40
    concept of middle class, 33, 37
    contributions to missionary fund, 65
    conversion, 50–54
    depression, 51–54
    Edwards's influence, 34, 39, 44–46
    Emerson's influence, 32
    enthusiasm for "system", 37
    establishment of Mount Holyoke, 3,
        11–12, 25, 32, 39, 45
    family background, 31
    on gender role, 23
    and Grant (Polly), 52
    gravesite, 3–4
    and labor-saving devices, 38
    and mainstream society, 46–47
    Mount Holyoke curriculum, 42, 43
    on Mount Holyoke's tuition, 39
    nurturing of missionary zeal, 62–65
    opposition to "belle ideal", 13
    as representative of Calvinist tradition,
        25
    students, 7, 22, 35, 38, 62, 139–42
    on teaching, 22–23, 31
    thirst for knowledge, 42
    and women's education, 11–12, 14, 16–
        17, 30, 47
    *See also specific students and
        geographic locations for missionary
        work*

Maharashtra (India), 87–112, 140, 160n.
    8
Mahars, 105–6
Maines, Sir Henry, 36
Makhanya, Sibusisiwe, 123, 133
Malik Kassim Meerza, Prince, 70
Mann, Margaret, 42, 43
marriage
    Hindu ceremony, 109
    Lyon's views, 46–47
    Nestorian, 72, 82
    Zulu customs, 129, 130
Mather, Cotton, 15, 18
Matthews, Z. K., 169n. 32
Mayhew, Thomas and Matthew, 18
Mead, Sidney, 24
Melville, Herman, 147n. 20
Methodist Church, 4
middle class, 33, 37
Middle East, 86
Mill, John Stuart, 103
Missionary Herald, 64, 65, 78, 124
Missionary Review, 101
Missionary Society, 66
missionary work. *See* foreign missionary
    work; *specific geographic locations*;
    specific missionaries
Modak, R. V., 105
Moore, Abigail, 42, 62, 71, 91, 97, 102–3

Mount Holyoke, 3
  alumnae, 47, 62; in Africa, 114–21, 124–28; in India, 90–103; in Persia, 62–64
  anti-Catholic sentiment at, 39–41
  communal organization, 32–33, 50
  curriculum, 42, 43, 70
  domestic work at, 38–39, 41
  family life at, 35
  female missionaries, 6
  laying of cornerstone, 45
  missionary zeal at, 62–65
  and Nestorian students, 70–72
  public endowment, 11–12, 25
  spiritual experiences at, 41
  tuition, 39
  See also Lyon, Mary; *specific alumnae*
mourning rituals, 72–73
Mpande, King, 114–21
Munger, Maria, 98
Munger, Sendol, 98, 101, 107
Muslims, 68, 75, 78, 80–84, 107–8, 165n. 75
mystics, female, 57–58

Natal, 112, 114, 120–28, 132–34, 137, 140
Native Home Missionary Society, 137
negritude, 123
Nestorians, 64, 68–87, 140, 158n. 27
Nestorius, Bishop, 79, 80
New Divinity thought, 11, 12, 16–20, 23, 25, 28, 29, 32, 41, 56, 139–41
Newell, Harriet, 5, 22, 90, 127
Newell, Samuel, 5
Ngidi, Mbiana, 137
Nguni people, 171n. 70
Nikant, Daji, 89
Northampton (Mass.), 30
Norwegian missionaries, 120
Noyes, John Humphrey, 33–35
Nurallah, Amir, 81

objectification, 135–36
Oneida Community, 32, 33–35, 37
Oopadesh Chundrika, 104
Osborne, Sarah, 17
Owen, Francis, 116

Pandharpur (India), 106–7
pantheism, 93
Parsons, Talcott, 36

patriarchal family, 88, 131
Patwardhan, Leelabai, 110
Percival, John, 20
Perkins, Justin, 64, 65, 69, 70, 72, 79, 159n. 29
Persia, 62, 64, 68–86, 140
piety, 150n. 44. *See also* female piety
polygamy, 82, 118, 129
Pomeroy, Lydia, 63–64
Poona (India), 110
Powar, Bhagoba, 106
pride, 27
Protestantism, 4, 25
  and Catholicism, 39–40
  in Hawaiian Islands, 20
  self-examination, 49
  See also conversion
Prubhakur, 104
public speaking, 13
public welfare, 14
Pundalik, 106–7
Pundit, Vishnu Shastri, 109
Puritanism, 148–49n. 34, 150n. 44
  myth of morbidity, 24–26
  and Republican Motherhood, 15–16
  and suffering and redemption, 58
Putnam, Lovina, 52–53

racial stereotyping, 135
Raghonata, Babaji, 98
Ramabai, Pandita, 110
Ramakrishnapunt (convert), 101
Ranade, Mahadev Govind, 166n. 80
Read, Caroline, 98
Read, Hollis, 98
reading, 119, 135, 136
redemption, 44–46, 49, 52, 58, 139
religion
  alternative movements, 25
  and education, 14
  and public welfare, 14
  and science, 42, 43
  and social and intellectual change, 36
  See also specific religions
Republican Motherhood, 11, 12–13, 26, 28, 29, 32, 103, 139
  and Hinduism, 88, 91, 109
  and Nestorians, 68–69, 78
  Puritan roots of, 15–16
Retief, Peter, 117, 119

Rhodesia, 127
Rice, Mary, 68, 73, 78
Rig-Veda, 109
Roman Catholic Church. *See* Catholic
    Church
Rood, Alvina Virtue Pixley, 124, 126
Rood, David, 126
Rowlandson, Mary, 58–59
Rush, Benjamin, 13
Ryan, Mary P., 24

Saiving, Valerie, 26–27
Sanders, Elizabeth, 147n. 20
Sangale, Krishnaraw Ratnaji, 108
sannyasa, 92
Sanum (Nestorian woman), 76–78
Savitri (legendary character), 92
Sawtell, Mr., 65–66
Schreuder, Hans, 120, 121
Science, 41–44
Scott, Ann Firor, 26
self-denial, 26–28
self-examination, 49, 50, 73
self-interest, 17, 23
self-pity, 50
self-sacrifice, 5–6, 15, 16, 23, 49, 68, 113,
    141–43
sewing, 125
sex
    in Hawaiian Islands, 20
    and sin, 15
    in Zulu culture, 129–30, 132–33
Shaka, King, 115, 116–17, 118, 167–68n. 12
Shakta rituals, 105
Shedd, William A., 85
Shepstone, Theopholis, 133–34, 135
Shimon, Mar, 73, 81
Shivaji, 107
sin, 15, 23, 26–27, 149n. 39
Sklar, Kathryn Kish, 24, 25, 30
slavery, 17, 120, 141
Smith, Eli, 80, 86
Smith-Rosenberg, Carol, 24
social change, 141–42
social organizaion, 87–88
soul, 93
South Africa, 134. *See also* Natal;
    Zululand
Speer, Robert E., 86
Spoford, Sophia, 124

Star of the East (Buchanan), 55
Stiles, Ezra, 17
Subjection of Women, The (Mill), 103
suffering, 15, 57–58, 75
syncretism, 89
Syriac language, 74–75, 77

Tajol-Saltaneh, 83
Taylor, Nathaniel William, 24
teaching, 22–23, 30–31
Thomas, Saint, 79, 89
Thurston, Persis, 66
Tilak, Lakshmibai, 110
Tolman, Susan, 65, 66
Tonnies, Ferdinand, 36
Tracey, Ira, 65
Tswana people, 135

Unzondelelo, 137
Urmiyah (Persia), 68–85

veils, 83
Vidyasaga, 109
Vilakazi, Absolom, 123, 132
virtue, 150n. 44
Voortrekkers (Boers), 117, 120, 121, 134

Watts, Isaac, 43
Whaples, Elizabeth, 66
White, Amanda, 42, 51
White, Hannah, 30
Whitefield, George, 16
Wilder, Abbie Temperance Linsley, 124,
    126–27
Wilder, Hyman, 127
Wilder, Jane, 94–95, 96, 101, 102, 164n. 49
Wilder, Royal, 94–95, 100, 101–2, 107,
    163nn. 41, 44, 164n. 49
Willard, Emma, 26
Williams, Tirzah M., 66
Wilson, Woodrow, 85, 86
Wingate, Sarah, 53
Winthrop, John, 15
Wirth, Louis, 36
women
    African, 113, 114–15, 123
    antebellum New England and
        missionary, 6–7, 21–23, 27–28, 48,
        140, 142
    "belle ideal", 12, 13

boarding schools, 29
education of, 11–12, 13, 14, 16–17, 26, 30, 47, 139, 143; in India, 88, 94, 97, 100, 103, 109–1; Nestorian, 69–72
female piety tradition, 4, 5–6, 88, 90–91, 141
feminist distaste for self-denial, 26–28
foreign missionary work, 5, 7, 148n. 27
Hindu, 90, 94, 98, 109–11, 113
maternal role, 12, 13, 113
Nestorian and Muslim, 82–84, 113
and Puritanism, 15
self-sacrifice, 5–6, 15, 141–43
support of Hopkins, 17–18
teaching as career, 30–31
Zulu, 113, 114–15, 123, 125, 129–33, 138
See also gender roles; *specific missionary workers*

Women Invited to War (Adams), 14
Wood, Gordon, 36, 37
Wood, Lucy, 102, 162n. 33
Wood, William, 97, 102, 162n. 33
Woods, Leonard, 5
World Their Household, The (Hill), 23
writing, 119, 135, 136

Yohanan, Mar, 69, 70, 72, 75, 158n. 27

Zingian race, 135
Zulu Congregational Church, 137
Zulu culture, 125, 129–30, 131–33, 134, 136, 137, 170n. 48. *See also* women, Zulu
Zululand, 112–21, 134
Zulu-land (Grout), 126
Zulu language, 124, 135